Soviet and East European Studies

INDIA'S ECONOMIC RELATIONS WITH THE USSR
AND EASTERN EUROPE, 1953 TO 1969

Soviet and East European Studies

EDITORIAL BOARD

The National Association for Soviet and East European Studies exists for the purpose of promoting study and research on the social sciences as they relate to the Soviet Union and the countries of Eastern Europe. The Monograph Series is intended to promote the publication of works presenting substantial and original research in the economics, politics, sociology and modern history of the USSR and Eastern Europe.

FIRST BOOKS IN THE SERIES

A. Boltho, *Foreign Trade Criteria in Socialist Economies*
Sheila Fitzpatrick, *The Commissariat of Enlightenment*
Donald Male, *Russian Peasant Organisation before Collectivisation*
P. Wiles, ed., *The Prediction of Communist Economic Performance*
Vladimir V. Kusin, *The Intellectual Origins of the Prague Spring*
Naum Jasny, *Soviet Economists of the Twenties*
Galia Golan, *The Czechoslovak Reform Movement*
Asha L. Datar, *India's Economic Relations with the USSR and Eastern Europe, 1953 to 1969*

INDIA'S
ECONOMIC RELATIONS
WITH THE USSR AND
EASTERN EUROPE
1953 TO 1969

ASHA L. DATAR

CAMBRIDGE
AT THE UNIVERSITY PRESS
1972

Published by the Syndics of the Cambridge University Press
Bentley House, 200 Euston Road, London NWI 2DB
American Branch: 32 East 57th Street, New York, N.Y.10022

© Cambridge University Press 1972

Library of Congress Catalogue Card Number: 76–178285

ISBN 0 521 08219 6

Printed in Great Britain
at the University Press, Aberdeen

CONTENTS

FOREWORD

A fatal motor accident in March 1971, in which Miss Asha Datar was involved as a passenger, ended her promising career at the age of thirty. She was then in the Professional Trainee Programme of the World Bank gaining experience in the subject matter of this book through missions to African countries on the negotiation and use of development assistance.

Having taken a first degree in politics at the University of Bombay, she read philosophy, politics and economics at St Anne's College, Oxford, on a scholarship awarded by the Oxford Society, and went on to write the thesis from which this book developed. The preparation of her doctorate – gained in 1970 – was undertaken while on the staff of the Oxford University Institute of Economics and Statistics, and completed in her own time while working in Washington. Miss Datar's economics tutor, Miss Peter Ady (St Anne's) and her supervisor for the doctorate, Miss Nita Watts (St Hilda's) were her principal sources of encouragement and instruction. She also took into account observations by her University examiners, Lord Balogh (Balliol) and Mr Michael Kaser (St Antony's).

APPENDIXES

TABLES IN THE TEXT

UNITS OF MEASUREMENT

Unless otherwise stated, values cited in the text are those before the devaluation of June 1966, viz. Rs.4·75 = U.S. $1; the subsequent exchange rate was Rs.7·5 = U.S. $1.
Weights and measures are in metric tons.

ABBREVIATIONS

AICC	All India Congress Committee
AID	Agency for International Development (U.S.A.)
CMEA	Council for Mutual Economic Assistance (Comecon)
Congress	U.S. Congress (refers to the Senate and House of Representatives)
Consortium	India Consortium (group of friendly governments formed in 1958 to co-ordinate aid)
Constitution	The Constitution of the Republic of India 1950
CPI	Communist Party of India
CPU	Committee on Public Undertakings (India)
DGCIS	Director General of Commercial Intelligence and Statistics (India)
DLF	Development Loan Fund
EC	Estimates Committee
ENI	Ente Nazionale Idrocarburi (Italy)
Eximbank	Export–Import Bank (U.S.A.)
HEC	Heavy Engineering Corporation (Ranchi)
HMBP	Heavy Machine Building Plant
IBRD	International Bank for Reconstruction and Development (World Bank)

ICICI	International Credit and Investment Corporation of India
IDA	International Development Agency (U.N.)
IFC	Industrial Finance Corporation of India
IJMA	Indian Jute Mills Association
IMF	International Monetary Fund
ISI	Indian Statistical Institute
NCAER	National Council of Applied Economic Research
NPCI	National Productivity Council of India
OECD	Organisation for Economic Cooperation and Development
ONGC	Oil and Natural Gas Commission
PL 480; PL 665	Public Law 480; Public Law 665, of the United States Congress (on commodity aid deliveries by the Government of the United States); on the Cooley Amendment to the former see p. 210.
RBI	Reserve Bank of India
STC	State Trading Corporation
SUNFED	Special United Nations Fund for Economic Development
UNCTAD	United Nations Conference on Trade and Development
USGPO	United States Government Printing Office

1

INTRODUCTION

The purpose of this study is to evaluate the contribution to India's development made by economic and technical co-operation with the USSR and other East European countries (henceforth referred to as the East European countries only). While the subject of this study is an assessment of the costs and benefits *to India* of this debtor/creditor relationship, it is to be expected that the case study will throw light on some issues which are of common interest and concern to other developing countries also. The issues are (i) the role of external finance in a country's development effort (i.e. the difficulties in matching availabilities with requirements), (ii) the terms and conditions of aid and (iii) the special advantages or disadvantages associated with establishing trade and credit relations with the centrally planned economies.

If the volume of aid offered was the chief determinant of its impact on development, the aid received from the centrally planned economies[1] would not be all that important. Together they gave only about 8 per cent of the total external official finance utilised during the period 1951/2 to 1968/9. Even looking at 'economic cooperation' rather than aid, while the share of East European countries in India's external trade has increased, it still constitutes only 20 per cent of the total external trade. It is worthwhile examining the impact of this aid on the Indian economy for two reasons. First, the continued economic cooperation between a mixed economy and centrally planned economies is a rather unusual phenomenon. Second, because of the cold war situation in the 1950s, the Soviet aid programme precipitated a re-examination of aid policies by other donors. This indirect benefit was equally, if not more, important to the developing countries than actual aid offered by the East European countries.

[1] In this study 'centrally planned economies' and 'the East European countries' mean Bulgaria, Czechoslovakia, East Germany (GDR), Hungary, Poland, Rumania, USSR and Yugoslavia (where, however, planning operates within a market); 'socialist countries' includes all these and China.

This study deals with India's trade and credit relationship with East European countries rather than just 'aid'. While trade and aid have different meanings and are to be distinguished in common usage, they are used interchangeably in East European literature. Indeed trade is considered as a special kind of aid.

The definition of aid is a controversial question. It is used to cover a multitude of transactions involving the transfer of resources – funds, commodities and skills – to the developing countries.[1] It is not proposed to review the growing literature on aid or to choose one definition: 'aid' means different things to different people. To donors the important factor is the sacrifice involved in giving aid, i.e. the opportunity cost of real or financial resources released.[2] To recipients what matters is the net benefits from a so-called unilateral transfer – not just the so-called grant 'element'.[3] Since one of the purposes of this study is to find out how much of what is called aid is really beneficial, defining aid flows is equivalent to prejudging the issue.

The East European countries consider trade as aid, which is hence also treated in this study; but there are, further, two good economic reasons why East European aid cannot be treated in isolation from trade. First, the East European countries commit themselves to accepting repayment in goods. Second, since 1958/9 all the commercial and non-commercial transactions between India and East European countries are covered by comprehensive non-convertible currency payment arrangements. Any currency balances accumulated can only be used to buy goods and services from the partner country. Net benefits from this arrangement depend upon the quality, prices and volume of goods that India buys and sells. If she cannot

[1] In its annual reports on aid to the developing countries (61) the OECD includes grants, loans and government suppliers' credits in the official flow of funds. On the defined terms of OECD official development assistance of OECD and the USSR, see Kaser (38, pp. 476–8).

[2] Pincus (67, p. 308) makes the point that a donor does not view a foreign loan as aid if its terms and conditions approximate those on the domestic capital market. However, it is still 'aid' for the recipient if his alternative borrowing rates are higher. See Carter (14) for an assessment from the aspect of the benefits accruing to the USSR from aid.

[3] Ohlin (60) developed a formula for measuring the grant equivalent in various loans, based on interest rate, grace period and maturity.

INTRODUCTION 3

purchase the goods she wants, the benefits from this arrangement may be lessened. In other words, if exporting to a country
does not involve a commitment to buy an equivalent amount
from that country and vice versa, the two questions of trade and
aid can be treated separately. But, given the payment arrangement India has, the answer to the question whether and how
India benefits from the availability of credit from the East
European countries really depends upon an examination of
India's trade and balance of payments with them. However,
trade is only one dimension of Indo-East European economic
cooperation. Two other dimensions are equally important, if
less tangible. First, since foreign exchange is a scarce resource,
by tying credits to specific projects or sectors, donors may have
influenced sectoral priorities and policies. Second, as mentioned
before, Soviet aid has influenced the availability of finance from
other donors. Western countries, especially the United States,
certainly interpreted it as a challenge and another move in the
cold war and reacted to it as such. This reaction is best summarised in the words of Dwight Eisenhower, then President of
the United States, 'If the purpose of Soviet aid to any country
were simply to help it overcome economic difficulties without
infringing its freedom, such aid would be welcomed as forward-
ing the free world purpose of economic growth. But there is
nothing in the history of international communism to indicate
this can be the case. Until such evidence is forthcoming, we and
other free nations must assume that Soviet Bloc aid is a new
subtle, long range instrument, i.e. directed towards the same
purpose of drawing its recipient away from the community of
free nations, and ultimately into the Communist orbit.'[1]

To study this three-dimensional relationship, the main
questions discussed in the subsequent chapters are:

(i) How much credit, in the sense of unilateral transfer of
goods instead of exchange, has India received? In a comprehensive trade agreement the deficit on current account should
equal net capital receipts. However, India might have been
accumulating idle currency balances and such balances would
represent a waste of credit finance. It is worth asking whether
such 'waste' was a serious problem because other developing
countries have also faced this problem in their economic

[1] U.S. Department of State (89, p. 1).

relations with the USSR. In fact, one of the charges levelled against the Soviet Union's trade and credit programme has been its supposed inability to deliver the goods.[1] If the criticism is justified, the utility of non-convertible payment arrangements is questionable.

(ii) What is the true worth of this aid? Since all the past credits have been tied to imports for particular projects from the creditor country, the nominal value of aid will have to be discounted for any costs associated with bilateral trade and the tying of aid.

(iii) Were India's exports to these markets in repayment of aid additional to her exports elsewhere? If India's exports to the East European countries increased at the expense of her other markets, there would be no net gain in foreign exchange earnings apart from the temporary addition to India's resources during the period between receipt of aid and repayment, and possibly higher unit prices for exports in these and/or other markets. But if the aid agreements enable exports greater than could otherwise be realised, the benefit to India is clearly increased. These bilateral trade agreements may be self-defeating if they result in trade diversion. Conceivably, they might even reduce India's total foreign exchange earnings. The question how far they actually did so is to be examined.

(iv) To what extent were the prices of India's exports and imports comparable to those she got from the rest of the world? If India paid a higher price for her imports than would have been paid to alternative suppliers, this might have been neutralised by a higher price for her exports. What really matters is the import purchasing power of her exports.

(v) The prices of exports, however, may be important in themselves, if the prices received in bilateral trade affect India's exports elsewhere.

(vi) Did the project financed from such credits have a high priority in the development plan and did it deserve the priority it received? Since the East European countries offered a 'package deal' (i.e. including technical know-how and personnel with machinery and equipment), better planning and speedier,

---

[1] The studies on Soviet aid and trade in the 1950s emphasised the USSR's inability to export goods on time. See Allen (3), and various contemporary U.S. Department of State booklets.

more efficient implementation of the projects receiving credits from the East European countries might be expected. In practice, it is found that there was inadequate project planning, resulting in an escalation of project costs. Whenever these can be attributed to the collaborators, they are treated as reducing the real value of aid.

(vii) The impact of the availability of credits from East European countries on sectoral priorities and the distribution of investment between public and private sectors is worth examining.

(viii) The impact of the availability of finance from East European countries on the aid efforts of other countries will also be investigated.

Before getting down to discussing these questions it will be useful to review the main trends in the international aid effort. This will clearly bring out the interplay between various forces, such as the attitude of India and the donors towards aid. Towards the beginning of the 1960s there was a greater willingness among donors to treat external funds as an integral part of resources available for investment. India's attitude towards dependence on foreign funds and aid changed in the late 1950s. To understand fully India's economic relations with the East European countries, it is necessary to view them within the context of the changing international scene and the economic and political developments in India.

On the international scene, the main actors are the United States and the Soviet Union, the principal protagonists in the cold war. There are four landmarks in U.S. aid policies. The first phase ended in 1948, when communist forces entered Greece in the arena of civil war. During this time, Europe was struggling to restore its economy with scant American support. While the USSR was also busy recovering from the war, it was also consolidating its gains in Europe. The cold war tensions came to a head with the invasion of Greece and President Truman initiated his famous Point-4 programme in Congress: the Marshall Plan for Europe was launched in 1950. The primary motive behind extending money and technical assistance at this time was to enable countries to stand up to the threat of communism and the main effort was directed towards Europe. Promoting economic development was only an incidental by-product of the scheme aimed at protecting the United States and others; it is significant that the aid authorising act was entitled the Mutual Security Act. And even from the discussions in hearings on the annual authorisation and appropriations, it is quite clear that defence support and economic aid were indistinguishable.[1]

The second landmark was the Korean War. The industrialised countries did not properly appreciate the importance of the developing countries until the outbreak of hostilities in Korea. In his message to Congress in 1952, President Truman underlined the importance of developing countries as markets and as suppliers of raw materials. In fact, he went to the extent of saying that to ensure production at full capacity in American factories, foreign aid was essential.[2]

In the literature on U.S. aid, various reasons are mentioned to support the case for providing capital to developing countries. Thus Brown and Opie, in a book published in 1953, said, 'The interest of the U.S. in extending assistance to the underdeveloped countries is compounded of a humanitarian impulse to aid the less fortunate, a desire to promote sound and expanding world trade, the necessity of increasing supplies of raw materials and the firm determination to forestall the spread of communism. But the role of the U.S. in assisting underdeveloped countries is conditioned by its belief in the value of the democratic form of political organisation and in certain basic principles of economic philosophy that are embedded in the American system.'[3] Even Brown and Opie do not emphasise the role of aid in promoting development as such.

Since the primary motive behind the U.S. aid programme was to strengthen the countries anxious to fight communism, it was natural that those who refused to align themselves in this crusade should suffer. While India did receive substantial amounts of grants and surplus commodities from the United States before 1954, the U.S. Government and Congress made no secret of their displeasure with Indian neutrality, and on

[1] See the Annual Discussions on Mutual Defence Security Act 1951–5.
[2] These views were expressed by President Truman in his speech to the Newspaper Guild, 28 June 1950, and by Henry Bennet speaking for the Technical Cooperation Administration and are quoted in an article by J. Rippie, 'Historical Perspective' (97, p. 13).
[3] Brown and Opie (13, p. 83).

occasions Congress reduced the aid appropriations requested. The American reaction is understandable, for the Indian Government was challenging the very core of the proposed defence mechanism – the military alliances. It is interesting though, that in the pre-1954 period, American policy makers did not feel embarrassed to let it be known that economic aid was dependent on good behaviour, i.e. commitment and concrete action to oppose communism.[1]

In his book on foreign aid, Andrew Westwood describes how the United States faced awkward situations in countries like Indonesia and Iran because of the supposed requirement imposed by the American Congress that all recipients of American aid, except under the Point-4 programme, should in effect declare their alignment with the 'Free World'. In practice the recipients of economic aid were required only to declare their adherence to the principles of the United Nations,[2] but even this was treated as a string and became a source of irritation to the neutral developing countries.

During the 1950s, it was the U.S.A. who gave most bilateral assistance to independent governments. Great Britain and France concentrated mainly on meeting the needs of their colonies and former colonies.[3] Until the USSR entered the picture, the United States was virtually the only donor making capital available to developing countries. She therefore had a strong bargaining position.

The third landmark was the Soviet Union's entry into the aid-giving business. The USSR's emergence as a competitor and its success among the developing countries led to some soul-searching in the United States. The prevalent opinion was that the theatre of war had changed, while the Russian desire for domination had not, and that the United States must devise weapons to cope with this type of economic warfare.[4] It is fair

[1] The objectives and methods of the aid programme were closely scrutinised in Congress and the anti-communist bias of the aid programme is clear from the hearings before the Senate Foreign Relations Sub-Committee.

[2] Westwood (95, p. 33).

[3] For a history of international aid in the 1950s see Little and Clifford (44); Friedman, Kalmanoff, (27, ch. 2); and Pincus (80, 81).

[4] The economic activities of the Sino–Soviet bloc became a very fashionable subject for discussion among political scientists. The bias of American authors is evident even in the various titles of works on the subject, *Soviet Economic Warfare*, *Sino–Soviet Offensive in the Less Developed Countries*, *The Challenge of Co-existence*.

to point out that individuals – economists, political scientists, Congressmen, Administration officials – might have been interested in offering aid even before the USSR took the 'offensive', but their views were not translated into policies. The re-orientation of the American aid programme which was manifested in many ways – establishment of the Development Loan Fund (DLF), support for concessionary terms of loans and for international coordination of aid, including IDA – might not have received Congressional backing but for the argument advanced that development aid would be a new and more suitable weapon to cope with the new type of warfare. The biggest bonus of the Russian presence was that 'disinterested aid' became very popular and neutrality became acceptable as a political stance. Since 1957, the United States has taken a continuous interest in providing aid to India and has co-operated with the World Bank to coordinate international aid efforts.

The fourth landmark was a new American policy, offering long-term development loans on a continuing basis and integrating external funds into the planning process. It was not crystallised and formalised until President Kennedy moved into the White House. In his aid message to Congress in 1961, he tacitly recognised that a reason why the American aid programmes had not been more successful in the past was the lack of emphasis on a long-term programme and he urged a commitment by the United States to this. He said, 'Uneven and undependable short-term finance has weakened the incentive for long-term planning and self-help by the recipient nations which are essential to serious economic development. The lack of stability and continuity in the programme – the necessity to accommodate all planning to a yearly deadline – when combined with a confusing multiplicity of American aid agencies within a single nation abroad – have reduced the effectiveness of our own assistance and made more difficult the task of setting realistic targets and sound standards. Piecemeal projects, hastily designed to match the rhythm of the fiscal year, are no substitute for orderly long-term planning. The ability to make long-range commitments has enabled the Soviet Union to use its aid programme to make developing countries economically dependent on Russian support – thus advancing the aims of world communism.'[1] The American aid programme has not lived up to the standards set by President Kennedy, and the hope for a 'decisive' turnaround in the fate of the less developed countries in the development decade has not been realised.[2]

This study does not review foreign aid policies of other donors, because while they have made substantial contributions, aid from other sources (apart from the United Kingdom) really started in the 1960s, within the framework of the Indian Consortium. Although these countries are treated as a group, it is not implied that they had identical views on aid policies or foreign aid objectives. However, the purpose of reviewing American aid policies is to show how the international climate changed in favour of long-term development aid in the 1950s. In this context, the two most important entities are the U.S.A. and the World Bank. The World Bank assumed importance, first, because it was the most important agency giving development loans in the early 1950s, and second, because it took the leading role in organising the Indian Consortium in 1958, and itself gave loans on concessional terms.

There was also an interesting reversal in the World Bank's position. In the early 1950s, several developing countries sought to establish a special U.N. fund (SUNFED) to give loans on concessionary terms, but the Bank did not favour that proposal. In the late 1950s, however, the Bank established its own affiliate to provide such funds – the International Development Agency (IDA).

The USSR's rediscovery of the road to Paris via Peking and Calcutta[3] became evident after Stalin's death. Whatever her specific motives and objectives in cultivating the friendship of the developing countries, there was a fairly standard pattern for winning friends and influencing people. The USSR concentrated its efforts on a few developing countries, opening trade with them and offering them credits. The occasion chosen was usually when a country was in serious economic difficulties, i.e. when it could not find markets for its major exports – Egyptian cotton, Burmese rice, Icelandic fish. The USSR then

---

[1] The Message of the President to Congress, quoted in Goldwin (29).
[2] This hope was expressed in the same 1961 aid message to Congress.
[3] Lenin had observed soon after the Revolution that the road to Paris lies through Calcutta and Peking.

offered to buy the goods, sometimes at a premium.[1] The opening of trade relations was accompanied by an exchange of
cultural and goodwill missions and visits of political dignitaries
and offers of economic missions. The USSR was using economic
relations as a part of its wider objective of establishing close
relations with the developing countries, but the international
situation was such that, while promoting its cause, it could in
fact claim truthfully that it was only helping the developing
countries to achieve their own aspirations of economic and
political independence of the West. Whether this independence
would bring about changes favourable to the USSR – in social
systems and political institutions – is another question.

In dealing with the developing countries the USSR had certain
advantages, such as its ability to move quickly to respond to
changed situations and its lack of a colonial past. In fact, the Soviet
spokesmen could sympathise with the developing countries, pointing to the fact that the USSR had also suffered at the hands of
Western countries in the 1920s. Khrushchev, in a speech made at
the Aswan Dam, referred to the lack of support and the consequent hardships the USSR had to suffer at the hands of Western
powers. In fact, he listed this as one of the motives for the Soviet
Union's economic cooperation with the developing countries.[2]

Just as the United States learnt from the USSR's experience
later, the latter had learnt from the initial reactions of developing countries and its programme was tailored accordingly.

The chief characteristics of Soviet economic cooperation are:

1. Emphasis on 'equality' between partners. The newly
liberated countries were very sensitive about inferior status.
The Soviet spokesmen therefore emphasised that it was an equal
partnership. One consequence of this was that they offered not
'humiliating charity', i.e. grants, but businesslike loans.

2. Coordination between trade and aid policies. They looked
upon this cooperation as a means of finding markets for
machinery and equipment and obtaining raw materials from
developing countries. The reasons for this are partly economic

---

[1] The Sino–Soviet bloc's economic activities in the underdeveloped countries
have been described in the pamphlets and booklets produced by the U.S. Department of State and various Congressional Committees (see e.g. 87, 88, 89 and 90).
[2] Khrushchev's speech (49).

necessity and partly political expediency. R. L. Allen has pointed out that, since the USSR has concentrated on the development of heavy industry since the Revolution, the internal cost structure has changed in such a manner that it is advantageous to increase exports of machinery and import raw materials, especially agricultural products.[1] From this point of view, developing countries would be suitable trading partners for the socialist economies. It does not follow from this either that economic considerations were predominant in the Soviet Union's decisions to establish trade relations with developing countries or that any particular deal was profitable. Many American writers sought to argue in the fifties that, because the USSR opened relations with particular countries (Ghana, Egypt, Burma, Argentina) in the wake of its difficulties with Western countries, the USSR's trade was the result of political opportunism and not economic necessity.[2]

There is no necessary contradiction between the two, however. The choice of a particular source of supply may be dictated by political expediency, but the need may still be genuine. The choice of trading partners should not be confused with the composition of trade, or the necessity or desirability of obtaining certain goods from abroad.

The main attraction of the East European credits for developing countries was that the former were willing to accept repayment in kind. They were far ahead of others in recognising the need for linking trade and aid policies.

3. 'Non-interference' in the internal affairs of developing countries. The USSR scored a propaganda victory by underlining the fact that it offered no advice – political or economic – regarding development strategy priorities and policies. At a conference in Dar-es-Salaam, a Soviet Academician said, 'The cooperation between the socialist and the liberated countries is a vivid demonstration of the fact that the countries of the capitalist economic system and the socialist countries can not only live in peace, but can develop excellent business relations. This cooperation between equals rules out any sort of interference in the internal affairs of other states or any violation of their national sovereignty.[3]

[1] Allen (3, ch. 3).   [2] See U.S. State Department booklets (87, 88, 89, 90).
[3] Martynov (49, p. 70).

4. Aid with 'no strings' attached. This is somewhat different from the previous point. The 'no strings' argument was aimed at American reluctance to give aid to non-aligned countries or countries friendly to the USSR. Thus, Martynov says, 'When the socialist countries grant aid to the liberated countries, they never object to those countries accepting credits from the Western countries.'

5. All East European aid was tied to projects and to the country of origin.

6. The East European aid was mainly directed towards the public sector industries. Since one of the objectives of Soviet policy is to reduce Western economic domination, it is natural that their credits should be directed at challenging the monopoly of Western firms. In explaining how Soviet aid can remove the obstacles to development, Martynov says, 'Industrialisation is the most complicated problem for the liberated countries at their present stage of development. This is not only due to the almost complete absence of internal capacities for producing machines and equipment, to the shortage of investment funds, to the shortage of specialists and skilled workers and to poorly surveyed natural resources, but also to the opposition of international monopolies.'[1] In a policy pamphlet produced by the Soviet economic mission to the U.N. the same point is made, that the Soviet Union contributes to liberation from economic domination by supporting industrial development.[2]

7. The East European countries first adopted the practice of announcing credits well in advance of the plan, thus facilitating the integration of external and domestic resources.

8. It is interesting that the character of the East European aid programme has changed little over the years, and that the countries concerned have not responded to new situations with new techniques.

The preceding discussion of the foreign aid policies of major donors shows how the international aid climate changed over a relatively short period – between 1955 and 1958. The change was due to a number of factors. The impact of the increasing debt service burden and the unfavourable prospects for exports

[1] See Martynov (49, p. 70).
[2] USSR mission to the U.N. (91, pp. 2–3).

of primary products were increasingly realised. However, there is some truth in Khrushchev's boast that Western aid is a special form of Soviet aid.[1]

While as a result of rivalry among donors, external official funds became available for long-term planning from 1950 to 1960, the Government of India on its part also changed its attitude towards external finance and resigned itself to the fact that substantial and continuing external support would be necessary to implement the programme for industrialisation. The change in attitude towards external assistance was a function of the success of Indian foreign policy and of the foreign exchange situation.

Before launching the programme of industrialisation, India's foreign exchange position was comfortable, but it deteriorated very rapidly. Table 1 brings out how foreign exchange requirements rose much faster than foreign exchange earnings.

From 1950/1 to 1960/1 imports rose from Rs.6,500 million to Rs.11,400 or by 75 per cent and further to Rs.19,040 million in 1968, or by 67 per cent. During the same years, exports were Rs.6,010 million, Rs.6,600 million and Rs.13,600 million respectively, i.e. they increased by some 10 per cent and 106 per cent respectively. Table 1 also shows that, while savings and investment as a percentage of net domestic product were equal in 1950/1, and savings were only marginally less (7 per cent of net national product) compared to investment (7·6 per cent of net national product) in 1955/6, domestic investment exceeded domestic savings by 3·7 per cent in 1960/1, by 2·8 per cent in 1965/6 and by 2·5 per cent in 1968/9, and this gap was filled from external resources.[2] The pattern of proposed financing shows both an increasing dependence on external resources from the First to the Third Plan and a desire for self-reliance, in that only 1·3 per cent of the proposed investment will be financed from external resources in 1973/4.

Just one example can bring out the tremendous foreign exchange difficulties faced. Even during the Second Plan, exports were only about 60 per cent of total imports. For the Third

---

[1] A speech by Khrushchev quoted by Tansky(78, p. 5).

[2] Because of devaluation in June 1966, the rupee value of external loans increased in 1968/9 compared to the pre-1966 period. In fact the relative decline in external assistance (measured in dollars) was more marked than shown by the figures here.

Table 1 *Domestic product, saving, investment and foreign trade, 1950/1 to 1980/1*

	1950/1	1955/6	1960/1	1965/6	1968/9	1973/4	1978/9	1980/1
Net domestic product at factor cost: thous. million Rs. [a]	159·6	188·1	208·6	259·7	290·7	383·3	517·0	582·0
Growth rate [a]		3·4	4·0	2·6	3·9	5·7	6·2	6·1
Mid-year population: millions [a]	357	390	433	487	527	596	666	690
Growth rate [a]		1·8	2·1	2·3	2·7	2·5	2·3	1·7
Per capita net domestic product: Rs. [a]	447	482	528	533	552	643	776	844
Growth rate [a]		1·5	1·8	0·2	1·2	3·1	3·9	4·2
Income from agriculture and allied activities: thous. million Rs. [a]	101·6	117·4	135·7	127·7	148·6	189·5	234·0	254·0
Growth rate [a]		2·9	2·9	−1·3	3·0	5·1	4·3	4·2
Income from mining, manufacturing and construction thous. million Rs. [a]	24·9	29·7	38·2	51·9	55·0	80·6	126·0	150·0
Growth rate [a]		3·6	5·2	6·3	2·0	7·9	9·3	9·1
Income from other activities: thous. million Rs. [a]	33·1	41·0	54·7	80·1	87·1	113·0	157·0	178·0
Growth rate [a]		4·3	5·9	7·9	2·8	5·4	6·8	6·4
Investment–income ratio (per cent) [b]	5·0	7·6	11·5	13·6	11·3[c]	14·5	16·7	17·7

External resources–income ratio (per cent)[a]		0·6	3·7	2·8	2·5[c]	1·3	−0·3	−0·3
Saving–income ratio (per cent)[e]								
(i) Household	5·0	7·0	7·8	10·8[f]	8·8	13·2	17·0	18·0
(ii) Corporate	3·1	5·1	5·3	6·3	6·4	7·6		8·4
(iii) Government	0·8	0·7	1·5	3·3	1·4	4·5		8·2
Imports (thous. million Rs.)[g]	6·5	6·8	11·4	14·1	19·0	22·2	26·8	29·5
Exports (thous. million Rs.)[g]	6·0	6·0	6·5	8·1	13·6	19·0	26·5	30·2

[a] Compound annual rate of growth over the previous column.

[b] Investment figures from 1955/6 to 1965/6 have been taken from a report, 'Economic Recovery', Perspective Planning Division, Planning Commission.

[c] Differs from data available to the Reserve Bank of India, according to which external assistance formed 1·7 per cent of national income and hence investment–income ratio was 10·5 per cent.

[d] External assistance data up to 1965/66 are as reported by the Reserve Bank of India.

[e] The breakdown of saving–income ratio into household, corporate and government sectors up to 1965/6 has been worked out by the Reserve Bank on the basis of the ratio observed among these categories on the basis of data calculated by the Reserve Bank. Data on saving from 1955/6 to 1965/6 have been arrived at after deducting external assistance, as reported by the Reserve Bank, from investment, as available from the 'Economic Recovery' report.

[f] According to the Fourth Plan, 10·5 per cent.

[g] At current prices.

Note: Net domestic product and income is at 1968/9 prices.

Source: RBI Bulletin, July 1970.

Plan, however, the projected maintenance imports (admittedly underestimated at Rs.3,850 million) alone were in excess of projected exports during the plan.[1] In other words, any new investment with a foreign exchange component would have had to be financed by external capital inflows.

In light of the critical foreign exchange situation reached by 1958, the rescue operation organised by the World Bank in that year to cope with the foreign exchange crisis was well received in official circles. India's Finance Minister, commenting on the first meeting of the Consortium,[2] said in Loksabha, 'On the 13th August, 1958, I made a statement in this House on the "Foreign Exchange Situation". I referred therein to the Conference to be convened by the International Bank for Reconstruction and Development to discuss the Indian situation in respect of foreign exchange and the manner in which India could be helped ... There was a general recognition that the tempo of development that has already been built up in this country over the past few years should be maintained with due regard to financial and economic stability. I wish to mention here that the World Bank played a crucial role in bringing to successful fruition the discussions regarding our immediate requirements of external assistance ... I am glad to say that no conditions have been attached to this offer of assistance ... The friendliness shown at the Conference was backed by concrete indications of the assistance to be extended to us for carrying forward the Second Five Year Plan. In the main, these indications related to the credits to be made available over the immediate period ahead ending March 31, 1959, though our needs for the rest of the Plan period were taken note of. There was also a general recognition of the fact that an effective contribution towards India's economic advance could be made only if assistance ... could be made available sufficiently on a long-term or continuing basis.'[3]

The Finance Minister emphasised that there were no con-

---

[1] See *The Third Five-Year Plan*, section on exports and imports (126).

[2] Aid India Consortium. This is a group of Western governments including the U.S.A., Great Britain, Canada, West Germany (FRG), France, Italy, Japan, and the IDA, organised by the World Bank.

[3] Excerpts from the original statement made in Loksabha quoted by the Finance Minister on his visit to the United Kingdom, the United States and Canada, August–September 1958.

ditions attached to this finance, but even the willingness to treat external finance as an integral part of the long-term development programme represents a tremendous psychological change from the early years of independence. From the earlier view that receiving aid was humiliating, Indian statesmen had come to regard it as necessary in the transitional period, believing also that India was a deserving and worthy client.[1]

This coordination between donors and recipients can be indirectly inferred by a comparison between expected and actual inflows of external official finance. As table 2 below shows, the divergence between expectations and actual assistance received was much smaller in the Second Plan than in the First. In the Third Plan, expectations differed from actual receipts by only 1 per cent. The reason is that the size of India's requirements and likely availability were discussed beforehand between Consortium members and the Indian Government.[2]

The close coordination between donors and the Government of India represents a tremendous change in that even though policy advice offered by the Consortium countries may be interpreted as a 'string', the Indian Government came to accept it.

Table 2   *External assistance expected and received*

Percentages of total resources available

	First Five Year Plan	Second Five Year Plan	Third Five Year Plan	Annual Plans 1966/9
Original estimates	25.2	16.7	29.3	36.5
Actual	9.6	22.5	28.2	35.9

[1] This sentiment was expressed by the then Indian Ambassador to Washington B. K. Nehru, thus: 'India is unwilling to generate internally all the necessary capital to reach the point of take-off by the most obvious means: viz. by changing the institutional framework of Indian society through restricting seriously the individual liberties and democratic freedoms which we so proudly cherish and which give us so much strength. For India, the alternative to such restrictions is to receive, temporarily, greater assistance from other nations.'

[2] It is the normal practice of the World Bank to send a team ahead of the Consortium meeting to study recent economic developments in the country concerned and form a judgement about the borrower's requirements for external financing.

The acceptance of this 'aid and advice' package deal meant that the philosophy of planning also underwent a radical change.

The East European countries did not offer policy advice as such. Nonetheless, it is worth examining whether the establishment of economic relations with the East European countries affected India's approach to planning. The term 'approach to planning' may mean different things. For example, it may mean (a) the attitude towards planning *per se*, i.e. whether planning for development is necessary and desirable, (b) the goals of planning, (c) the strategy and (d) the tools of planning.

From the timing of the first two decisions, it is clear that the establishment of economic relations with the East European countries had little to do with the commitment to long-term planning or the objective of achieving a more equitable income distribution. Even before achieving independence there was a planning committee in Congress (National Planning Committee) chaired by Nehru himself, which advocated the desirability of long-term planning and prepared some studies. Nehru attached great importance to the establishment of a planning commission, which was set up at around the same time the constitution was adopted, long before Indo-East European cooperation began. This was when the cold war was being intensified and the USSR exploded her first hydrogen bomb. It is unlikely that the United States was very enthusiastic about the adoption of centralised planning by India, and Britain was not in a position to provide massive financial assistance.

Among the objectives of planning, emphasis on equitable distribution of income and equal opportunities is closely associated with socialist thinking. Again this objective was adopted long before the Second Plan was formulated. The constitution[1] listed this objective in 1950.

The important, perhaps decisive, factors in Indian planning were Nehru's personality and convictions. His thinking was undeniably influenced by his visit to the USSR in 1927 and by the impact which the Russian Revolution and USSR's subsequent history made on him and his generation.[2] His pre-

[1] Constitution of the Republic of India, chapters on directive principles of state policy.　　　[2] Mahalanobis (46, p. 1) makes this point.

independence efforts to produce a blueprint for a plan bear testimony to his genuine conviction that planning was essential to solve the twin problems of unemployment and poverty.

The phrase 'socialist pattern of society' gained currency in the mid-fifties at the time when Indo-Soviet relations were being consolidated, but the underlying principle – public ownership of the means of production – had been advocated by Nehru long before. In one of his speeches on economic policy, Nehru pointed out that National Congress 'accepted this principle about 17 years ago – the nationalisation of ownership or control of defence and key industries and public utilities – and I do believe that such industries will have to be nationalised some time or other'.[1]

When the Second Plan was prepared and the strategy of developing heavy industry in the public sector was adopted, the USSR offered a credit for a steel plant, but there was no expectation of a continuous flow of funds from the socialist countries. At this stage, China was at least as influential in India as the USSR, and China was not giving any credits.

Since the USSR was the first country to adopt centralised planning as the tool for development, it is natural that Indian planners should have studied the Russians' experience and learnt from it. There are many similarities between the Mahalanobis two-sector model and the Soviet-type model. The influence is noticeable in both the strategy of industrial development and the tools of planning.

In a recent book about the socialist planning experience and its applicability to the developing countries, C. Wilber outlines the Soviet-type model. The preconditions of this model are: severance of any colonial bond, elimination of economic domination by foreign capitalists and a redistribution of economic and political power. The institutional characteristics include collectivised agriculture, public ownership of enterprises, comprehensive central planning, centralised distribution of essential materials and capital goods and a system of administrative controls and pressures on enterprises to ensure compliance with the plan. The strategy of development encompasses a high rate of capital formation; priority of basic capital goods industries; bias in favour of modern, capital-intensive technologies in key

[1] Nehru (55, pp. 110–11).

2

processes combined with labour-intensive techniques in auxiliary operations, and import substitution policy in international trade; utilisation of underemployed labour for capital formation and heavy investment in human capital.[1]

The Mahalanobis two-sector model also emphasises high rates of capital formation and gives high priority to building up heavy industry in the public sector. Two lines of thought dominated Mahalanobis' thinking. Given the capital output ratio, the rate of growth of income depends upon the increment of invested income. This was a familiar approach to growth, which had already been adopted by Harrod and Domar[2] and was not necessarily a socialist scheme.

The second predominant theme in Mahalanobis' thinking was that the rate of development in the long run depends upon the pattern of investment. Thus he says, 'The capacity to invest (without import of capital goods) in any one year is determined by the pattern of volume of production of capital goods in the previous year. The rate of expansion of the basic industries, therefore, sets a limit to the rate of growth of the economy as a whole and may constitute a second limiting factor.'[3] Therefore, the strategy recommended was import substitution by investment in heavy industries. This has been described as a Soviet-type industrialisation by Rosenstein-Rodan,[4] and it has been suggested that the adoption of this strategy may be partly due to the fact that Mahalanobis had close contacts with Russian economists and was impressed with the Soviet thinking on industrialisation.[5]

While Mahalanobis himself, and Nehru, who was equally enthusiastic about heavy industry, may have been impressed by what they saw in the USSR, the basic reason why Nehru thought the USSR's experience was relevant to India was his firm commitment to the goal of economic independence and his belief that development had to be financed by Indian efforts. Thus, in a speech called 'Bullock Cart, Motor Lorry, Jet Plane'

[1] Wilber (96, p. 13).
[2] See Harrod (30) and Domar (24).   [3] Mahalanobis (46).
[4] Rosenstein-Rodan in (1, p. 245). In his essay he classifies two types of industrialisation, one adopted by the USSR and the other in the West. The latter was characterised by its adherence to the principle of the international division of labour.
[5] Bhagwati and Chakravarty (9, p. 7).

he justified heavy industries thus: 'if we industrialise we have
to have certain basic, key, mother industries in the country ...
out of which other industries grow. If we do not do that, we
shall remain dependent upon others.'[1] In this context he pointed
out that, even in Japan, capital industries were developed first.[2]

Without entering into the controversy about whether
Mahalanobis was influenced by the Feldman model or whether
he arrived at his conclusions independently, it is worth pointing
out some striking similarities. In describing the Feldman model,
Domar says that the economy is divided into two sectors.
Category 1 produces capital goods, category 2 consumer goods
and the division is complete. The implications therefore are
that 'in the closed economy the rate of investment is rigidly
determined by the capital coefficient and the stock of capital in
category 1. Similarly the output of consumer goods is determined by the stock of capital and the capital coefficient of
category 2. Hence the division of total output between consumption and investment at any given moment depends on the
relative productive capacities of the two categories and not on
the propensity to save, though the latter can reassert itself by
causing an underutilisation of the capital stock in one category
or another, a waste ruled out in the model. The division of total
investment (that is, of output of category 1) between the two
categories is, however, completely flexible. Indeed, the fraction
of total investment allocated to category 1 is the key variable
of the model.'[3]

Mahalanobis also approached the problem of maximising
long-term growth as one of maximising the output of the capital
goods industries, but did not treat the question of the economy's
saving propensity independently. As Bhagwati and Chakravarty
point out, Mahalanobis made the savings rate a rigid function
of certain structural features, such as the capacity of the
domestic capital goods industry and the capital output ratios
of the capital goods sector and the consumer goods sector.[4]

While the similarities between the two models are undeniable,
it would be a gross oversimplification to conclude that the
planners adopted the strategy of industrialisation because the
USSR offered credits. The policy makers – especially Nehru –

[1] Nehru (56, p. 61).   [2] Nehru (56).
[3] Domar (24, p. 229).   [4] Bhagwati and Chakravarty (9, p. 6).

may have genuinely believed that India was facing a similar situation to that of the USSR on the verge of industrialisation, and that therefore the Soviet model was more relevant. One may agree or disagree with the emphasis on economic independence and the planners' assessment of export prospects. The justification of the strategy should not, however, be confused with the motives.

As Wilber points out, the USSR has opened a new era of forced economic growth in agriculturally overpopulated countries.[1] Many of the developing countries are characterised by a stagnant agricultural sector and a small industrial sector dominated by foreign investors and are anxious to force the pace of industrialisation. Spulber points out that the possibility of automatically fulfilling 'realistic capital formation targets by planning in physical terms, in countries with defective statistical information and unresponsive price mechanisms' is also an added attraction.[2]

It is tempting now to attribute the Indian planning strategy to Soviet influence because the perspective of planning has changed and some of the decisions which may have been justified then do not appear to be so with hindsight.

It would not be valid to say that the strategy of building up heavy industries for capital accumulation and cottage industries to meet the demand for consumer goods was the result of copying the Soviet experience. There were good reasons for developing cottage industries, such as their employment potential, relatively low capital and foreign exchange requirements and, most important, Mahatma Gandhi's philosophy. Support of village industries was a long-standing commitment of the Congress party and may have won more converts to planning among Congressmen whose sympathies were not socialist.

Reference to cottage industries brings out another reason why the Soviet experiment may have been considered particularly suitable. People of Nehru's generation had watched the misery and unemployment during the depression. At least until the Second World War, Western countries could not claim to have solved the problem of unemployment. Nehru realised

[1] Wilber (96, p. 1).
[2] Spulber (77, pp. 127–8).

the importance of achieving full employment as an independent objective. Since the socialist countries had attained full employment, that may have been an added attraction for choosing Soviet-type industrialisation – saving up the scarce resources, capital and foreign exchange, for investment in capital goods industries, and using labour-intensive techniques for producing consumer goods.

Within the framework of overall objectives and strategy, the adoption of which was influenced more by domestic factors than inspiration from the USSR, the relative priorities of sectors and industries may have been influenced by the availability of East European credits because of the foreign exchange constraint. This question is discussed in detail in chapter 5.

Establishment of economic relations may have influenced the approach to planning by facilitating exchange of ideas regarding planning techniques. Again, just the fact that the USSR had the experience and expertise necessary for centralised planning may be more relevant than the establishment of economic relations as such. One important example of this influence is the importance attached to physical planning – working out commodity balances within the framework of a long-term perspective plan. Mahalanobis talks about the importance of financial planning and avoiding inflation. However, the tools for financial planning were not well developed and even a discussion of this subject is a relatively new development.[1] In the Mahalanobis model, the role of the pricing mechanism is ignored.

Moreover, Mahalanobis seems to have assumed that, if capital goods were available, investors would, in fact, want to invest in those industries and would have the financial resources available. Investment decisions in period $t+1$ would be determined by the output of investment goods industries only if these decisions were made or controlled by the state. Otherwise, in a closed economy, the capacity of investment goods industries would only impose a *ceiling* on investment.

Before turning to the main theme of the book, India's trade and credit relationship with the Eastern European countries, it is worth raising the question of possible political effects of this aid on India's internal and external policy, because these countries scored a tremendous propaganda victory by describing

[1] See Bhatt (10) and Divetia (23).

their aid as being without any strings and based on the principle of non-interference in the recipient's internal affairs.

The hypothesis is that the USSR did not interfere with Indian foreign policy or internal affairs. In that sense, Soviet aid was without strings. The argument is not that the Soviet Union did not interfere because of altruistic motives, but that it suited her interests best. Eldridge, in his recent study of the politics of foreign aid to India, rightly argues that Indo-Soviet relations were dominated by foreign policy considerations and that the USSR did not actively support the Communist Party of India (CPI).[1]

Indo-Soviet political relations can be appreciated fully only against the background of the new, i.e. post-Stalin, foreign policy towards the developing countries and the role assigned to India and India's own attitude towards international relations, especially with great powers. Indo-Soviet relations formed a part of the general campaign by the Soviet Union to make friends among the developing countries. Most of the newly liberated countries were still economically dependent on the West for markets, technical know-how and capital but were anxious to break free. Since the USSR had no foothold among these countries, it was no sacrifice to express sympathy with their aspirations for independence. On the contrary, reducing Western influence among these countries was a desirable development. Therefore, the aspirations of developing countries for economic independence coincided with the USSR's interest. The policies advocated by newly liberated developing countries were threatening the vested interests of Western powers, and it was natural that they should try to protect their interests. In so doing, however, they exposed themselves to charges of interference, whereas all the USSR had to do was to side with the developing country.

The description given above is very general and obviously the USSR has tailored its strategy and tactics to local circumstances. Generally speaking, however, the goal of Soviet policy was to promote friendly relations with the developing countries and this necessarily involved supporting the local bourgeoisie – the leaders of the movement for independence – who generally formed the government. Again, supporting the nationalist

[1] Eldridge (25, p. 50).

bourgeoisie did not necessarily mean that the USSR was not interested in promoting the interests of the local communist party, but that that was a secondary objective.

While Indo-Soviet relations conformed to the general pattern, India was given special treatment for the following reasons. First, India was one of the first countries under colonial rule to gain independence and take an independent stand on world matters. Her views were very close to those advocated by the Soviet statesmen. Secondly, because of her size and stable leadership, and the policies advocated by the Indian Government – consistent opposition to imperialism and colonialism – the country had earned a special place among the developing countries. Thirdly, because of her geographic location and the Soviet Union's concern about communist China, the USSR may have been anxious to have India on her side. The Sino-Soviet conflict did not start till the late 1950s, but the Russian statesmen may have expected some trouble from a strong China.

Since the USSR was anxious to establish her good faith among developing countries by demonstrating that she did not intend to interfere in the internal affairs of the country concerned, it was in her interest to make sure that India was not only acting completely independently, but was seen to be acting independently. India's reputation as an independent non-aligned country was in itself an asset for the USSR because the two governments saw eye to eye on many world problems. At least until Nehru's death, India's stand on many matters carried some weight with other developing countries. From the Soviet Union's point of view it was desirable to have India criticise Great Britain and France in the Suez crisis, for example, or the United States in the first Cuban crisis. In a sense, India had nothing to gain by opposing these powers, which provided financial assistance, whereas the USSR was obviously an interested party and its criticism would not be accepted in the same manner as Indian criticism.

It is interesting to mention in this context that Indo-Chinese relations became strained around 1958 – before the rift between the USSR and China was acknowledged. However, the Soviet Union and other East European countries made no effort to withdraw any credits. On the contrary, the USSR and Czechoslovakia announced new credits to be utilised for projects during the Third Plan. Similarly, after the 1962 Indo-Chinese border dispute, the Russians did not refuse to sell defence equipment but agreed to set up a MIG-21 factory in India. To this day, the USSR remains an important supplier of defence equipment.

On India's side, the establishment of economic relations with the USSR and other East European countries did not represent a fundamental departure in foreign policy or a sharp break with past practice.[1] One of the basic tenets of foreign policy was non-alignment and opposition to military alliances, and the government had maintained that position since independence. In a speech made by Nehru in the Constituent Assembly[2] in 1948, he emphasised that non-alignment was the best policy for India.[3] An AICC resolution passed in 1948 presents a good, if rather self-righteous, summary of how the ruling party viewed foreign policy.

At the annual session of the Indian National Congress, the party adopted a resolution that 'the foreign policy of India must necessarily be based on principles which have guided the Congress in the past years. These principles are the promotion of world peace, the freedom of all nations, racial equality and the ending of imperialism and colonialism ... It should be the constant aim of the foreign policy of India to maintain friendly and cooperative relations with all nations and to avoid entanglements in military or similar alliances which tend to divide the world in rival groups and thus endanger world peace.'[4]

India's stand on non-alignment is too well known to need any elaboration, but a brief review will show the direction of Indian foreign policy. In line with its policy of establishing friendly relations with the USSR, diplomatic relations were established in 1947 and India was the second non-communist country to grant recognition to China's new communist government in 1950. The Government of India advocated China's admission

[1] The background material used to discuss Indian foreign policy is foreign policy debates in Loksabha, Nehru's speeches on foreign policy, texts of documents concerning Indian Foreign Policy, 1947–64, and U.N. debates on Kashmir, Goa and Hungary, and the books by Karunakaran (36) and Rajan (69).

[2] An assembly formed for preparing the Indian Constitution.

[3] Nehru (55, pp. 211–20).

[4] This resolution of the All India Congress Committee (AICC) is quoted from Varma (92, p. 1).

to the U.N., opposed its condemnation in Korea as an aggressor, and sought to bring about peace in Korea. If friendship with the socialist countries did not develop before 1954, the problem was lack of opportunity and not lack of will.

It is undeniable that after 1956 India moved much closer to the USSR than before, but this friendship with the Soviet Union did not represent a fundamental departure in India's policy either towards the USSR or towards others; nor was it influenced by the Russian's willingness to offer credits. This hypothesis is supported by the fact that even though communist China did not offer any credits, India was quick to recognise China. Indeed India had to accept China's claim to Tibet in 1954, and was willing to pay this price to keep up its idealistic stance in foreign policy.

Between 1954 and 1956, Indo-Soviet cooperation increased very rapidly, backed by exchanges of ideas, goodwill missions, and visits by senior political dignitaries of both countries. The socialist countries were among the first to accept Prime Minister Nehru's famous five principles of 'Panchshil' – admittedly only because it suited their own ends. Nonetheless, the fact that China and the USSR were willing to accept 'peaceful co-existence' with other nations gave this doctrine wide circulation and enhanced India's prestige in the world.[1] During his visit to India in 1955, Marshal Bulganin went as far as to say 'Soviet-Indian relations based on the famous five principles convincingly confirm the correctness of the thesis of possibility of peaceful co-existence and friendly cooperation of states with different socio-political systems.'[2] In fact, the joint communique issued at the end of Nehru's visit to the USSR in 1955 extended the third principle of non-interference in each other's internal affairs to include 'for any reasons of an economic, political or ideological character'.[3]

In the 1950s its financial credits were not big enough to give the USSR any leverage in Indian politics, but nevertheless the Soviet Union's friendship was very important. The geography and politics of the Indian sub-continent, with its division between India and Pakistan, are such that if one country draws

[1] For a detailed description of Indo–Soviet relations during the period 1954–6, see Rajan (69).
[2] Bulganin (cited in 119, p. 494).   [3] *Ibid.* p. 486.

close to one super-power, the other is likely to make friends with
the adversary. After independence there was a feeling in India
that the Western powers favoured Pakistan. This feeling was
partly generated by the Kashmir problem, a brief summary of
which is perhaps in order.[1] The Indian Government took the
matter to the United Nations. After the ruler of Kashmir,
supported by the National Conference, an organisation led by
Sheikh Abdullah and having a large following in Kashmir, had
signed a treaty of accession with the Government of India
following a request for military aid, Kashmir had been attacked
by raiders supported by the Pakistan Government. The Indian
Government approached the U.N. to first ensure cessation of
hostilities; Pakistan wanted a plebiscite to be conducted, supervised by an international commission. The Indian Government
counterproposed a return to peaceful conditions *first*, to be
followed by a plebiscite supervised by an international commission but administered by the Kashmir administration. The
cease-fire was arranged after much discussion in 1949, but the
international commission did not obtain the withdrawal of
Pakistan forces from Kashmir. Since then, accepting the *status
quo*, Pakistan has brought up the question of a plebiscite at
regular intervals in the Security Council.

Against this background and the support given by Britain
and the United States to Pakistan's position, the Government
of India was concerned about the repercussions of Pakistan's
joining an American-sponsored military alliance. Indian statesmen felt that Pakistan would exploit her membership to gain
further support for a plebiscite in Kashmir. What the Indian
Government needed was a friend in the Security Council to
veto any unacceptable resolutions. The USSR used her veto
many times on India's behalf. The USSR's popularity was due
to the unequivocal stand Bulganin and Khrushchev took on the
Kashmir issue during their visit in 1955. Eldridge in his
book, while emphasising the limitations of a public opinion
survey, points out that after the Bulganin and Khrushchev visit
there was a marked pro-Soviet trend and that the public
attitude was much more influenced by the outsiders' stand on

[1] For a history of the Kashmir problem, see Karunakaran (36, ch. 6), debates in Loksabha on Kashmir problems and debates in the Security Council
(84).

Kashmir and Goa than by foreign aid.[1] It is interesting to note in this connection also that there was some tension following the 1965 Indo-Pakistan war and subsequent wooing of Pakistan by the Soviet Union.

The fact that Nehru, as the chief architect of foreign policy, cherished a friendship with the USSR, did not mean as is often suggested, that his policy became pro-Soviet. There is one concrete case in which the Government of India's stand in the U.N. was apparently affected by its anxiety not to offend the USSR, viz. the U.N. debates on the Hungarian crisis. The criticism was that there was a sharp contrast between Indian reaction to the Suez and to the Hungarian crises. Indian condemnation of the USSR's actions was not forthright and India abstained from voting for certain U.N. resolutions – especially the one on 4 November 1956.

The Indian Government's policy on the Hungarian question and the U.N. vote on 4 November were, however, something of a special case, part of the explanation lying in Nehru's mistrust of reports by the Western press. One of Nehru's reservations was in the inability of the Indian Government to verify the facts in the Hungarian situation: there was no senior Indian diplomat present in Budapest when the events occurred and the Government of India had to rely on the Western press and Marshal Tito.[2] Nehru's reaction when expressed was quite clearcut and unambiguous. His views were expressed rather late – on 5 November (the crisis started in the third week of October). He said in a speech at the Ninth General Conference of UNESCO at New Delhi, 'We see today in Egypt as well as Hungary both human dignity and freedom outraged and the force of modern arms used to suppress peoples and to gain political objectives.'[3] Four days later, at an AICC meeting, he supported the right of the Hungarian people to decide their form of government without external pressure.

If Nehru was willing to take the risk of offending the USSR in public, it is at first glance difficult to see why India voted against some resolutions in the General Assembly on 4 and 9

[1] Eldridge (25, pp. 91–2).
[2] *The Hindu*, 6 November 1956, quoted in Rajan (69).
[3] *The Hindu*, 10 November 1956, report on the AICC resolution, quoted in Rajan (69).

November. A plausible explanation may be the personality of the chief Indian delegate, Krishna Menon. A more likely explanation is, however, that the Indian Government was worried about the suggestion that the withdrawal of foreign forces be accompanied by a general election held under U.N. auspices.[1] Hence, the concern for dealing with a member state as though it were struggling for its independence. The five-power 9 November resolution, for example, called for U.N.-supervised elections in Hungary and this was probably the main factor. Menon added in a discussion on this resolution that no member who was supporting the proposal that the United Nations should hold elections in Hungary would like a similar move in respect of his own country.[2] Nehru in his defence of this vote in Parliament perhaps went a step further and said that the motivation and object behind it was 'to run down India because India had taken a strong line in the U.N. about various matters'. Nehru was probably worried that Pakistan might use this vote as a precedent in re-opening the Kashmir question. Pakistan had been pressing for a plebiscite in Kashmir but this was unacceptable to the Government of India.

To sum up then, economic aid was not offered or withdrawn as a price for good or bad behaviour. If the USSR and India shared common views on many subjects it was because of the anti-colonial, anti-capitalistic bias of India's policy makers and the desire for economic independence, which coincided with the USSR's interests. After India became independent of Great Britain in 1947, freedom was automatically interpreted as freedom from Western political and economic domination. This ideological bias was reinforced by the politics of the subcontinent – the fact that Pakistan became a military ally of the NATO countries whereas India was only a friend, at best. Geographical factors also played a part in this relationship. It is precisely because of the need to behave just as a good friend and no more that the USSR's scope for direct action in internal politics has been limited. In fact, the history of the Indian communist party (CPI) shows that the USSR not only did not

[1] Excerpts from Menon's speech to the General Assembly Emergency Supplementary Session, 569th Meeting, p. 44. Quoted in Rajan (69).

[2] Debates in the General Assembly, 571st Meeting of the General Assembly O.R. II, Emergency Supplementary Session, pp. 68 and 75, quoted by Rajan (69).

exert any pressure on the Indian Government, but did not hesitate to side with the latter, thus embarrassing the CPI. For example before Soviet statesmen blessed Indian foreign policy in 1955, the CPI had been very critical of it and had to reverse its stand.[1] What must have been equally embarrassing was the fact that none of the Indian communist leaders were held in such high esteem in the USSR as Nehru. Nor were they admitted to the inner circles of the communist leadership.

In discussing the possible political effects of economic cooperation with the Soviet Union, the question can be treated at two levels: first, government policy towards, say, the CPI or right-wing groups; second, whether cooperation with the USSR changed public opinion or altered the fundamental balance of power in such a manner as to promote the cause of parties advocating socialist principles.

At the first level the question is relatively easy. The CPI always functioned as an independent party in India and as such participated in elections, and there has been no change in policy. During Nehru's time government policy towards the CPI was consistent. Nehru openly ridiculed its loyalty to other powers. The CPI was not granted special favours because of Indo-USSR friendship. In response to popular unrest at Kerala, the government imposed President's rule, even though the communist controlled government had not requested help. Recently the central government reacted to a crisis in West Bengal (another communist-controlled state government) in the same manner.

The other question, however, is much deeper, and cannot be answered so easily. It is this author's opinion, however, that, while the USSR may have made a favourable impression on public opinion, foreign policy was not an important issue in any of the elections. Also, to ensure friendship with the USSR it was not necessary to have a communist government. The Congress Government was friendly with the USSR. Therefore the fortunes of political parties depended much more on their stand on local issues, leadership and organisation.[2] Looking back at

---

[1] For the CPI's attitude to foreign policy, see Overstreet and Windmüller (62) and foreign policy debates in the Loksabha (118).

[2] Many people in India believe that the USSR has contributed significantly to the finances of the CPI, and therefore to its success in elections. There seems to be no concrete evidence, but the success of this operation depends on its being kept secret.

the history of general elections it is undeniable that the CPI has improved its position significantly – especially in West Bengal and Kerala. However, its success has been very uneven, depending upon local circumstances, and the USSR's aid policies have had little to do with it.

The possible political effects of Indo-Soviet aid were mainly in two directions. First: the impact of availability of credits from the USSR on the policies of other donors, discussed partly in this chapter and partly in the next. Second: by making available credits for industries in the public sector, the pattern of investment between public and private sectors was influenced to some extent. The resultant income distribution in favour of the public sector may have had some political consequences, but it is too early to assess these effects.

In other words, the political effects of Indo-Soviet economic cooperation will result from the influence it may have had on economic decisions. These questions are discussed in subsequent chapters.

Appendix 1.1 *India's economic assistance agreements with the East European countries*[a]

Name of credit	Amount of credit	Amount utilised up to 31 March 1966	Balance available for Fourth Plan
(1)	(2)	(3)	(4)
USSR			
Bhilai credit	647·4	647·4	—
Industrial enterprises credit	595·3	443·8	151·5
Drugs credit	95·2	94·6	0·6
1st credit for Third Plan projects	1,785·8	1,332·5	453·3
Barauni credit	119·1	116·1	3·0
2nd credit for Third Plan projects	595·3	173·6	421·7
Bokaro credit	1,058·2	12·8	1,045·4
	4,896·3	2,820·8	2,075·5
Poland			
1st Polish credit	153·0	109·6	43·4
2nd Polish credit	155·0	3·8	151·2
3rd Polish credit	105·0	—	105·0
	413·0	113·4	299·6
Yugoslavia			
Yugoslav credit	214·3	97·1	117·2
	214·3	97·1	117·2
Czechoslovakia			
1st Czech credit	231·0	126·1	104·9
2nd Czech credit	400·0	—	400·0
	631·0	126·1	504·9
Total	6,154·6	3,157·4	2,997·2

[a] In millions of pre-devaluation rupees.
Source: Ministry of Finance, *External Assistance*, 1965/6.

Appendix 1.2 *Projects financed with East European countries' credits* (in Rs. million)[a]

Name of credit (1)	Amount of credit (2)	Name of project (3)	Allocation (4)	Contracts placed (5)	Amount drawn on 31 May 1967 (6)
1st Polish credit	241·0	1. Machine tools project expansion of Praga Tools	2·5	2·5	2·5
		2. Boilers for power project – Paras and Bhusaval	38·1	38·1	38·1
		3. Barauni power project	64·1	64·1	64·1
		4. Sudamdih coal mine project	62·3	62·3	37·1
		5. Monidih mine	39·6	39·6	8·0
		6. Gidi coal washery	27·5	27·5	27·5
		7. Escorts scooters and motor cycles project	5·5	5·5	5·2
		Total	239·6	239·6	182·5
2nd Polish credit	244·1	1. Deep coal mines	55·0	7·6	7·1
		2. Factory for manufacture of mining machinery and coal washery etc.	n.a.	—	—
		(a) Sudamdih	0·2	0·2	—
		3. Zinc smelter project (dropped)	2·7	2·7	—
		4. Two cellular concrete factories	20·8	10·4	—
		Total	78·7	20·9	7·1

3rd Polish credit	165·4	Two 125 Mw sets for Nagpur power station	92·9	92·9	—
Yugoslav credit	337·5	1. Ships			
		(a) three Konkan passenger ships	24·1	24·1	24·1
		(b) four Motor cargo ships	66·1	66·1	65·6
		(c) Bulk carriers	85·7	85·7	30·3
		2. Equipment for power projects			
		(a) Periyar, Sholayar I and II (Parambikulam) and Kodayar	18·6	18·6	8·3
		(b) Yamuna – I Stage	18·4	18·4	16·8
		(c) Kalakote	19·7	19·7	17·3
		(d) Kanpur	32·1	32·1	31·8
		(e) Kandla	9·3	9·3	9·3
		3. Equipment for development of fisheries industries Marine diesel engines	8·0	8·0	8·0
		4. Crane for: Upper Sileru power station	1·1	1·1	1·1
		Total	283·1	283·1	212·6
1st Czechoslovak credit	363·8	1. 1st Phase of III Stage of foundry forge plant, Ranchi	94·2	94·2	80·9
		2. Heavy machine tools project, Ranchi	52·3	52·3	55·4[b]
		3. High pressure boiler project, Tiruchirapalli	45·0	45·0	44·5
		4. Heavy power equipment plant, Hyderabad	86·9	86·9	81·2
		5. Tools, jigs and fixtures	29·2	8·4	—
		6. Heavy plates and vessels works	40·3	14·5	—
		7. Components for turbo blowers and compressors	20·6	20·6	—
		Total	368·5	321·9	262·0

Appendix 1.2 *Projects financed with East European countries' credits—contd.*

Name of credit	Amount of credit	Name of project	Allocation	Contracts placed	Amount drawn on 31 May 1967
2nd Czechoslovak credit	630·0	1. Expansion of the high pressure boiler plant at Tiruchi	33·1	—	—
		2. Expansion of the heavy power equipment plant at Ramachandrapuram	33·1	—	—
		3. (a) Ajmer machine tool factory	} 63·0	8·4	—
		(b) Bhavnagar machine tool factory		—	—
		4. Additional foundry and forge facilities:			
		(a) Wardha	} 141·8	—	—
		(b) Jabalpur		8·3	—
		5. 2 × 110 Mw thermal power station, Ennore	133·5	133·5	—
		6. Factory for the manufacture of tractors and power tillers	23·6	—	—
		7. Components:			
		(a) HPEP (Hyderabad)	} 179·4	106·4 }	} 87·5
		(b) HPBP (Tiruchi)		38·8	
		(c) HMT (Ranchi)		17·7	
		Total	607·5	313·1	87·5

a In post-devaluation rupees.
b This includes utilisation on account of tools, jigs and fixtures under item 5.
Source: Ministry of Finance, External Assistance: 1964/5 and 1965/6. Estimate Committee 4th Loksabha, 1967–68. *Report on Utilisation of External Assistance.*

Appendix 1.3 *Projects financed with Soviet credits* (in Rs. million)[a]

Name of credit	Date of agreement	Amount of loan	Projects	Contracts placed	Amount drawn up to 31 March 1968
(1)	(2)	(3)	(4)	(5)	(6)
Bhilai credit	2.2.65	1,019·6	Bhilai steel plant	1,019·6	1,019·6
Credit for industrial projects	9.11.57	937·5	1. Heavy machine building plant	254·7	246·2
			2. Coal mining machine plant	156·8	151·3
			3. Ophthalmic glass project	19·2	17·5
			4. Korba coal mining projects	84·4	81·6
			5. Neyveli thermal power station	219·1	217·7
				734·2	714·3
Credit for drugs projects	29.5.59	149·9	Drugs projects	149·9	149·7
First credit for Third Plan projects	12.9.59	2,812·4	1. Expansion of Bhilai steel plant	952·9	903·2
			2. Expansion of Neyveli thermal plant	131·5	130·8

Appendix 1.3 *Projects financed with Soviet credits—contd.*

Name of credit	Date of agreement	Amount of loan	Projects	Contracts placed	Amount drawn up to 31 March 1968
			3. Singrauli power station	229·5	219·1
			4. Expansion of HMBP	113·7	102·7
			5. Kotah precision instruments projects	34·8	24·9
			6. Expansion of coal mining machinery plant	36·2	36·2
			7. Expansion of Korba thermal power station	174·7	170·7
			8. Barauni oil refinery	67·7	70·7
			9. Heavy electrical plant	237·8	153·8
			10. Exploration of oil and gas	519·8	509·3
				2,498·6	2,321·4
Barauni credit	28.9.59	187·5	Barauni oil refinery	187·5	183·3
Second credit for Third Plan projects	21.2.61	937·5	1. Bhakra right bank hydro-electric power station	91·6	91·6
			2. Koyali oil refinery	127·3	126·9
			3. Coal washery at Kathara	46·5	44·7
			4. Refractories plant	2·5	2·5
			5. Exploration, development and production of oil in Cambay, Ankleshwar and in other areas	256·6	155·1

	Date	Credit		
6. Production of pumps and compressors – preparation of technical-economic report			2·5	0·2
Additional projects agreed for financing under savings from Soviet credits			527·0	421·0
1. 5th unit for Bhakra right bank power station			15·6	14·0
2. Kerala precision instrument plant			5·0	1·2
3. Expansion of refineries				
(i) Barauni			13·1	11·4
(ii) Koyali			14·0	5·9
4. Compressors and pumps project			3·8	3·8
5. Steel foundry for railways			2·3	2·1
6. Sixth blast furnace at Bhilai			74·3	39·4
7. Working drawings, etc. for Neyveli thermal power expansion. (400 Mw to 600 Mw)			4·1	1·4
			132·2	79·2
Bokaro steel plant	25.1.65	1,666·7	1,666·7	245·6
1. Lower Sileru hydro-power station	10.12.66	2,500·00	27·5	—
2. Neyveli thermal power station (400 Mw to 600 Mw)			139·2	133·8
			166·7	133·8
Total		10,211·1	7,082·4	5,267·9

Bokaro credit

Credit for Fourth Plan projects

a Post-devaluation rupees.

Appendix 1.4 *Scope of credits from East Europe*

(1)	(2)	(3)	(4)	(5)	(6)	(7)	(8)
Name of credit	f.o.b. value of machinery and equipment %	Freight %	Insurance %	Documentation etc. %	Technicians' salaries Foreign %	Technicians' salaries Local %	Credit finance of third country imports %
USSR credits	100	100 when shipped in Soviet vessels	100 when shipped in Soviet vessels	100	100	nil	Does not arise
1st Polish credit	100	nil	nil	nil	nil	nil	nil
2nd Polish credit	100	nil	nil	100	100	nil	nil
3rd Polish credit	100	nil	nil	100	100	nil	nil
1st Czechoslovak credit	100	nil	nil	nil	nil	nil	nil
2nd Czechoslovak credit	100	nil	nil	nil	nil	nil	nil
1st Yugoslav credit	80	nil	nil	nil	nil	nil	1st 10% met fully. Subsequent to be shared equally
2nd Yugoslav credit	85 for ships 90 for capital goods	100 when shipped in Yugoslav vessels	nil	nil	nil	nil	1st 10% met fully Subsequent to be shared equally
Bulgarian credit	85	nil	nil	nil	nil	nil	100
Hungarian credit	85	nil	nil	nil	nil	nil	nil

Appendix 1.5   *Bilateral payment arrangements with East European countries*

| Country | Payment | | Final settlement of balances | | | |
| | | | Exchange settlement | | Offset settlement | Automatic transfer- |
	Sterling	Rupees	Sterling	Rupee/ Sterling	Rupees	ability
1. Bulgaria	—	Jan. 1954 to Dec. 1973	Apr. 1956 to Dec. 1959	Jan. 1954 to Dec. 1955	Jan. 1960 to Dec. 1973	June 1953 to Dec. 1953
2. Czechoslovakia	—	Nov. 1953 to Dec. 1968	Nov. 1953 to Dec. 1960	—	Jan. 1961 to Dec. 1968	Mar. 1949 to Oct. 1953
3. East Germany	—	Oct. 1954 to Dec. 1968	Oct. 1954 to Dec. 1959	—	Jan. 1960 to Dec. 1968	—
4. Hungary	Apr. 1949 to Dec. 1953	Jan. 1954 to Dec. 1970	—	Apr. 1949 to Dec. 1958	Jan. 1959 to Dec. 1970	—
5. Poland	Jan. 1951 to Dec. 1955	Apr. 1956 to Dec. 1973	Jan. 1951 to Dec. 1959	—	Jan. 1960 to Dec. 1973	July 1949 to Dec. 1950
6. Rumania	—	Mar. 1954 to Dec. 1973	Mar. 1954 to Dec. 1958	—	May 1959 to Dec. 1973	—
7. USSR	—	Dec. 1953 to Dec. 1970	Dec. 1953 to Dec. 1958	—	Jan. 1959 to Dec. 1970	—
8. Yugoslavia	—	Nov. 1953 to Dec. 1968	July 1953 to Mar. 1956	Apr. 1956 to Mar. 1959	Mar. 1959 to Dec. 1968	Dec. 1948 to June 1953

Source: Indian trade agreements with other partners, cited in 6, p. 35.

2

A COMPARISON BETWEEN AID FROM EAST EUROPEAN AND OTHER COUNTRIES

A comparison between the funds given by the East European countries and others can serve three purposes. First, it helps in the appreciation of the differences between their attitudes and programmes regarding terms of repayment, and end use of aid. Second, it shows how the other countries reacted to the programme introduced by East European countries. Third, it highlights the rigidity of the credit programme adopted by the East European countries. While other donors, mainly the United States, the United Kingdom and the World Bank Group, have responded to the changing requirements of the Indian economy, the nature and direction of the East European programme has changed very little. If the East European countries do not have the flexibility or ability to cope with changing import requirements, their willingness to give credits may have little practical value in the years to come.

This chapter is divided into two sections: first, a comparison of terms of aid and second, an assessment of the influence of the East European aid programme on other donors. To recapitulate history briefly, external official funds utilised in the Third Plan amounted to more than ten times the funds utilised in the First Plan.[1] At the same time the proportion of grants to total assistance fell from 55 per cent in the First Plan period to 22.5 per cent in the Second and 5 per cent in the Third Plan period. Consequently the debt service ratio increased very rapidly, especially in the 1960s, reaching 28 per cent of India's export earnings in 1968/9.

The general trend was towards the 'softening' of loan repayment terms from the Second to the Third Plan. While there has been a variation in the terms of aid offered by different countries at different times, there was a clear recognition of India's

[1] See Appendix 2.1, pp. 76–9.

difficult foreign exchange situation in the 1960s. The latest experiment in coping with the foreign exchange situation is 'debt relief'. The USSR and other East European countries, however, have not changed the terms of their credits nor offered other concessions.

The USSR was the first donor to accept the principle of giving development loans on concessional terms. The concessional element depends on the rate of interest, amortisation period and currency of repayment. The USSR merely offered low interest rates. When other donors also accepted the principle of concessionary loans they offered larger amounts at nominal interest rates and with longer amortisation periods. The total loans authorised from other countries at interest rates of $2\frac{1}{2}$ per cent or less amounted to Rs.7,580 million up until 1965/6, compared to Rs.5,265 million from the East European countries. The actual receipts from other countries were twice as much as from the East European countries.[1]

Since 1965 the United Kingdom has given interest-free loans worth U.S. $220 million. The total receipts from IDA up to the end of 1969–70 amounted to Rs.6,456 million, compared to Rs.3,085 million from the USSR.

However, a comparison between nominal interest charges on different loans does not do full justice to the softening of terms after 1960.[2] Interest payments for a number of years were waived on many loans and therefore the effective interest rate[3] – that which makes the sum of all the future annual interest payments equal on a 'present value basis' to the credit originally received – is lower than the nominal interest rate. Some important examples are:

(1) The United States gave a wheat loan of Rs.903·0 million at an interest rate of $2\frac{1}{2}$ per cent but agreed to postpone 18 semi-annual instalments of interest and principal without additional interest payments. This postponement implies an effective interest rate of 2 per cent per annum.

(2) All the PL 480 loans signed since the inception of the Third Plan have an effective interest rate of between $\frac{3}{4}$ per cent

---

[1] See Appendix 2.2, pp. 80–3.
[2] For a comparison between Soviet and Western terms see Kaser (38).
[3] This is similar to the internal rate of return.

and $2\frac{1}{2}$ per cent. The total value of loans authorised up to the end of 1969/70 amounted to Rs.17,030 million (post-devaluation rate of exchange).

(3) On all U.S. AID loans granted before 1963 the nominal interest rate was only $\frac{3}{4}$ per cent per annum. This was raised to 2 per cent in 1963/4 and to $2\frac{1}{2}$ per cent after October 1964. But because the interest paid during the first ten years of the duration of these loans, granted in 1963/4 and from October 1964 respectively, is only $\frac{3}{4}$ per cent and 1 per cent, the effective interest rate is even lower. The effective interest rates on these loans are 1·69 per cent and 2·125 per cent per annum respectively. India was granted Rs.6,793 million in AID loans during the Third Plan – more than the total amount granted by all the East European countries during the period 1951 to 1965/6.

(4) The interest rate charged on British loans negotiated before 1964 was linked to the treasury rate, but because interest payments during the first seven years were waived, the effective interest rate on a loan with $6\frac{1}{2}$ per cent interest was only $3\frac{1}{2}$ per cent.

A trend towards the softening of terms can be seen also in longer amortisation periods. The average amortisation period was greater during the Third Plan than throughout the Second Plan. Table 3 shows that only 3·7 per cent of the official credits received had amortisation periods longer than 25 years during the Second Plan, but this percentage had risen to nearly 40 per cent during the Third Plan. The trend has continued in the past four years, and 'debt relief' has been introduced as a new element.

During the Third Plan the credits with relatively shorter maturity periods were official suppliers' credits from Belgium, France, Italy and official loans from Czechoslovakia, Poland, Yugoslavia and the USSR. In theory, most of the East European credits are to be repaid in eight years and Russian credits in twelve years. In practice, the repayment of principal does not start until a year after the final invoice for machinery and equipment for each project is received. Since East European projects take three to four years to complete, the amortisation period is usually longer – ten to twelve years from the date of first drawing on the credit for any project instead of eight, and fourteen to seventeen years instead of twelve.

Notable exceptions to this general pattern were the credits for Bhilai and Bokaro. In the case of Bhilai, the repayment started a year after the receipt of the invoice for each instalment of equipment, and not after the invoices for all the equipment had been received. These two credits constituted 33 per cent of the total credits granted by the Soviet Union during the period 1956/7 to 1965/6. This arrangement therefore meant that India started repaying the credit even before the project was completed and production had started.

Table 3 *Official development credits authorised during the Second and Third Plans, arranged according to the period of maturity*

Period of maturity in years	Second Plan	Third Plan
	(as % of total credits utilised)	
0–6	6·0	0·4
7–10	9·7	9·3
11–14	32·6	8·6
15–19	24·0	15·5
20–23	23·3	16·2
24–25	0·7	10·8
Over 25	3·7	39·2

Notes: (1) Development credits only. (2) PL 480 and PL 665 not included (total value was Rs.15,983 million). (3) Official assistance only.
Source: Computed from the details of loan agreement. See Ministry of Finance, *External Assistance*, 1965/6.

The comparison of interest rates and amortisation periods above shows that compared to the U.S. or IDA, the East European countries do not give softer terms of repayment. However, this comparison does not show, as Klaus Billerbeck alleges,[1] that the East European countries' loans are closer to 'private suppliers' credits' than to 'official assistance from the other countries'. For one thing, the interest rate on private or official suppliers' credits is high, ranging from 5 per cent upwards, and there is usually a down payment of 15 to 20 per cent. Secondly, when Western donors have offered loans for industrial enterprises in the public sector, their terms have been similar to those offered by the East European countries.

[1] Billerbeck (11, pp. 8–16).

For example, the loans for two other steel plants – Durgapur (U.K. banks) and Rourkela (West Germany) – carry a high interest rate and have short amortisation periods. Table 4 shows the terms of credits received for prospecting and refining petroleum and building pipelines. The East European loans compare favourably with any Western credits available for that particular purpose. Or again the Industrial Credit and Investment Corporation of India (ICICI) has received loans from the World Bank at interest rates of 4 to 6 per cent with amortisation periods of ten to fifteen years. When the Eximbank of the U.S.A. gave loans to American concerns in India, these credits were relatively short – ten to fifteen years – and the interest rates much higher than $2\frac{1}{2}$ per cent. All the credits received for shipping in India, either from East European countries or others, carry similar terms of repayment. If these are classified as 'external assistance' the East European credits qualify for the same description for they cannot be considered as private suppliers' credits any more than can these other official loans for industrial enterprises.

For a country faced with a severe foreign exchange shortage, repayment in local currency would be a special concession. Most of the credits India received were repayable in convertible currency. Excluding commodity assistance, credits worth Rs.2,730 million from non-East European donors were classified as repayable in rupees. The description 'repayable in rupees' was originally applied to the credits received from the East European countries as well and was advertised as a novel feature.

If the creditor country purchases in India goods and services which India would not have exported anyway, or for which India would not have been paid in foreign currency, then such a repayment is really repayment in rupees because it does not involve any sacrifice of foreign exchange. However, as applied to most of the loans India received, this description is invalid because it refers to the unit of account and not to the mode of payment.

There are two types of loans generally included in this category. First, loans from East European countries which are more accurately described as repayment in kind. To be accurately described as repayable in rupees, in the sense that there was no foreign exchange cost involved, it must be shown that India could not have exported these goods elsewhere. This question is considered in chapter 4.

The second category consists of loans made from counterpart rupee funds generated from the sale of agricultural commodities or raw materials, which are deposited in India and re-lent to India for development projects agreed upon by both the parties concerned. The most important donor is of course the United States, but Canada and Denmark have also provided loans of this type. The Reserve Bank of India has classified loans worth Rs.2,731 million as repayable in rupees, excluding PL 480 commodity assistance.

The United States will not demand repayment in convertible currency on any loans made to India under PL 480 agreements which were signed before March 1966. Until March 1966, India had received Rs.3,512 million in the form of grants and Rs.7,408 million as loans, and the U.S. reserved Rs.1,838 million for its own use. The amount reserved for embassy expenditure in India amounts to payment in foreign currency. But otherwise counterpart funds are really credits – 'repayable in rupees'.

Both East European and other credits are meant to finance imports of goods. However, when the PL 480 counterpart funds are re-lent to the Indian Government and the new credits are spent on locally produced goods, this feature – local cost financing – is a very welcome one because it helps to utilise the domestic capacity created in manufacturing industries. As most donors look upon the credits given to the less-developed countries as a way of promoting their own exports, they are reluctant to finance expenditure in local currency. By granting credits which are spent on domestically produced goods the United States has attended to one of India's special problems – that of encouraging local production whilst utilising project-tied assistance. The USSR has financed purchases in local currency in other countries but not in India. The USSR credits have helped utilisation of domestic capacity but in another way, i.e. by specifically tying repayment to exports.

Having discussed the terms of repayment, let us see how the terms of payments have affected the net inflow of funds.

Table 5 shows the ratio of debt repayments to gross assistance utilised up to 1965/6. This table is also divided into two

Table 4 *External loans received for oil exploration, pipelines and refining* (in Rs. million)

Date of agreement	Amount (Rs. million)	Purpose	Period (years)	Interest %	Repayments Commencing	Ending	Amount drawn up to March 1969 (Rs. million)
U.K.							
June 1959	40·0	Naharkotia pipeline	6½	6½	6.64	12.66	40
September 1964	20·0	Capital and other equipment for drilling operations of Oil India Ltd.	25	6½a but 3½ effective	3.10.71	31.10.89	—
France							
September 1961	37·0	Oil exploration with ONGC for equipment and services	10	6	5% down payment, balance in equal instalments over a period of 10 years from the date of final delivery or completion of assembly		

Italy						
1962/3	214·3	Pipelines from Barauni to Delhi, technical assistance, oil exploration equipment	10	6	5% on the date of signing the contract, 3% a year after signing the contract. 92% in half yearly instalments starting two years from signing the contract	53·26
Rumania						
October 1968	55·9	Technical assistance, design plant and equipment for Gauhati refinery	7	2½	Principal a year after the completion of deliveries	
USSR						
September 1959	330·0	Oil exploration and equipment, Barauni and Koyali refineries	12	2½	Same as above	313·1
September 1959	39·5	Barauni				39·5
February 1961	80·1	Koyali				80·1

[a] Interest payments waived for the first seven years.

Source: External Assistance, 1965/6, and Ministry of Finance.

Table 5 *Development aid received and repayments: total, 1951/2 to 1965/6, and by country, 1955/6 to 1965/6 (in Rs. million)*

	Second Plan 1955/6 to 1960/1							Third Plan 1961/2 to 1965/6							Total 1951/2 to 1965/6		
	Total credits utilised	Total grants utilised	Total aid	Repayment of principal	Repayment of interest	Total repayment	(6) as % of (1)	Total credits utilised	Total grants utilised	Total aid	Repayment of principal	Repayment of interest	Total repayment	(13) as % of (10)	Total aid utilised	Total repayment	(16) as % of (15)
	(1)	(2)	(3)	(4)	(5)	(6)	(7)	(8)	(9)	(10)	(11)	(12)	(13)	(14)	(15)	(16)	(17)
Austria								47·0		47·0					47·0		
Belgium								48·9		48·9	3·6				48·9		
Britain	1,218·5	4·3	1,222·8		25·1	25·1	2·1	1,704·2	8·0	1,712·0	292·5	437·4	729·9	42·6	2,935·3	755·0	25·7
Canada	157·1	603·0	706·1	16·4	19·4	35·8	5·0	115·4	543·6	659·0	95·3	26·8	122·1	18·5	1,616·1	157·9	9·7
Czechoslovakia								126·1	4·0	130·1					130·1		
Denmark								6·0		6·0					6·0		
Federal Republic of Germany								2,197·3	19·1	2,216·4	1,033·8	435·8	1,469·6	66·3	3,473·3	1,638·6	47·1
France	1,250·8	6·1	1,256·9	55·8	104·9	160·9	12·8	209·8		209·8					209·8		

3

Italy								116·5		116·5					116·5		
Japan	160·1	3·5	163·6		2·6	2·6	1·6	882·2	1·3	883·5	82·1	94·7	176·8	20·0	1,047·1	179·4	17·1
Netherlands								95·1		95·1					95·1		
Poland								113·4		113·8			1·1		113·4	1·1	
Sweden									25·8	25·8					25·8		
Switzerland								60·4		60·4	1·1				60·4		
USSR	748·5	38·1	748·4	167·3	19·3	186·6	23·7	2,072·3	49·6	2,121·9	371·8	153·6	525·4	24·8	2,870·4	712·0	24·9
U.S.A.	1,536·6	5,916·7[a]	10,316·4	68·4	122·0	190·4	1·9	7,961·7	8,777·1[a]	16,738·8	666·0	1,078·3	1,744·3	10·5	25,884·6	2,013·3	7·8
Yugoslavia								97·1		97·1	1·1		1·8		97·1	1·8	
IBRD	2,227·9		2,227·9	90·3	182·0	272·3	12·0	1,233·6		1,233·6	392·0	491·9	883·9	71·0	3,799·7	1,276·9	33·6
IDA								2,006·3		2,006·3					2,006·3		
Australia		74·4	74·4						70·3	70·3					196·7		
New Zealand		29·0	29·0						51·3	51·3					51·3		
Norway		18·7	18·7						6·2	25·8					25·8		
Grand total	7,299·5	7,054·5	14,334·0	398·2	474·4	872·6	6·1	19,093·3	9,603·7	28,697·0	3,090·8	2,914·7	6,005·5	20·9	45,067·7	7,077·4	15·8

[a] The figures include PL 480, PL 665 assistance as well as funds in the currency of a third country, but exclude: (1) Supplier's credit other than those forming a part of Consortium Aid. (2) Rockefeller Foundation grants. (3) Assistance under Title II and III of PL 480. (4) Technical assistance in the form of experts, trainees etc., where granted in kind, without payment or offsetting against credit. (5) Certain *ad hoc* grants in the form of equipment and supplies where the value is not known.

Note: (i) The figures refer to development credits only. Receipts and payments of defense credits are excluded. (ii) The grand total includes other credits and payments not specified here. (iii) Columns (15) and (16) refer to all development credits received and all repayments from 1951/2 to 1965/6. The main donors during 1951/2 to 1955/6 were U.S.A. and World Bank.

Sources: Ministry of Finance, *External Assistance*, 1965/6 and the *Explanatory Memorandum to the Central Government Budget.*

sub-periods 1955/6 to 1960/1 and 1961/2 to 1965/6 to show how
debt servicing as a percentage of gross aid utilised increased
from the Second to the Third Plan. The period since 1965/6
is treated separately below, because as a result of devaluation
the debt/service ratio increased sharply.

Table 6   *Ratio of debt service to gross assistance utilised for major
donors*

Country	1956/7 to 1960/1	1960/1 to 1965/6	Total, 1951/2 to 1965/6
	(%)	(%)	(%)
U.S.A.	1·9	10·5	7·8
Canada	5·0	18·5	9·7
Japan	1·6	20·0	17·1
USSR	24·0	24·8	24·9
Other East European countries	24·9	22·9	23·9
U.K.	2·1	42·6	25·7
IBRD	12·0	70·2	33·6
Federal Republic of Germany	19·1	66·3	47·1
Total[a]	6·1	20·9	15·8

[a] Including other donors, notably IDA.
Source: Ministry of Finance, *External Assistance,* 1965/6, and the *Explanatory Memorandum to the Central Government Budget.*

With a slightly different division into sub-periods, table 6
summarises the information in table 5 and shows that in the
first period 1956/7 to 1960/1 the ratio of debt repayments to
the total assistance utilised was highest for East European
countries and lowest for the U.S.A. and Japan. The exception-
ally low ratio for the U.S.A. reflects the fact that the U.S.A.
gave big grants and re-lent a large amount of counterpart
funds realised from the sale of surplus agricultural commodities
on very generous terms. The picture looks substantially different
if loans only are compared, because the terms offered by most
Consortium members were stiffer than those granted by the
East European countries until 1958/9. However, the provision
of grants by the latter has had the effect of softening the overall
net effect on the ratio of debt service to total assistance utilised.

The United States, Canada and Japan therefore transferred more resources, as a percentage of gross assistance given, than the Soviet Union whereas the United Kingdom, the IBRD and the Federal Republic of Germany transferred less. But the true ratio for the IBRD would be closer to that of the U.K. and the USSR if adjusted for the over-estimate on account of earlier loans. West Germany's debt service/assistance utilised ratio is, however, extremely high.

Another interesting feature is that while the net transfer from the USSR, as a percentage of total assistance utilised, is the smallest, during the period 1956/7 to 1960/1 the USSR appears in a more favourable light due to two factors – the sharp drop in the contribution of grants (excluding PL 480 counterpart funds) and the relatively hard terms of repayment on loans negotiated during the Second Plan. The consequence was that the ratio of overall debt service to gross disbursement increased from 6·1 per cent in the Second Plan to almost 21 per cent during the Third.

Table 7 sets out an alternative ratio, that is, the past repayments as a percentage of credits utilised (grants and commodity assistance being excluded), which indicates an altogether different ranking, viz. the USSR has the second lowest ratio of debt service utilised after Japan. The purpose of the table for the present study is only to show the pattern of future payments if no grants are forthcoming from important donors and to argue for softening the terms of loans.

Since devaluation, the debt servicing burden, as a percentage of either gross assistance received or export earnings, has increased very sharply. This is a general phenomenon, but the difference between East European countries and Consortium countries is that the latter have rescheduled debt repayments.

Between 1966/7 and 1968/9, the net inflow of aid as a percentage of gross disbursement (excluding food aid) fell from 62 to 48 per cent.[1] Even including food aid, the ratio of net aid to gross aid disbursements fell from 75 to 59 per cent. For the other East European countries as a whole the ratio of debt service to total assistance utilised rose from less than 25 per cent in the pre-devaluation period to 37 per cent in the post-devaluation

[1] Ministry of Finance (115, 1968/9, table xv, p. 53).

Table 7 *Repayments as a percentage of development credits utilised from major donors* (in Rs. million)

Country	Second Plan		Third Plan		1951/2 to 1965/6	
	Credits	Repayments as % of credits utilised	Credits	Repayments as % of credits utilised	Credits	Repayments as % of credits utilised
U.S.	1,536·6	12·4	7,961·7	21·8	9,498·3	47·1
U.K.	1,218·5	2·0	1,704·2	42·8	2,922·7	25·8
West Germany	1,250·8	12·8	2,197·3	66·5	3,448·1	47·5
IBRD	2,227·9	12·0	1,233·6	70·2	3,799·9	33·6
Japan	160·1	1·7	882·2	20·9	1,042·3	17·2
USSR	748·5	24·9	2,072·3	24·8	2,820·8	24·9

Source: Ministry of Finance, *External Assistance*, 1965–66, and the *Explanatory Memorandum to the Central Government Budget.*

period. However, in the case of the USSR, the debt service reached between 75 and 80 per cent of gross aid received. Over the period 1966/7 to 1969/70 there has been little net inflow of resources from the USSR. In fact, if defence credits are included, there has probably been a net outflow. But unlike the Consortium countries, the USSR did not consider it necessary to give debt relief, the explanation apparently being that it feels that its loans already carry concessional terms. The Consortium countries, however, reacted differently. During the period 1967/8 to 1969/70, these countries together made available a sum of U.S. $272 million for debt relief.

The lack of response by the Soviet Union to India's current foreign exchange problems is a good illustration of the rigidity of the USSR's credit programme. Another illustration is the fact that so far the USSR has shown no inclination to 'untie' its credits. Aid can be tied to purchases in the aid-giving country or to a specific type of project or both. If the projects selected for financing by donors have a high priority in the recipient country's development programme, there is little danger of a distortion of priorities. Similarly, if the creditor country can provide credit-financed imports at competitive prices, there is no cost involved in tying credits to purchases in the country of origin. However, when a country like India is trying to match the aid available from various countries to its requirements, 'tying' creates problems. As donors have their preferences about the end use of funds it has not been always possible for India to get supplies from the cheapest source or to get precisely what it wanted. Consortium members made an effort to meet India's special requirements during the Third Plan by granting her non-project loans, but the East European credits have been tied both to specific projects and to purchases in the country of origin and it is reasonable to ask how much of the former group's aid was effectively free of ties.

Apart from commodity assistance from the United States very little of the assistance India received during the period 1956/7 to 1960/1 was non-project. For the subsequent period, the data available (table 8) does not distinguish between donors: in 1961/2 to 1965/6 59 per cent of the total loan agreements signed was for projects only and 54 per cent during 1966/7 to 1969/70. However, as already stated, the East European percentage being 100 throughout, the proportion for others must have been sharply falling.

Table 8   *Non-project aid as a percentage of total official development loans, 1961/2 to 1965/6 (including East European countries) (in Rs. million)*

	1961/2	1962/3	1963/4	1964/5	1965/6	1966/7 to 1969/70
1. Total amounts of loan agreements	3,924·1	5,968·9	4,587·0	4,929·9	4,153·4	19,180
2. Non-project element	1,169·0	2,747·6	1,833·4	1,433·7	2,512·2	8,822
3. Non-project aid as percentage of total loans	30	46	40	29	60	46

Note: Row 1 includes East European countries, which, however, have not granted any non-project assistance. Row 2 is hence virtually confined to the Consortium countries.

Source: (1) Estimates Committee (1967/8), 11th Report, p. 47. (2) Government of India, *Economic Survey*, 1967/8 to 1969/70, sections on external aid.

Not all non-project credits are free of ties: some loans may be reserved for a particular commodity. But the importance of non-project loans is that they help to ensure full utilisation of capacity created with the help of project loans. The shortage of foreign exchange has resulted – particularly in the 1960s – in under-utilisation of capacity in many industries. Not until 1966 did the USSR grant suppliers credit to finance the imports of spares and components necessary for Soviet-aided projects. However, since even this facility has not resulted in the accumulation of a trade deficit in the period 1966/7 to 1969/70, it seems that India has not used suppliers' credit much.

It should be pointed out that credits to the East European countries are not the same as 'tied' credits from others, because if purchases of credit financed goods are tied to the country of origin, the creditor country is committed to buying Indian goods as repayment. In other words, the yardstick for measuring price costs of tied credits is not merely import prices but the terms of trade. If the prices paid for imports are 15 per cent higher than the world import prices and if export prices received are also 15 per cent higher, then the effective prices paid for imports are not really higher. The effective cost of tying in the case of East European countries would be the difference between the terms of trade with the rest of the world and with the East European countries.

Since a significant motive for giving aid is export promotion, it is not surprising that the main part of official assistance was tied to imports from the donor country. As table 9 shows, only 22 per cent of the total assistance utilised during the entire period 1951/2 to 1965/6 was not tied to purchases in the country of origin. Details for assistance granted by countries in the period 1966/7 to 1969/70 are not available, but it is likely that, apart from loans given by the international organisations, something like the same proportion prevailed.

Table 9 *Official development assistance tied and untied, 1951/2 to 1965/6 (from all countries)* (in Rs. million)

	Total assistance value	Of which			
		Tied		Untied	
		Value	(%)	Value	(%)
Up to First Plan:					
Authorised	3,650	3,080	84·4	570	15·6
Utilised	1,960·	1,620	83·7	340	17·3
During Second Plan:					
Authorised	14,200	10,540	74·3	3,660	25·7
Utilised	8,910	5,920	66·8	2,990	33·2
During Third Plan:					
Authorised	24,940	20,670	82·9	4,270	17·1
Utilised	20,260	16,740	87·6	3,520	12·4
Total:					
Authorised	42,790	34,290	80·0	8,500	20·0
Utilised	31,130	24,280	78·0	6,850	22·0

Note: Excluding U.S. commodity assistance.
Source: Estimates Committee, 11th Report, p. 40.

The above discussion shows that, while other donor countries tied most of their credits either to a project or to purchases in the country of origin, East European countries were tied both ways. Therefore, assuming East European countries paid the same prices for exports as others, the costs of tying may be higher in their case.

In a recent study on the subject, Jagdish Bhagwati says, 'An analysis of the limited general evidence available points to the conclusion that the direct costs alone of aid tying are equivalent to a significant proportion of the value of tied aid, and almost certainly amount, on the average, to as much as one-fifth of the value of tied aid.'[1]

While all tied aid is more expensive than untied aid and there is no evidence that the East European countries charge higher (monopolistic) prices than others, it seems that the cost of tied credits from the East European countries may be higher than those from other countries. The reason for suspecting higher costs is that there is little room for mitigating the effects of tied aid by following ideal procurement policies and exploiting switching possibilities.

Professor Bhagwati summarises the costs associated with tying thus, '... source tying will generally impose costs, inclusive of "monopolistic" pricing by suppliers, even when ideal procurement policies are followed. Moreover, these costs are likely to be accentuated when the donor countries also specify the end use, by project or otherwise, of source tied aid. These costs will vary with (i) the flexibility, in substitution, that the recipient country enjoys through access to more than one source of foreign funds; (ii) the extent to which such exploitation of substitution possibilities is permitted by the donor countries; and (iii) the willingness and ability of the recipient country via optimal procurement and related policies, to exploit such substitution and competitive possibilities as exist.'[2]

In the case of most East European credits to India, the credits were offered for industrial projects in the public sector. It is not possible to say whether India could have negotiated credits for a different purpose to begin with. In any case the only other alternative means of finance for most of these projects was private suppliers' credits. Other donors were generally reluctant

---

[1] Bhagwati and Chakravarty (9, p. 3).   [2] *Ibid.*, p. 33.

to provide finance for the type of projects for which East European credits were available. It should also be remembered that the choice was restricted to what the partner country could offer, i.e. whether the equipment was suitable to India's requirements or not.

One more factor that makes tied credits from the East European countries more expensive is that there is only one supplier of equipment. Since the creditor and the supplier are the same India does not even try to get a lower price from them. Of course, firms in the Western donor countries may collude and quote one price and this in fact has been the general practice in case of tied credits, but at least it may be possible to exercise choice in equipment produced by different firms. Even this possibility is ruled out in the case of East European credits, since there is no competition within the country.

Another aspect of the rigidity of East European credits which is often mentioned is the time lapse between the authorisation and utilisation of credits. The East European countries' credits are characterised by the long delay between announcement of a credit and the actual disbursements, and part of the reason is that the rate of disbursement on project tied credits depends upon the progress of the project. If the projects financed by the East European credits take, on the whole, a longer period to go into operation, the gap between authorisation and utilisation increases. Moreover, the East European countries followed the practice of announcing credits well in advance, i.e. the credits for the Third and the Fourth Five Year Plans were announced in the preceding plan periods. Therefore statistics on authorised credits give a misleading comparison because delay between authorisation and utilisation of East European credits is longer for Consortium members (see table 10). Thus, no less than Rs. 2,250 million of the total authorisations announced during the Second Plan period were intended to be utilised for projects in the Third Plan. Similarly the USSR credit of 300 million roubles and a number of smaller East European credits authorised in 1966/7 will finance industrial projects in the Fourth Plan.

Even after extracting these special cases the rate of utilisation of East European credits is slower than that of Consortium credits.

Table 10 *Comparison of development assistance authorised and utilised from Consortium and East European countries, 1956/7 to 1965/6 (in Rs. million)*

| | Consortium members | | USSR and East European countries | |
	Authori-sation	Utili-sation	Authori-sation	Utili-sation
	(1)	(2)	(3)	(4)
1956/7 to				
1960/1	21,439·8	13,419·9	3,766·7	760·0
1961/2	4,111·4	3,120·0	—	246·0
1962/3	6,317·0	4,104·7	159·0	330·0
1963/4	4,676·2	5,347·2	20·0	525·2
1964/5	5,837·4	6,400·0	1,519·8	809·4
1965/6	6,252·7	7,052·6	42·1	540·4
Total	27,194·7	26,024·5	1,740·9	2,451·0
1966/7	10,745	9,792	3,375	525
1967/8	6,952	11,056	121	601
1968/9	9,373	7,729	—	862

Source: Economic Survey, 1969/70, tables 7.2 and 7.3.

Table 11 *Development assistance from Consortium and East European countries (authorised and utilised for 1961/2 to 1965/6) (in Rs. million)*

	Total available	Utilisation	Utilisation as % of authorisation
Consortium members[a]	35,000	26,024·5	74
USSR and other East European countries (including Bokaro)	3,740·9	2,451·0	65

[a] Including the amount 'in the pipeline', which means that the government concerned had agreed to provide a particular sum but the money had not been earmarked for anything specific and was not utilised during the particular year.

Source: Appendix 2.1 and 2.2, pp. 76–83.

Table 11, however, still does not explain why the rate of utilisation should be so slow if the credits had been announced well in advance and the two governments had some time to work out the project. The bulk of Rs.3,740 million should have been utilised at least in the five years of the Third Plan. Part of the answer may lie in two considerations. In the first place the East European countries undertake a feasibility study of their own. In all cases the time required for negotiations, preparation and approval of feasibility studies as well as for supplying equipment exceeded the estimate. Orders cannot be placed until the feasibility study has been accepted and detailed engineering and designing have been completed. Secondly, enterprises, which rarely have reserve capacity, cannot deliver goods immediately; this can often result in another two or three years being lost. These institutional difficulties are perhaps unavoidable in the dealings between a 'mixed' and a 'socialist' economy, where production and investment decisions are made differently.

A comparison between Consortium assistance and East European credits would not be complete without referring to technical assistance (see table 12). The term 'technical assistance' is applied to any inflow of goods and services which results in increasing the productivity of the resources employed in production. Although both the East European and Consortium countries offer assistance meant to increase productivity, the operation and nature of the assistance offered by the two donor groups are quite different.

First, most of the 'technical assistance' received from the East European countries is not in the form of grants, as table 13 shows. India received approximately Rs.1,980 million from various donors in cash in addition to the services of 3,550 foreign experts and training for 11,550 Indian students abroad. Among the East European countries, only Czechoslovakia gave a cash grant of Rs.6 million and the USSR gave equipment for a mechanised farm (though it is not included in this table). Apart from these small grants all technical assistance from the East European countries is paid for. The payment for these services is either charged against the development credit for the project or paid out of India's export earnings. For instance, under the terms of the Soviet credits the salaries of foreign

Table 12   *Technical assistance in cash and kind received from foreign governments, the U.N. and Ford and Rockefeller Foundations*

	Technical assistance in kind		Cash grant for equipment (Rs. million)	Remarks
	Foreign experts in India	Scholarships to Indian trainees		
Australia	63	1,050	71·0	
U.K.	224	2,153	298·2	
Canada	47	801	0·6	
Czechoslovakia	8	23	21·0	
West Germany	25	20	—	
France	38	419	—	
Japan	56	235	—	
Netherlands	—	425	1·2	
New Zealand	18	116	2·5	Cash is equivalent of expert services.
U.S.A.	1,271	4,542	1,840·0	
U.N.	1,800	1,700	40·3	
Rockefeller Foundation	—	49	33·2	Includes 25 travel grants and 24 fellowships.
Ford Foundation	—	—	367·5	To finance services of foreign technicians, to train Indians abroad and to import equipment.
Total	3,550	11,553	2,723·0	

Note: Unless otherwise specified, cash payment is in addition to the services of experts.
Source: Ministry of Finance, *External Assistance*, 1965/6.

Table 13 *Payments for technical assistance on certain projects financed by East European countries* (in Rs. million)

	Report (project)	Working drawings (designs)	Foreign technicians	Training Indian technicians	Miscellaneous (technical assistance)	Total stated payments
Pharmaceuticals:						
Rishikesh	1·08	2·0				3·08
Hyderabad	1·32	2·1				3·83
Madras	4·70	8·5				11·20
Phyto-chemical	8·50					8·50
Refineries:						
Gauhati	7·80				2·80	10·60
Barauni	3·08	7·59			1·18	11·85
HEC:						
HMBP	(22·60)[a]		24·0			54·10
Coal mining	13·50		17·0	7·5	15·40	51·90
Foundry forge[b]			(49·0)[c]	6·0		49·00
Heavy machinery	38·70					38·70
Bhilai	25·00					25·00
Bokaro	25·00	36·00				61·00

[a] Includes drawings, designs etc.
[b] Payment for detailed project report is not known.
[c] Includes payment to the collaborators for project reports, consultancy etc.
Note: This table does not show the total payments for technical assistance to the East European countries but only such payments for the most important projects for which data are available.
Source: Various reports of the Committee on Public Sector Undertakings.

technicians and payments for documentation are eligible for credit financing,[1] but otherwise separate arrangements are made for payments.

Second, just as all development credits for the East European countries are tied to projects, the technical assistance they offer is for the specific projects, though there are a few scholarships which offer opportunities for students to be trained in various fields comparable with the Fulbright or Commonwealth Scholarships and travel grants.

When the services of foreign technicians are spread over different fields, it is difficult to quantify the contribution of this type of technical assistance. On the other hand, when foreign technicians work on a specific project or train Indian technicians for a specific job, it is easy to demonstrate their usefulness. It is argued, with some justification, that this in-job training is more suitable to India's needs, because the problem of utilising the skills thus acquired does not arise. But a comparison between East European and other technical assistance is not fair because the scope of technical assistance from the two sources is quite different. There is no doubt that there is some waste involved in the study and travel grants made available under various Commonwealth and American schemes. However, India does need a variety of skills and the waste involved in the general schemes springs from the absence of detailed manpower planning and not from the fact that the principle is wrong.

Billerbeck has suggested that it is more appropriate to compare the technical assistance supplied by East European countries with the services – technical know-how and expertise – provided by private concerns to their overseas branches.[2] This comparison is valid in that India pays for whatever services are received but on the other hand, no private enterprise would undertake the sort of elaborate training programme that the USSR did in Bhilai: 686 engineers and skilled workers were trained in the USSR and 4,500 workers and 500 engineers in India by the Soviet side; the highest number of Soviet engineers at any one time was 843 and had been reduced to less than 100 in 1961.[3] In general, the Soviet side not only trained Indian personnel for positions of responsibility but were willing to let them

---

[1] See Appendix 1.4.   [2] Billerbeck (11, pp. 8–10).   [3] See (11).

COMPARISON 65

work in designing and drawing and, for example, accepted their blueprint for such an intricate plant as a coal washery. In the case of the Gauhati refinery, some cost saving was effected by preparing some of the drawings in the refinery rather than importing them.[1] Bokaro is one exception in that the Soviet side refused to use the report prepared by the Indian consultants and did not utilise the skilled staff available in India.

Table 14   *Grants as a percentage of total assistance*

	From the U.S.A.[a]	From all countries
First Plan 1950–6	50	55
Second Plan 1956–60	33	22
Third Plan 1960–5	3	6

[a] Excluding food supplied under PL 480 and PL 665.
Source: Ministry of Finance, 164, 1969/70, table 7.3.

Table 14 shows that the payments for project tied technical assistance came to nearly 10 per cent of the credits utilised. In addition India paid Rs.50 million for the salaries of foreign technicians.[2] There may well have been other payments and the true cost of technical services rendered may be nearer to 15 per cent of the development credits utilised. This is a sizeable percentage.

As has already been shown, the East European countries were not important donors in the sense that discontinuation of East European credits would have posed serious financial difficulties for India. Even in the field of industrial development, they contributed less than 20 per cent of the total external funds made available. Nonetheless, the availability of these credits has been an important factor because of the reactions it produced among other donors. By introducing competition in the aid-giving business, the USSR forced others – especially the U.S.A. – to review aid policies and programmes and India was one of the main beneficiaries. The argument, however, applies either way. Perhaps the USSR would not have been interested in India except for the interest shown by the

[1] Committee on Public Sector Undertakings (103, p. 49).
[2] Columbia School of Law (18, p. 162).

United States. What India benefited from was the 'cold war'. The USSR gets credit because had it not chosen India as a 'friend' the latter would not have received much attention from others.

The contrast between the volume of funds made available before and after the USSR offered to set up a steel plant is indeed striking. During the First Five Year Plan India received external public funds worth Rs.2,017 million. This amount went up to Rs.14,302 million during the Second Plan, a sevenfold increase. The Rs.28,688·5 million utilised during the Third Plan was twice the sum used in the Second Plan. Moreover, the sum of Rs.2,017 million includes a wheat loan from the United States which was more in the nature of emergency food aid than development finance. Only the loans from the World Bank, worth Rs.338 million[1] during the First Plan, can be treated as funds for development proper.

It may be argued that the increase in the volume of funds after 1955 was due to other factors, such as the deterioration in India's foreign exchange position, and that the volume of funds received before 1955 was small because India did not need much. In fact, however, the original plan estimates show that 25 per cent of the public sector outlay was expected to be financed from external sources, compared to the 9·6 per cent that actually materialised.[2] The demand for external funds increased because of the industrialisation programme, but the USSR's emergence as a donor definitely influenced external supply conditions.

The USSR learnt from the mistakes of Western donors and was guided by three principles: to give loans rather than grants; to charge lower interest rates; and to accept repayment in kind. It may be argued that the first is not significant. The Soviet Union benefited from this arrangement rather than India. Interest rates charged on a loan are not very meaningful *per se*. When a credit is tied to a project and to the country of origin the advantage gained from a concessional interest rate can easily be wiped out by the higher prices charged for equipment provided. The significance of the 'apparent' concessions by the USSR lies more in the fact that it challenged the prevalent view

[1] See Appendixes 2.1 and 2.2.
[2] *RBI Bulletin*, July 1970 (22, p. 1108, table 9).

on development – that the developing countries could afford to borrow what they needed at the current interest rate.

Rightly or wrongly, a great deal was made of the 'virtue' of giving loans rather than grants, both by American writers and by the Soviet statesmen. Consequently, after the Soviet entry into the arena of development aid, the emphasis of the U.S. aid programme on grants changed: the percentage of loans to the total funds received from the U.S.A. rose significantly from the First to the Second Plan.

The only loan from the United States during the First Plan, moreover, was an emergency food loan to purchase wheat; all funds made available for development were on a grant basis. The practice of other countries initially was similar but all moved towards loans rather than grants: as a result, the proportion of grants in total assistance dropped between the First and the Third Plans from 55 to 5·5 per cent. Similarly, after the USSR adopted the practice of non-convertible amortisation, viz., 'repayment in rupees' (see p. 46), India obtained such loans from the U.S. and Denmark worth Rs.2,787 million.

Perhaps the influence of the East European countries on other donors is most evident in the field of industrial development. The USSR made available the first official credits for industrial projects in the public sector; such credits were made for drugs, oil refineries and heavy engineering industries. In each of these cases, the offers were followed by offers from Consortium donors, but mainly for the use of private firms. The volume of official funds available for industrial development increased during the successive plans (see table 15).

Table 15 *Development loans authorised and utilised for industrial development* (in Rs. million)

	First Plan	Second Plan	Third Plan
Authorisation	193	7,390	15,266
Utilisation	23	2,554	12,836[a]

[a] Estimated.

Source: RBI, *Report on Currency and Finance* 1965/6, Statement 83.

East European practice affected that of other countries, however, in divergent ways: on the one hand it influenced aid offers away from grants towards loans, but because its interest charges were lower than those on loans offered by others, the latter had to reduce their rates. Thus replacing grants by loans hardened the terms, whereas lowering interest rates had the opposite effect.

Apart from the United States' wheat loan in 1951, the interest rate paid on all loans before Bhilai was the commercial interest rate. The principle of concessionary interest rates was not accepted in the U.S.A. until the establishment of the DLF in 1957, following an inquiry of the U.S. Congress into the success of the USSR's economic relations with the developing countries. As table 16 shows, interest rates were not brought down to 2·5 per cent or below until 1960. The DLF did introduce loans at interest rates varying between 3 and 5 per cent. While the World Bank did not, itself, lower the interest rates on its loans, its affiliate, the International Development Association (IDA) was established, which gave credits worth Rs.2,660 million at a nominal interest rate.

Table 16   *Loans at 2½ per cent or lower interest from East European and other countries authorised and utilised during the Second and Third Plans* (in Rs. million)

	Total amount utilised			Total amount authorised	
	All countries	East European countries	Others	East European countries	Others
	(1)	(2)	(3)	(4)	(5)
Second Plan	748·5	748·4	—	3,490·8	—
Third Plan	9,255·3	2,268·3	6,987·0	1,775·0	9,578·8

Notes: (1) Development credits only. (2) PL 480 and PL 665 are not included (value was Rs.15,983 million). (3) Official assistance only.

Source: Computed from the details of Loan Agreement. See: Ministry of Finance, *External Assistance,* 1965/6.

The initial effect of the availability of East European credits was to break the monopoly of private foreign investors in, for example, steel, the oil industry and pharmaceuticals. The fact that the position of foreign investors was being challenged roused the interest of governments in the Consortium group, which made funds available for the use of private firms in the same industries.

The Government of India wanted a steel plant in the public sector as early as 1952. The World Bank was informally approached about a loan for the project, but the government was informed by the Bank that it would not consider a loan for a public sector steel project.[1] This was because the Bank felt that the public sector should only do what the private sector could not or would not do. The government thereafter started negotiations with some Western firms and did get credits for two steel plants from West Germany and the United Kingdom, but the governments were not involved. The German firms gave a supplier's credit for a very short period which was later refinanced by the government.

The USSR came to India's rescue later in the case of the Bokaro steel plant. Initially India had approached the United States for a fourth steel plant in the public sector. The administration was sympathetic to the idea because many people felt that there was no monument to the U.S. aid effort in India. Moreover, the British and the German plants had run into difficulties. An American team of experts and technicians came to India to do a technical-economic survey of the project, and a preliminary report was prepared. These negotiations had been going on for more than two years when a committee of private citizens, appointed by President Kennedy, brought out a report taking a firm stand against helping enterprises in the public sector. The Clay Committee argued that, while the United States could not force its system of free enterprise upon others, it would be unreasonable to expect the U.S. to support the public sector.[2] This report was favourably received in the U.S. Congress. The Bokaro steel plant was in the public sector and the Government of India was reluctant to allow equity participation from private American and Indian firms. Rather

---

[1] Loksabha Secretariat (117). In reply to a question asked about financing a steel plant in the public sector, the Minister concerned stated that the World Bank had been approached informally.   [2] Clay Committee (16).

than have its request turned down by the U.S. Congress, the Government of India decided to withdraw the request for a loan. Even though the USSR had already given its quota for the Third Plan, it expressed its willingness to finance the Bokaro steel plant.

The pharmaceutical industry and the exploration for and refining of petroleum were listed under Schedule B in the Industrial Resolution of 1956, which meant that the public sector was expected to take a leading part in the future development of these industries. Their characteristic is that they are dominated by a few giant companies, are highly profitable and require advanced technical know-how. It was not until the East European countries had offered to cooperate with the government that these companies showed any willingness similarly to collaborate.

The pharmaceutical industry in India was completely dominated by foreign firms in the fifties, and the prices of drugs were very high. The major branches of this industry are antibiotics and sulphonamides, but hardly any were produced in India before the 1950s. At the time of the Pharmaceutical Enquiry Committee report in 1954, manufacturing still consisted largely of encapsulating and packing. For the Government of India, this was quite unsatisfactory, and it started the production of penicillin and a few other drugs with technical assistance provided by the World Health Organisation. Pharmaceuticals is one of the industries which is most heavily protected by patents, which foreign firms guard very zealously. India could only have broken this monopoly by seeking technical know-how from the East European countries. The USSR offered to set up five plants to manufacture antibiotics and surgical instruments in the public sector in 1955/6. American firms considered this as a challenge and brought pressure upon the Government of India to let an American firm, Merck and Co., into the industry.

The full story came out in a debate on an agreement between the Hindustan Antibiotics Co. and Merck and Co., in the Loksabha. The American firm was given a royalty payment of $2\frac{1}{2}$ per cent on domestic sales after tax and 5 per cent on sales abroad in return for the technical know-how provided for the production of penicillin and streptomycin. According to General

Sokhey,[1] who went to the USSR as a member of the negotiating team, the Soviet authorities had already given the Indian firm the formulas, strains and instructions for the development of streptomycin and dihydrostreptomycin. In spite of this the Hindustan Antibiotics Co. agreed to pay a royalty to Merck and Co. for the same formulas and not to pass them on to other firms in India.

If the USSR had really offered India the technical know-how then the agreement with Merck and Co. was an unnecessary import. India had to make this concession because American firms were very anxious that the industry should not be taken over by the USSR. Apart from the danger of the political pressure which they might have brought to bear, they offered the incentives of lower import prices for drugs and a reduction in the cost of streptomycin and dihydrostreptomycin in India. The Minister concerned pointed out this part of the agreement as being an advantage.

The history of these negotiations with the USSR shows how the Soviet Union's willingness to help set up the industry enabled India to get marginal concessions from private foreign firms. The prices of these products were coming down in the U.S.A. in 1958 due to overproduction. However, India would not have benefited from this price reduction had the USSR not been interested in setting up a plant. The Indian pharmaceuticals industry has not proved successful, but that is a different issue.

However, India benefited by breaking the monopoly of private firms in the field of exploration for petroleum. In the post-independence period, India signed agreements with three Western firms to set up refineries in India. These companies had complete freedom regarding the prices and the source of supply of crude oil. Therefore they had no interest in, nor any incentive to prospect for, oil in India. Even if India had persuaded other companies to prospect for crude oil in India the existing refineries could and would have refused to take it. In 1959/60 the USSR offered to sell its own crude oil to India at a discount of from 15 to 20 per cent below the world market

---

[1] Loksabha Secretariat (117). Mr Parulekar as M.P. made a speech in Loksabha when the Hindustan Antibiotics and Merck and Co. contract was being discussed, 19 April 1959.

price, but India was unable to accept this offer because the existing plants refused to refine it. Rumania and the Soviet Union then offered to set up plants in the public sector to refine any imported or indigenous crude oil.

In spite of the Government of India's earlier efforts, Western firms were not interested in investing in oil exploration and production in India. In December 1953, an agreement was signed with Stanvac (U.S.) for joint exploration in an area of 10,000 square miles in West Bengal. The government participation was limited to 25 per cent of the expenses or a maximum of Rs.25 million. Y. Yershov,[1] a Russian author, says that, though the agreement was signed in 1953, Stanvac had already been carrying out a geological and airborne magnetic survey which indicated considerable oil-bearing areas in West Bengal. In support of his contention he says that *The Statesman* of 5 December 1953 quoted well-informed circles as saying that the survey had revealed the existence of large oil deposits in that area. A year earlier the newspaper *Imorza*[2] carried an interview with a Stanvac spokesman who declared that a preliminary survey of the areas bordering on the Bay of Bengal had revealed the existence of considerable oil deposits.[3] The company drilled some ten wells but progress was slow and in 1960 Stanvac stated in an official communique that it was terminating operations in West Bengal.

At Naharkotia, Assam, an oilfield located as early as 1923 was not being exploited, on the grounds that the strata were 3.2 km. deep. This reason was regarded with some suspicion because there were oil wells in the U.S.A. (Wyoming) nearly 7 km. deep. It was not until 1953 that drilling began at Naharkotia, and the production of crude was delayed for another five years, on the grounds that transport facilities were not ready. The Estimates Committee severely criticised this delay.[4]

The argument is not that the Western oil companies were deliberately following anti-Indian policies, but that they just did not find it actually or potentially lucrative enough to develop oil production in India, for oil refineries in India had

---

[1] Yershov (98, p. 50, n. 2).
[2] *Imroza* is published in Pakistan.
[3] Yershov, *ibid.*
[4] Quoted in the Bureau of Petroleum Information, *A Handbook on the Petroleum Industry in India* (99).

complete freedom regarding their source of supply. India was a large and growing market and it was against the refining companies' interest to discover or develop new fields in India when the world supply situation was such that petroleum companies were taking steps to control rather than to expand output in the fifties. If they had found considerable oil reserves in India, the Government of India would have brought pressure on them to refine domestic crude oil and they would have lost yet another market for their existing sources. Another deterrent may have been the costs of exploration in India. The companies would have had to start by making detailed geological surveys, and they might reasonably have preferred to concentrate on areas where some preliminary work had been done already and the costs of further exploration were therefore lower.

The Soviet Union not only offered to help in prospecting for crude oil but actually produced results. The oil potential in Cambay was put at 30 million tons, and oil in commercial quantities was discovered at Ankleshwar. To process this oil, the USSR and Rumania offered technical and economic assistance to set up refineries in the public sector in 1958 and 1959. At this stage no Western firms would have been interested in co-operating with the government. When the original agreements with Burmah–Shell and Stanvac were negotiated they were reluctant to offer any equity capital to the public sector in India. After the USSR had built two refineries in the public sector, however, foreign firms became interested and the government was offered two refineries at nearly half the price of the first USSR refinery. Goldman described the events as follows: 'There was considerable evidence to indicate that the Indians had paid an exorbitant price for Russian help. By the time the Indians had decided to build a third refinery at Koyali, the Western firms realised the seriousness of the situation and began to make counter efforts. In addition, once the cartel had been broken, other Western firms decided to enter the field. Consequently, Philips Petroleum Company of Bartlesville, Oklahoma, won the right to build the fourth refinery for the Indian Government at Cochin in Madras. Their plan called for an initial capacity of 2·5 million tons. This provoked bids from ENI (the Italian state-owned oil corporation) and other

Western firms. Thus, for the first time, India was permitted the luxury of competitive offers.'[1]

India benefited further from the competition between private firms and the East European countries, as the Soviet Union brought down the cost of the refinery at Koyali. The Soviet Union is very sensitive about its image among the developing countries and once it was known that the prices of Western refineries were much lower than those from the USSR it responded quickly. Even though India paid a higher price for a refinery from the Soviet Union, this was necessary in order to attract participation in the public sector from Western firms, which was achieved in the form of credits from the United Kingdom and France for building pipelines and for prospecting.

The comparison between the aid programmes of East European countries and others brings out clearly the fact that the former have acted as a supplementary source of finance which is relatively small, and that, were the USSR to cut off its aid tomorrow, it would impose no great financial strain. The Soviet Union's emergence as a donor has not reduced India's dependence on the West, but it has made her a more attractive candidate for aid. This 'aid-inducing effect' of the East European countries has proved invaluable. The comparison has also brought out the fact that the only innovation in the aid programme of the East European countries since 1954 is the provision of supplier's credits since 1967 to pay for spares and components. If the East European countries are not willing to consider loans for other purposes – apart from setting up heavy industry in the public sector – it is worth asking the question whether these loans are worth negotiating. As the *Economic Survey*, 1969/70, points out, 'the Indian economy has now developed to a stage at which a considerable part of the capital equipment required not only by industry but also by power, transport, communication, agriculture and other sectors can be fabricated within the country with import only of components and raw materials' (p. 41).

In so far as external loans continue to be project tied, this problem – whether to utilise domestic capacity created and to forgo a foreign credit – will have to be faced, irrespective of the source of finance. The problem is that most of the progress

[1] Goldman (28, pp. 98–9).

in import substitution has been in fields which interest foreign donors. The problem will be felt in negotiating East European credits, because the Soviet-aided enterprises, such as the heavy machine building plant, are grossly underutilised. A liberalisation in the USSR's credit policies would go a long way in enhancing its value as a creditor.

Appendix 2.1 *Authorisation of external assistance classified by source, 1951/2 to 1969/70 (in Rs. million)* [a]

Source (1)	Total (2)	Up to First Plan (3)	During Second Plan (4)	During Third Plan (5)	1966/7 (6)	1967/8 (7)	1968/9 (8)	1969/70 April–September (9)
1. Consortium members		3,035	21,524	26,947	10,745	6,952	9,373	2,723
(a) Loans repayable in foreign currency		1,475	6,803	20,856	6,842	4,438	8,033	2,401
(b) Loans repayable in rupees		146	2,268	460	180	—	—	—
(c) Grants		1,245	1,146	1,125	655	85	624	160
(d) Other assistance (PL 480/665 etc.)		169	11,307	4,506	3,068	2,429	716	162
Distribution by country								
(i) Austria Loans		—	—	85	35	34	7	—
(ii) Belgium Loans		—	—	114	—	28	94	—
(iii) Canada Loans		—	157	328	408	522	208	447
Grants		323	571	851	577	72	528	111
Total		323	728	1,179	985	594	736	558
(iv) Denmark								
(a) Loans repayable in foreign currency		—	—	13	19	30	40	—
(b) Loans repayable in rupees		—	—	9	—	—	—	—
(c) Grants		—	—	—	—	—	—	8
Total		—	—	22	19	30	40	8

(v) France	Loans	—	—	720	225	—	450	—
(vi) West Germany	Loans	—	1,331	3,066	473	469	469	435
	Grants	—	21	7	18	6	36	36
	Total	—	1,352	3,073	491	475	505	471
(vii) Italy	Loans	—	—	809	233	—	41	98
(viii) Japan	Loans	—	354	1,304	319	344	212	—
	Grants		4	1	—			—
	Total	—	358	1,305	319	344	212	—
(ix) Netherlands	Loans	—	—	228	83	83	68	—
(x) Sweden	Loans	—	—	22	35	—	109	—
	Grants	—	—	38	20	—	—	—
	Total	—	—	60	55	—	109	—
(xi) United Kingdom	Loans	—	1,227	2,370	591	594	648	135
	Grants	4	4	10	1	1	49	
	Total	4	1,231	2,380	592	595	697	135
(xii) U.S.A.								
(a) Loans repayable in foreign currency		903	1,129	7,682	1,901	2,146	4,749	363
(b) Loans repayable in rupees		146	2,268	451	180	—	—	—
(c) Grants		918	546	218	39	6	11	5
(d) Other assistance (PL 480/665 etc.)		169	11,307	4,506	3,068	2,429	716	162
	Total	2,136	15,250	12,857	5,188	4,581	5,476	530
(xiii) IBRD	Loans	572	2,605	1,357	225	188	—	304
(xiv) IDA	Loans	—	—	2,758	2,295	—	938	619
2. USSR and East European countries	Total	647	3,741	1,714	3,375	121	—	—
	Loans	647	3,729	1,672	3,350	113	—	—
	Grants	—	12	42	25	8	—	—

Appendix 2.1 (contd.)

(1) Source	(2)	(3) Up to First Plan	(4) During Second Plan	(5) During Third Plan	(6) 1966/7	(7) 1967/8	(8) 1968/9	(9) 1969/70 April–September
Distribution by country								
(i) Bulgaria	Loans	—	—	—	—	113	—	—
(ii) Czechoslovakia	Loans	—	211	400	—	—	—	—
	Grants	—	—	4	—	—	—	—
	Total	—	211	404	—	—	—	—
(iii) Hungary	Loans	—	—	—	250	—	—	—
(iv) Poland	Loans	—	147	214	—	—	—	—
(v) USSR	Loans	647	3,191	1,058	2,500	8	—	—
	Grants	—	12	38	25	8	—	—
	Total	647	3,203	1,096	2,525	—	—	—
(vi) Yugoslavia	Loans	—	180	—	600	—	—	—
3. Others	Total	135	123	322	113	76	47	—
	Loans	—	65	163	—	—	16	—
	Grants	135	58	159	113	76	31	—
Distribution by country								
(i) Australia	Grants	111	22	124	89	76	31	—
(ii) New Zealand	Grants	17	17	9	2	—	—	—
(iii) Norway	Loans	—	—	—	—	—	16	—
	Grants	7	19	26	22	—	—	—
	Total	7	19	26	22	—	16	—

	Loans						
(iv) Switzerland	—	65	163	—	—	—	—
GRAND TOTAL	3,817	25,388	28,983	14,233	7,149	9,420	2,723
(i) Loans repayable in:							
(a) Foreign currency	2,122	10,597	22,691	10,192	4,551	8,049	2,401
(b) Rupees	146	2,268	460	180	—	—	—
(ii) Grants	1,380	1,216	1,326	793	169	655	160[b]
(iii) Other assistance (PL 480/665 etc.)	169	11,307	4,506	3,068	2,429	716	162

[a] Post-devaluation rupees.
[b] Wheat assistance amounting to Rs.38 mn. was also authorised by the European Economic Community under the International Grains Agreement.

Note: In addition to the above authorisations, debt relief in the form of re-scheduling or postponement was provided as under:

	1966/7	1967/8	1968/9	1969/70 (April–September)
Japan	1·9	4·6	12·6	14·7
Canada	—	0·5	0·7	—
U.S.A.	—	—	6·6	6·6
IBRD	—	11·3	11·3	11·3

Source: Government of India, *Economic Survey*, 1969/70.

Appendix 2.2 *Utilisation of external assistance classified by sources, 1951/2 to 1969/70 (in Rs. million)* [a]

(1) Source	(2)	(3) Up to First Plan	(4) During Second Plan	(5) During Third Plan	(6) 1966/7	(7) 1967/8	(8) 1968/9	(9) 1969/70 April–September
1. Consortium members	Total	1,955	13,420	26,066	9,792	11,056	7,729	4,257
(a) Loans repayable in foreign currency		1,241	5,331	15,051	5,709	7,396	6,232	3,330
(b) Loans repayable in rupees		23	1,168	1,564	95	41	74	—
(c) Grants		640	1,473	919	748	510	577	109
(d) Other assistance (PL 480/665 etc.)		51	5,448	8,532	3,240	3,109	846	818
Distribution by country								
(i) Austria	Loans	—	—	47	36	32	30	9
(ii) Belgium	Loans	—	—	49	—	19	16	95
(iii) Canada	Loans	—	157	115	112	179	290	132
	Grants	197	603	544	665	455	481	75
	Total	197	760	659	777	634	771	207
(iv) Denmark:								
(a) Loans repayable in foreign currency		—	—	—	21	29	15	8
(b) Loans repayable in rupees		—	—	6	5	Negligible		—

(c) Grants — Total	—	—	6	26	29	15	8
(v) France — Loans	—	—	210	69	338	137	16
(vi) West Germany — Loans	—	1,199	2,197	613	676	582	176
Grants	—	6	20	16	6	36	18
Total	—	1,205	2,217	629	682	618	194
(vii) Italy — Loans	—	—	117	1	15	544	351
(viii) Japan — Loans	—	160	882	267	402	554	138
Grants	—	4	1	—	—	—	—
Total	—	164	883	267	402	554	138
(ix) Netherlands — Loans	—	—	95	62	84	47	63
(x) Sweden — Loans	—	—	—	15	13	21	—
Grants	—	—	35	22	1	—	5
Total	—	—	35	37	14	21	5
(xi) United Kingdom — Loans	—	1,219	1,704	882	806	549	243
Grants	—	4	8	1	5	47	2
Total	—	1,223	1,712	883	811	596	245
(xii) U.S.A.							
(a) Loans repayable in foreign currency	903	368	6,395	2,101	2,964	2,679	1,252
(b) Loans repayable in rupees	23	1,168	1,558	90	41	74	—
(c) Grants	443	856	311	44	43	13	6
(d) Other assistance (PL 480/665 etc.)	51	5,448	8,532	3,240	3,109	846	818
Total	1,420	7,840	16,796	5,475	6,157	3,612	2,076
(xiii) IBRD — Loans	338	2,228	1,234	245	228	193	81
(xiv) IDA — Loans	—	—	2,006	1,285	1,611	575	751

Appendix 2.2 (*contd.*)

Source		Up to First Plan	During Second Plan	During Third Plan	1966/7	1967/8	1968/9	1969/70 April–September
(1)	(2)	(3)	(4)	(5)	(6)	(7)	(8)	(9)
2. USSR and East European countries	Total	—	761	2,450	525	601	862	393
	Loans	—	749	2,408	515	590	862	393
	Grants	—	12	42	10	11	—	—
Distribution by country								
(i) Bulgaria	Loans	—	—	—	—	—	—	—
(ii) Czechoslovakia	Loans	—	—	126	126	74	161	51
	Grants	—	—	4	—	—	—	—
	Total	—	—	130	126	74	161	51
(iii) Hungary	Loans	—	—	—	—	—	—	—
(iv) Poland	Loans	—	—	113	9	18	14	19
(v) USSR	Loans	—	749	2,072	336	464	565	321
	Grants	—	12	38	10	11	—	—
	Total	—	761	2,110	346	475	565	321
(vi) Yugoslavia	Loans	—	—	97	44	34	122	2

3. Others	Total	62	122	161	239	115	58	10
	Loans	—	—	60	70	31	22	10
	Grants	62	122	101	169	84	36	—
Distribution by country								
(i) Australia	Grants	52	74	70	160	78	31	—
(ii) New Zealand	Grants	3	29	5	2	1	—	—
(iii) Norway	Grants	7	19	26	7	5	5	—
(iv) Switzerland	Loans	—	—	60	70	31	22	10
GRAND TOTAL	Loans	2,017	14,303	28,677	10,556	11,772	8,649	4,660
(a) Loans repayable in foreign currency		1,241	6,080	17,519	6,294	8,017	7,116	3,733
(b) Loans repayable in rupees		23	1,168	1,564	95	41	74	—
(c) Grants		702	1,607	1,062	927	605	613	109[b]
(d) Other assistance (PL 480/665 etc.)		51	5,448	8,532	3,240	3,109	846	818

[a] Post-devaluation rupees.
[b] In addition, wheat assistance amounting to Rs.26 million was provided by the European Economic Community.

Source: Government of India, *Economic Survey*, 1969/70.

3

BALANCE OF PAYMENTS AND NET INFLOW OF FUNDS FROM THE EAST EUROPEAN COUNTRIES

In the period for which sufficient data are available for reconstructing India's balance of payments with the East European countries, viz. 1953/4 to 1965/6, India had comprehensive trade and payments agreements with each of the East European countries, under which the balances accumulated by a partner country could only be used for importing goods and services from the other partner. Since India was a net borrower during the period 1956/7 to 1968/9 it is reasonable to expect capital receipts to have been reflected in the current account deficit; if they were not, the explanation may be that India encountered difficulties in purchasing goods from Eastern Europe, and had to accumulate idle balances, which in effect constitute a waste of credit finance. An examination of India's trade with the rest of the world and with East European countries does reveal differences, even though India was a net borrower from both groups.

During the period 1950/1 to 1969/70 India's total trade with the world in both directions increased from Rs.12,500 million to Rs.29,600 million. During the same time trade with the East European countries increased from Rs.72 million to Rs.5,880 million, registering a much faster growth than India's trade with the world as a whole. However, there is an interesting contrast between India's trade with the world and India's trade with Eastern Europe. While India had sizable trade deficits on its merchandise trade account with the world every year during the decade 1956/7 to 1965/6, it had a surplus on its merchandise trade account with Eastern Europe, as shown in the published official trade statistics in four of these years.

After 1955, the flow of public capital funds (loans and grants) to India increased substantially. During the period 1956/7 to 1965/6, India utilised public loans and grants worth Rs.43,000 million. It is reasonable to expect that this flow would be reflected in the deficit on external trade, because external credits are generally made available for importing goods. Even though the credits from the Soviet Union, Poland, and Yugoslavia can also be used for paying for technical services rendered and shipping, these payments would not amount to more than 25 per cent of the credits utilised, and therefore net capital receipts would be reflected mainly in the merchandise trade account. However, India's net capital receipts from the East European countries of Rs.2,440 million during the period 1956/7 to 1965/6 are only partly reflected in the trade deficit during that period of Rs.680 million (see table 17).

Table 17 *Comparison of India's trade balance and net credits utilised, 1956/7 to 1965/6* (in Rs. million)

Country	1956/7 to 1960/1		1961/2 to 1965/6		Total: 1956/7 to 1965/6	
	Net credits utilised	Trade balances	Net credits utilised	Trade balances	Net credits utilised	Trade balances
Czechoslovakia		−88·5	−126·9	−249·5	126·9	−338·0
Poland		−65·1	112·3	−106·6	112·3	−171·7
USSR	561·5	+256·0	1,551·3	−341·9	2,122·3	−85·9
Yugoslavia^a		−61·9	97·3	−43·8	90·3	−105·7
Rumania	39·0	−29·7	−40·0	+42·4		+12·7
Sub-total	600·5	+10·8	1,840·8	−720·0	2,441·8	−70
Bulgaria		−6·4	28·1			−34·5
East Germany		+3·2		+45·6		+48·8
Hungary		−30·2		+27·0		−3·2
Sub-total		−63·1		+99·3		+36·2
Total	600·5	−22·6	1,840·8	−657·9	2,441·3	−680·5

^a The DGCIS import statistics for Yugoslavia are incomplete because they do not include imports of ships. The 1961/2 to 1965/6 import figures as published have been adjusted accordingly.

Note: Revised figures were used where available (especially for totals for receipts and repayments, 1956/7 to 1960/1).

Sources: 'Net credits utilised': The figures for 1956/7 to 1960/1 are taken from the *Explanatory Memorandum on the Budget of the Central Government*, 1961/2, Statements on receipts and repayments of foreign loans; those for the years 1961/2 to 1965/6 are taken from EC, 1967/8, 11th Report, 4th Loksabha, p. 143. Trade balances: DGCIS.

India utilised gross credits worth Rs.3,215 million from the East European countries during the period 1956/7 to 1965/6, while its total recorded imports from these countries were Rs.8,075 million. Therefore India apparently needed Rs.4,860 million to pay for its non-credit financed imports from Eastern Europe. As India's export earnings during the same period were Rs.7,450 million, it appears that after paying for current imports there were excess export earnings of Rs.2,570 million to pay for invisible and unrecorded imports. Looked at from a different angle, India had an apparent deficit of nearly Rs.630 million on its commercial trade, whereas the gross receipts of development credits amounted to Rs.3,215 million. The question therefore arises as to how these excess credits or excess export earnings were utilised. The explanation must be sought in debt servicing and other payments for invisibles and in the possibility of unrecorded imports.

When trade between India and another country is not regulated by any special payments arrangements, there is not necessarily any connection between the size of the Indian trade deficit and its capital receipts because, though aid may be tied to purchases within the donor country, India can use its export earnings to settle accounts elsewhere. Under the non-convertible payment agreements all transactions, commercial and non-commercial (including defence imports), can be settled with the balances accumulated, but these balances cannot be used for settling accounts with any third party. It is because of the comprehensive nature of these agreements and the provision that the excess balances have to be converted into technical credits until they can be eliminated by importing or by reducing exports that the size of India's current account deficit acquires significance. If an examination of India's balance of payments with the East European countries shows that it has not been able to finance a deficit on its current balance equal or nearly equal to the amount of net development (and defence) credits utilised, but has been giving its partners technical credits, it may be concluded that India could not exploit the balances to import.

It is worth finding out whether the USSR, the main creditor and the most important trading partner in this group, lived up to its obligations; that is, whether India's current account deficit was equal to credit receipts. It is possible that Hungary and Bulgaria were giving India technical credits while India was giving technical credits to the USSR. As the balances accumulated with the Soviet Union cannot be used to pay other countries, the technical credits given to the Soviet Union are a waste of credit finance.

If India gives technical credits to a lender country, it means in effect that the effective rate of utilisation of development credits by India is slower or that the rate of repayment of credits is accelerated. As the payment agreements with each East European country include all transactions, commercial and non-commercial, the question whether India's capital receipts are reflected in the current account deficit can only be answered by examining India's overall balance of payments with each of these countries. However, there are published data only on merchandise trade and development credit receipts payments. This is a convenient starting point: the rest of the balance has to be reconstructed.

Since 1962 India has been importing defence equipment against defence credits and/or grants from some East European countries and payments for defence equipment are made from export earnings. For security reasons, the Reserve Bank of India has not published even a summary statement of India's balance of payments with the East European countries. It has to be reconstructed by putting together the information available from different sources. Before constructing a balance of payments statement, however, the evolution of these special trade and payment agreements and the working of these non-convertible rupee payment agreements is explained below. This helps in understanding how currency balances are accumulated.

THE EVOLUTION OF TRADE AND PAYMENT AGREEMENTS[1]

The first trade agreement between India and any East European country was signed with Yugoslavia in 1948 and was followed by agreements with Czechoslovakia, Hungary, and Poland in 1949. These agreements were effectively agreements

[1] The characteristics of these agreements are summarised in Appendix 1.5, p. 41.

on trade quotas and there were no special payment arrangements. Payments were either made in sterling or could be converted into sterling. The first agreements containing special payment arrangements were signed in 1953. Between 1953 and 1956, each East European country in turn accepted the rupee as the unit of account in trade with India and it was agreed in principle that trade should be bilaterally balanced. However, if a surplus on either side developed in any year, the country concerned could demand settlement in sterling; and in the fifties settlements in convertible currency were quite common. Between 1959 and 1960, however, the agreements were revised and trading partner countries agreed not to demand the balancing payments in convertible currency but to hold rupee balances or on India's side to allow an overdraft on the partner country's rupee account until trade could be adjusted to absorb them.

Thus the surplus country has to give the deficit country a 'technical' or 'swing' credit as mentioned above, the purpose of which is to iron out short-term imbalances until accounts are restored to equilibrium. In the early fifties the agreements were annual but of late the pattern is a three- to five-year trade and payment agreement, implying that balances can be left outstanding for that period or – in effect – for longer. There are four characteristics of the present arrangements:

(i) *Payments in non-convertible rupees*

Under the present agreements payments for all transactions, commercial and non-commercial, are made in non-convertible rupees; but there is a clause that any outstanding balances can be settled by negotiations between the two countries. Therefore, a settlement in convertible currency has not been ruled out explicitly. However, no accounts have in fact been settled in convertible currency and balances have been carried over from one trade and payments agreement to the subsequent agreement period.

(ii) *Gold clause*

Though the unit of account is the rupee, the East European countries are protected against devaluation, because the exchange value of the rupee is fixed in terms of its gold content.

(iii) *No convertibility within the group*[1]

Until 1969 there was no convertibility within the group under the current arrangement, i.e. balances accumulated by India with one country could not be used to settle accounts with any other East European country; neither, for example, could Poland use a rupee surplus to make payments to the Soviet Union.

(iv) *No distinction between aid-financed and commercial transactions in trade accounts*

Though the payments for the credit financed and current imports come from different accounts, the two are not distinguished in the trade statistics. Therefore, the only way to separate aid and non-aid imports is to deduct the amount of net development credits utilised from the amount of total imports. Some development credits could, however, be used to pay for technical assistance and for shipping. Though it is not known whether India actually used these credits to pay for technical assistance and shipping, it is assumed here that 10 per cent of the amount of net credits utilised was so used. Therefore, out of the net credits utilised (Rs.600 million and Rs.1,840 million during the sub-periods 1956/7 to 1960/1 and 1961/2 to 1965/6) India had about Rs.540 million and Rs.1,655 million available for credit financed imports. India's total imports during these sub-periods were Rs.1,810 million and Rs.6,275 million. Therefore, India needed only Rs.1,210 and Rs.4,620 million to pay for current (recorded and unrecorded) imports and for net imports of services. As India's export earnings during the two periods came to Rs.1,785 and Rs.5,665 million, after paying for recorded non-aid imports, it had Rs.585 million and Rs.1,040 million left over respectively.

[1] This statement is valid for the period under consideration, but the transfer of balances from one East European country to another has subsequently been arranged. The *East–West Trade News*, 13 February 1969, noted that, to pay for imports from India, Bulgaria will transfer Rs. 15 million to Hungary, and Czechoslovakia will transfer Rs. 1·5 million to East Germany; it added that this was the first time India had allowed such an arrangement. However, the impression is gained from talks with Indian officials that India's East European partners – especially the USSR – have been reluctant to allow transferability within their group.

THE OPERATION OF PAYMENTS AGREEMENTS

The annual trade targets are fixed within the general framework of these agreements. The aim of these targets is to ensure a balance of total receipts and payments during each period under consideration. The trade targets are supposed to be devised in such a way that India's export earnings are sufficient to pay for commercial imports, repayments of development and other credits and any net payments on account of other current invisibles (including payments for defence imports). Thus if the agreements work as they should, India's trade deficit $M+M_1-X$ should equal $E-P-R-E_1-R_1$.

M = Imports (c.i.f.) excluding (combatant) defence equipment
M_1 = Imports of (c.i.f.) of (combatant) defence equipment
X = Exports f.o.b.
E = Development credits utilised
E_1 = Defence credits utilised
R = Repayment of principal of development credits
R_1 = Repayment of principal of defence credits
P = Net receipts/payments for current invisible interest payments, payments for technical assistance, transport freight and insurance

If $M+M_1-X<E-P-R-E_1-R_1$ the inequality is caused by net technical credits (T).

The need for India to give technical credit has arisen to a large extent from India's difficulty in finding acceptable imports to absorb her export earnings in Eastern Europe and from the slowness with which the East European countries have, on occasion, fulfilled export commitments. The difficulty in finding goods has two possible consequences. First, India may have had to import unnecessary goods. Secondly, India may have prepaid her debts. Though it is difficult to ascertain whether and to what extent India had to buy unnecessary goods, the debt repayment schedules can throw light on the question of timely or premature payment. The size of T is therefore only an approximate indication of the extent to which the real value of the development credits received by India falls short of their apparent value. It may understate the effective shortfall where either low priority imports have been accepted and/or the debt repayment burden has been accelerated.

COMPARISON BETWEEN INDIA'S TRADE BALANCE WITH AND NET CAPITAL RECEIPTS FROM EAST EUROPEAN COUNTRIES

It is easiest to start this discussion by comparing India's net capital receipts from each East European country with India's merchandise trade account with that country.

In the sub-period 1956/7 to 1960/1 most of the credits which India utilised were from the USSR, with a small credit from Rumania. In the period 1961/2 to 1965/6, India utilised credits from Poland and Czechoslovakia as well as from the USSR. Table 17 shows that in the cases of Poland, Yugoslavia, and Rumania the amount of net capital receipts is nearly equal to the deficit on the merchandise trade account in the period 1961/2 to 1965/6. In Czechoslovakia's case the latter is more than double the amount of net credits utilised, because the imports include non-combatant defence imports which were in fact wholly or partially credit financed, while the amount of credits utilised excludes receipts of defence credits.

For the East European countries excluding the USSR therefore, capital receipts are largely reflected in the trade deficit. However, India's experience with the USSR is very different. During the period 1956/7 to 1960/1, India had a surplus of more than Rs.250 million on her merchandise trade account (as indicated in the published official trade statistics) even though the net development credits utilised were about Rs.560 million. During the period 1960/1 to 1965/6 the size of India's trade deficit was much smaller (about Rs.340 million) than the amount of net development credits utilised (more than Rs.1,500 million). Since the USSR was the largest creditor, accounting for about 75 per cent of the development credits received from all East European countries, it is very important to find out why the capital receipts from that country did not enable India to accumulate a bigger trade deficit than she actually did.

The discussion above is based upon the data available from Indian sources. It may be argued that Indian import statistics are defective and may be misleading. Therefore, it is worthwhile to check whether Indian trade statistics tally with those of the partner countries from Eastern Europe, for both exports and imports.

Table 18   *India's trade with each East European country as shown in the reporting country's statistics, 1960–5*

Country	Exports reported from India (f.o.b.)	Imports recorded by the partner country (f.o.b.)	Imports reported by India (c.i.f.)	Exports reported from the East European country (f.o.b.)	Adjusted to c.i.f. (recorded f.o.b. 10%)
	(1)	(2)	(3)	(4)	(5)
Bulgaria	106·7	119·3	134·8	131·1	144·1
Czechoslovakia	681·2	690·3	930·6	964·9	1,057·9
East Germany	497·7	479·2	452·1	491·7	540·8
Hungary	324·1	422·2 (380·0)ᵃ	290·0	360·5	360·5
Poland	459·3	414·8	565·9	569·6	626·5
Rumania	164·4	199·3	122·0	159·5	175·5
USSR	2,933·5	2,744·8	3,275·0	4,283·2	4,711·5
Yugoslavia	494·6	496·5 (450·0)ᵃ	490·5	510·2	510·2

ᵃ Adjusted for f.o.b. valuation.
Note: Hungary and Yugoslavia record imports c.i.f. but all other countries record imports f.o.b.
Source: See Appendixes 3.2 and 3.3.

Table 18 shows that, despite the differences in timing, coverage and valuation, the figures for exports from India and imports into the partner country compare well, except for Hungary and the USSR. The figures from the two sources are not exactly identical but the differences are small enough to be put down to differences in coverage and timing and to errors and omissions. This is not the case with imports. Most East European countries record import statistics f.o.b., whereas the Indian import statistics are on a c.i.f. basis. The East European statistics have to be adjusted to include freight and insurance payments to make the two comparable. While the allowance made for freight and insurance varies from commodity to commodity, an average of 10 per cent of the f.o.b. value is generally used. After making this correction, the exports of East European countries are higher than the corresponding Indian figure, but this can easily be explained because the latter include payments for technical assistance – documentation etc. – which India does not. This, in addition to the differences in timing and valuation, provides an adequate explanation of the differences with all other countries except the USSR and Hungary.

In Hungary's case, imports and exports are both about 30 per cent higher than the corresponding Indian figures. The explanation must be either a different valuation or an exchange rate other than the official rate used here. No simple explanation will suffice in interpreting the Soviet Union's trade statistics. When the Soviet Union's exports to India and India's imports from the Soviet Union are both valued on a c.i.f. basis, the former are nearly Rs. 1,430 million greater than the former – too much to be explained by the usual sources of discrepancy. There are some peculiarities of the Indian and Soviet statistics which explain part of the discrepancy, such as the note pass system.

It is explained in the Technical Appendix 3.1 that at any one point of time the official Indian trade statistics (DGCIS) are incomplete because of the delays in recording government imports. To allow for this incomplete coverage 20 per cent of the last year's imports during the period under consideration should be added to the recorded figure.[1] As India's imports from the Soviet Union during 1965/6 were about Rs.900 million, the under-recording is about Rs.180 million. Therefore the figure for Indian imports from table 18 should be Rs.3,450 million and not Rs.3,275 million.

According to Soviet returns, India's imports of complete plant and equipment (item 16 in the Soviet commodity trade statistics) during the period 1961/5 amounted, after conversion at the official exchange rate, to Rs.2,000 million. From a survey of the technical assistance payments to the USSR for development aided projects, it appears that these payments amounted to about 10 per cent of the amount of the credit. If it is assumed that about 10 per cent of the price of the complete plant is paid for technical services, about Rs.200 million (of the price paid for the complete plant) would not be included in the Indian figure for imports. Therefore, the comparable figure for the

[1] See Appendix 3.1.

Soviet Union's imports should be Rs.4,511 million and not Rs.4,711 million.

The corrected figures of the Soviet Union's imports and Indian exports still show that the former are greater by Rs.1,060 million than the latter. There is no easy explanation of this gap. One possible hypothesis is that while the Indian trade statistics do not include combatant defence imports, the Soviet statistics do. The evidence available is rather ambiguous. The Soviet Union has an obvious interest in not revealing the magnitude of this trade, and therefore it is unlikely to be included in the published trade statistics. However, the defence equipment can be included under transport equipment or as miscellaneous items. That way, exports of defence equipment are recorded but are non-distinguishable from ordinary commercial exports. There is one good reason why the USSR may have started including defence equipment in merchandise exports. Even though it was a net creditor to the developing countries it often had trade surpluses with them, for instance with Burma and Argentina in the period 1955–7.[1] This proved embarrassing on two counts. The countries concerned themselves complained and various commentators in the Western countries, especially the United States, were quick to point it out. Tactically it may be a good move to include all the exports in published statistics. However, this is pure conjecture.

From the information available from the Indian side, it also appears that the size of defence imports is consistent with the unexplained gap between Russian and Indian figures regarding Indian imports and the Soviet Union's exports.[2] A comparison of the annual figures shows that the gap between Indian import statistics and Russian export statistics widens considerably after 1962 – when India started importing defence equipment on a large scale.

The other possibility is that the Indian Customs used different

---

[1] See U.S. Senate Report (86, pp. 14–18).

[2] The author personally discussed this question with the various government officials concerned with Indo–East European trade. From their experience they could not suggest any other explanation of this discrepancy between the Indian and Soviet Union trade statistics. They agree that it is a reasonable inference to suggest that the discrepancy is caused by unrecorded imports in the Indian statistics. The main category of goods which is deliberately left out of Indian Customs statistics is combatant defence imports.

prices to value the Soviet Union's imports from the valuation given on the invoice. When this point was raised with the government officials concerned, they thought that the discrepancy was too big to be explained by this sort of adjustment. The Customs do have their own valuation based on world market prices, but the need to make an independent estimate arises only because the private importers declare a false value either to avoid duty or to keep some foreign exchange abroad by getting the Reserve Bank of India to release more foreign exchange than is required to pay for imports. There is no incentive to build up balances in the East European countries, because these cannot be used to settle payments elsewhere. Therefore, although differences in valuation might cause some discrepancy between the Indian and Soviet statistics, it is unlikely to be of the order of Rs.1,000 million.[1] On the basis of the information available regarding the trade statistics of the USSR and India, the only plausible explanation of this large discrepancy is the treatment of defence imports. The amount of India's defence imports as estimated from Indian sources is somewhat smaller – Rs.750 million – than that estimated from the Soviet statistics – Rs.1,000 million. The explanation is partly the differences in timing and recording and partly the fact that no series of Indian trade statistics includes grant financed defence imports, and payments for technical assistance. India's balance of payments with the USSR is reconstructed accordingly, assuming that the inference about defence imports is correct, so that India's and the Soviet Union's accounts of Indo–Soviet trade are broadly similar and therefore Indian statistics do not present a misleading picture.

As mentioned earlier, a complete statement of India's balance of payments with each East European country is not available but has to be reconstructed from the data available from different sources. The methodology applied for estimating different items is discussed in the explanatory notes to table 20 (see pp. 103–5 and Appendix 3.1, pp. 108–17). Since the

[1] According to a State Department report quoted in the OECD study published in 1968 (61, p. 79) total military aid received was U.S.$610 million by the end of 1967. The figure quoted here is around U.S.$180 million (at the old exchange rate). The difference is due to two factors. First, the figures quoted here are only up to March 1966. Second, the figures shown here are net of repayment; the OECD study quotes a gross figure.

inference about the size of the defence imports is an important one, it is discussed in the text itself.

Table 19   *India's imports from the East European countries, 1961/2 to 1965/6* (in Rs. million)

	1961/2	1962/3	1963/4	1964/5	1965/6	Total
RBI (c.i.f.)	1,042·0	1,123·0	1,540·0	1,955·0	1,903·0	7,563·0
DGCIS (c.i.f.)	876·2	1,101·3	1,292·6	1,438·6	1,565·7	6,275·4
Difference	165·8	21·7	247·4	516·4	337·3	1,288·6

Sources: Data from RBI (128) and DGCIS (142), annual series. On 'difference' see text.

It is possible to isolate combatant defence imports because there are two series of Indian data on imports available. Table 19 shows the import figures from the two sources. The RBI figure for imports from the East European countries is higher by nearly Rs.1,290 million than the corresponding DGCIS figures. The two series differ in other respects as well, as in the inclusion of payments for technical assistance etc., but the residual is still Rs.850 million and most of this must be due to defence imports.

There were three main suppliers of defence equipment in this group – Yugoslavia, Czechoslovakia, and the USSR. India imported mainly non-combatant defence equipment from Czechoslovakia, which is recorded in the Customs statistics. This amount is Rs.125 million. It is unlikely that Czechoslovakia exported much more defence equipment than this. Yugoslavia did not provide combatant defence imports on a large scale either. Therefore, it was decided to allow Rs.50 million for imports of combatant defence equipment from Yugoslavia and to allocate the remaining Rs.750 million to the USSR.[1]

Table 20 shows that during the period 1956/7 to 1960/1 India's current account deficit was only Rs.125 million, whereas

[1] This is less than the Rs.1,060 million attributed to defence imports on the basis of the comparison of Soviet and Indian statistics above; but the discrepancy can probably be attributed to free grants of defence equipment and/or technical assistance not recorded by the RBI and other errors and omissions.

Table 20 *India's balance of payments with the USSR, 1956/7 to 1965/6 (in Rs. million)*

		1956/7 to 1960/1		1961/2 to 1965/6	
Current account		Receipts	Payments	Receipts	Payments
1. Merchandise imports (c.i.f.) (excluding defence imports)	A		920·0		3,280·0
2. Defence imports (c.i.f.)	E		—		750·0
3. Adjustment for incomplete coverage	E		180·0		180·0
4. Payments for technical assistance on development credit	E		150·0		330·0
5. Interest payments on development credits	A		20·0		160·0
6. Transport, insurance	E				
7. Exports f.o.b.	A	1,170·0	25·0	2,940·0	50·0
8. Total current account		1,170·0	1,295·0	2,940·0	4,810·0
9. Net current balance			−125·0		−1,870·0
Capital account					
10. Development credits utilised	A	750·0		2,070·0	
11. Repayments of development credits	A		170·0		350·0
12. Defence credits utilised	E			750·0	
13. Repayment of defence credits	A				550·0
14. Total capital account	A	750·0	170·0	2,820·0	900·0
15. Net capital balance			+590·0		+1,920·0
16. Net current and capital balance (net errors and omissions and technical credits)		465·00		+50·0	

Note: A means actual figures; E stands for estimated figures.

Sources: Rows 1 to 4 and 6, see pp. 103–7; row 5 (138); row 7 (137); rows 10 and 11 (137, 1965/6); row 12 (28, pp. 104–5); row 13, estimate by M. Kidron (Institute of Commonwealth Studies, Oxford University); row 16, row 15 *minus* row 9.

her net receipts on capital account were Rs.590 million. There is an unexplained gap of Rs.465 million. However, when India started importing defence equipment, this unexplained gap was reduced to Rs.50 million – probably representing only errors and omissions. It would be interesting to know how much of this unaccountable gap in the pre-1961 period is due to 'technical credits' given by India to the USSR. The other possible explanation is that other payments have been underestimated and/or not enough allowance has been made for the incomplete coverage of imports.

The payments for salaries of foreign technicians etc. may have been underestimated. If it is assumed that the payments amounted to 25 per cent of the credits utilised, instead of 20 per cent (see Technical Appendix 3.1), the additional amount is only Rs.35 million.

If it is assumed that the coverage of development imports in the fifties was even more inadequate than allowed for here and that most of the equipment imported for Bhilai was not recorded at all, part of the gap will be explained. Out of the Rs.600 million Bhilai credit, an allowance of Rs.180 million has already been made for unreported imports (see table 20). Out of the Rs.420 million left, let us assume that 50 per cent of the amount was never recorded.

Two factors, therefore, an underestimate of technical assistance payments and the incomplete coverage of imports, would account for Rs.245 million of the unexplained gap. Even then, there is no other explanation for the residual of Rs.200 million, and this is probably the amount of technical credits given by India to the USSR.

This hypothesis is supported by an examination of India's annual trade balances with the USSR and net receipts of development credits from the Soviet Union during the years 1956/7 to 1960/1 (see table 21) and by the difficulties experienced by other developing countries in obtaining goods from the USSR. A report on East European activities in developing countries prepared by the U.S. Department of State in 1958 observed that some of them had 'found themselves with substantial export balances with the USSR because the Soviets are unwilling or unable to provide the types of import goods which these countries wish to purchase. For example, Argentina and Burma both found themselves with substantial bloc trade credits which they could not use for the types and quantities of goods which they required'.[1] In the two years 1955 and 1966, Burma's exports to the USSR amounted to U.S.$26·6 million, whereas its imports from the USSR amounted to only U.S.$3·2 million, and Burma therefore had a trade surplus of U.S.$23·4 million.[2] Another report points out that because of its unsatisfactory experience with the Soviet Union, Burma not only requested a partial release from the commitment to ship rice but also got part of the credit balances transferred to Czechoslovakia. Uruguay also negotiated a similar arrangement to use its credit balances in third countries.[3]

However, India did not have this facility and probably had to accumulate balances, as brought out by table 21.

Table 21 *Comparison of the USSR's trade balances with India with net credits utilised, 1956/7 to 1965/6* (in Rs. million)

	Exports	Imports	Balance	Development credits utilised	Repayment of development credits	Net credit utilised
1956/7	155·0	169·0	−14·1	25·7	5·3	20·4
1957/8	166·6	244·7	−78·1	162·6	16·5	146·1
1958/9	259·0	172·1	+86·9	409·3	47·1	362·2
1959/60	303·8	171·9	+131·9	47·7	58·5	−10·8
1960/1	288·1	158·7	+121·4	102·5	58·9	+43·6
Sub-total	1,772·5	916·5	+256·0	748·4	58·9	561·5
1961/2	322·1	399·4	−77·3	245·7	76·6	169·5
1962/3	382·5	586·4	−203·9	324·3	112·7	211·6
1963/4	521·6	684·6	−163·6	472·9	111·7	361·2
1964/5	779·2	779·8	−0·6	649·7	125·6	524·1
1965/6	929·8	831·7	+98·1	379·7	94·6	284·9
Sub-total	2,934·6	3,261·9	−347·3	2,072·0	521·0	1,551·3

Sources: Exports and imports, *Monthly Bulletin of Statistics*, DGCIS, various issues. Development credits utilised and repayments thereof, *Explanatory Memorandum on the Budget of the Central Government*, 1961/2, and EC, 1967/8, 11th Report, 4th Loksabha; Ministry of Finance, *Utilisation of External Assistance*.

Note: Repayments include both principal and interest.

[1] U.S. Department of State (89, p. 43).
[2] *Ibid.* pp. 34–7, tables 6 and 7.
[3] U.S. Senate (86, p. 23).

During the years 1957/8 and 1958/9, India's net receipts of development credits amounted to Rs.510 million, while India had a nominal trade surplus of Rs.10 million. Not all capital receipts were available for importing equipment, because India had to pay for technical assistance as well as transport, freight and insurance. Supposing that India paid Rs.120 million (at 20 per cent of development credits utilised) for technical assistance, another Rs.20 million for other invisibles and the unrecorded imports amount to Rs.80 million (20 per cent of the total imports during the period), India still had Rs.290 million left over. And a significant amount of this, at least Rs.200 million, is probably the amount of technical credits given by India to the USSR.

If this credit had been settled within six months or so, it could be treated as an imbalance arising from leads and lags in payments. However, India continued to have a trade surplus of the order of Rs.250 million in the years 1959/60 and 1960/1 even though it was utilising additional development credits and had some balances outstanding from the previous years. It appears, therefore, that at least until 1961/2, India was giving back significant amounts to the USSR as technical credits. In fact 1962/3 is the first year when the deficit on India's merchandise trade account was equal to the amount of net development credits utilised, but in this year India paid Rs.40 million more than was due on the Bhilai credit and this practice continued at the Soviet Union's request for three years after 1962/3.

The official justification for pre-paying instalments of the Bhilai credit was that by so doing there was some saving of interest payments. From the trade balance it appears that imports were low. Therefore, the USSR suggested that Bhilai credit might be prepaid. Giving evidence before the Estimates Committee, a government representative explained the irregular patterns of repayment to the USSR thus, 'These were due to an arrangement whereby advance payment of repayment instalments was made to the USSR at their request which continued up to 1964/5.'[1]

---

[1] Estimates Committee (137, p. 223). The annual amounts of repayment of Bhilai credit are taken from the *Explanatory Memorandum to the Central Government Budget*.

According to the original arrangement, India would have had to pay about Rs.45 million of principal annually in the sixties. In fact, India paid Rs.226 million in the four years 1961/2 to 1964/5 or Rs.86 million more than she need have done. The trade and payment agreements are devised in such a way that India's export earnings should be enough to pay for imports which are not credit financed. If the agreements work as they should, India's total receipts should equal total payments. The preceding discussion shows that the inability to find enough goods and services to buy from the USSR before 1962/3 resulted in India's granting significant amounts of technical credits. The problem disappeared largely as a result of the payments for defence imports as well as the premature payment of Bhilai credit. However, this waste of finance before 1962/3 is not reflected in the regional balance of payments at all. On the contrary, India's balance of payments with the East European countries as a whole shows that the current account deficit was close to the net capital receipts.

Table 22 shows that during the period 1956/7 to 1965/6 India's net capital receipts were in excess of her current account deficit by more than Rs.700 million. Out of the excess capital receipts India gave Rs.90 million in 1956/7 to 1960/1 and Rs.150 million in 1961/2 to 1965/6 as technical credits, these being India's unused rupee balances. The rest, Rs.255 million and Rs.210 million respectively, must be put down to errors and omissions. The technical credits given by India during the two periods work out at 16 per cent and 8 per cent of the net development credits utilised.

If capital receipts are excluded from India's total imports, India needed only Rs.1,720 million and Rs.5,675 million respectively to pay for the current imports and other invisibles in the sub-periods 1956/7 to 1960/1 and 1961/2 to 1965/6. India's export earnings and net earnings on account of other current invisibles amounted to Rs.2,065 million and Rs.6,035 million respectively during the same sub-periods. Therefore, on her non-credit account, India had a surplus of Rs.345 million and Rs.360 million in the sub-periods 1956/7 to 1960/1 and 1961/2 to 1965/6, of which she was giving a part back as technical credits.

Table 22 *India's balance of payments with the East European countries (reconstructed), 1956/7 to 1965/6 (in Rs. million)*

		1956/7 to 1960/1		1961/2 to 1965/6		Total: 1956/7 to 1965/6	
		Receipts	Payments	Receipts	Payments	Receipts	Payments
Current account							
1. Merchandise imports (c.i.f.) (excluding defence imports)	A		1,810·0		6,275·0		8,035·0
2. Defence imports (c.i.f.)	E		—		800·0		800·0
3. Adjustment for incomplete coverage	E		360·0		250·0		610·0
4. Payments for technical assistance	E		150·0		430·0		580·0
5. Interest payments on development credits	A		20·0		170·0		190·0
6. Transport, insurance	E	280·0		370·0		650·0	
7. Exports (f.o.b.)	E	1,785·0		5,665·0		7,450·0	
8. Total current account	A	2,065·0	2,340·0	6,035·0	7,925·0	8,100·0	10,265·0
9. Net current balance			−275·0		−1,890·0		−2,165·0
Capital account							
10. Development credits utilised	A	805·0		2,410·0		3,215·0	
11. Repayments of development credits	A		185·0		410·0		595·0
12. Defence credits utilised	E			800·0		800·0	
13. Repayment of defence credits	E				550·0		550·0
14. Total capital account		805·0	185·0	3,210·0	960·0	4,015·0	1,145·0
15. Net capital balance		+620·0		+2,250·0		+2,870·0	
16. Net current and capital balance			345·0		360·0		705·0
17. Technical credits			90·0		150·0		240·0

Note: A means actual figures; E stands for estimated figures.

Sources: (Rows 1 to 4, and 6, see pp. 103–7; row 5 (138); row 7 (137); rows 10 and 11 (136, 1965/6); row 12 (28, pp. 104–5); row 13 estimate by M. Kidron (Institute of Commonwealth Studies, Oxford University); row 16, row 15 *minus* row 9.

EXPLANATORY NOTES TO TABLES 20 AND 22

Rows 1 to 3: Imports and adjustment for incomplete coverage[1]

At any given moment the Customs figures for imports are incomplete because there is an arrangement called the 'Note Pass System' whereby a government department can clear certain categories of imports without Customs inspection. As a result, these imports are not recorded at that time, and though the departments concerned are supposed to provide information concerning the value and nature of the goods involved etc., there are considerable delays before those imports are actually recorded. The problem of delays was more serious in the fifties. But since 1958 considerable efforts have been made to eliminate delays and bring the import statistics up to date.

From the literature available on the subject and discussions with various people dealing with Indo–East European trade statistics, it seems that the under-recording is greater in the case of the USSR than in the case of other East European countries and also that under-recording was a much more serious problem in the fifties than in the sixties. Therefore, it is necessary to make a separate estimate for the USSR and for other countries in both the pre-1960 and post-1960 periods.

The net technical credits given by India only partly reflect India's difficulties in finding enough goods and services to purchase, because technical credits are only the residual on which governments do not agree. At the end of each year, the two governments review the trade balance and adjust other items with a view to balancing payments and receipts. Had it not been for premature repayment of Bhilai credit, India's unutilised rupee balances during the period 1961/2 to 1965/6 would have been Rs.236 million (rather than Rs.150 million), which is more than 12 per cent of the net development credits utilised.

India's experience with the USSR is therefore in contrast to her experience with the East European countries as a group. By treating the countries as a group, the difficulties in finding goods to import from the USSR are obscured, because while India was accumulating currency balances with the Soviet Union, other countries were exporting more than they need have done. If there had been convertibility within the group India could have used her balances with the Soviet Union to pay the others. Since that was not allowed,

[1] For a more detailed discussion see Appendix 3.1, pp. 108–14.

the net advantages of utilising a credit from the Soviet Union were reduced and India was accumulating short-term debts from other countries.

From 1965/6 to 1969/70, the net receipts of development credits from the USSR have not been very significant, compared to Czechoslovakia for example (see table 23). If defence credits/ payments are included there has probably been little net transfer of

Table 23   *Receipts and repayments of development credits, 1966/7 to 1969/70* (in Rs. million, post-devaluation rates)

	1966/7	1967/8	1968/9	1969/70	Total
USSR					
Receipts	335·9	464·0	564·9	715·6	2,090
Payments	117·9	489·5	438·2	559·0	1,709
Czechoslovakia					
Receipts	127·1	74·3	161·3	84·0	446
Payments		13·6	45·7	63·2	122·5
Yugoslavia					
Receipts	25·9	34·4	6·7	6·5	73·5
Payments	11·8	18·7	21·2	34·6	86·3
Poland					
Receipts	8·7	9·8	21·5	50·7	90·7
Payments	7·9	19·0	19·0	19·0	65·0

Source: Explanatory Memorandum to the Central Government Budgets, Part II, 1970/1.

resources from the USSR. The annual repayments in the three years 1966/7 to 1968/9 have averaged more than Rs.400 million and will continue to be around that level for some years. Therefore, unless the rate of utilisation of new credits is accelerated considerably, there will be little new transfer of resources from the USSR in the coming years. The balance available for use at 31 March 1970 was Rs.3,662·7 million. but judging by past experience it is unlikely that this will be used up quickly. It is not unlikely that in the coming years credits from the USSR will be used only for repaying old debts and credit receipts will only mean that India's export earnings will be available mostly for importing current goods and services.

On the other hand, other East European countries, especially

Czechoslovakia, seem to have reached the same stage. India's trade deficit with Czechoslovakia during the period 1966/7 to 1969/70 was Rs.20 million, while her net credit receipts were Rs.324 million.

In the case of the USSR, 20 per cent of the total recorded imports during the period 1956/7 to 1960/1 and 20 per cent of the imports in the year 1965/6 should be added to the recorded imports during the two periods. For other East European countries, an allowance of 20 per cent of the value of the recorded imports in the period 1956/7 to 1960/1 and 10 per cent of the imports in the year 1965/6 is sufficient. In the latter period a certain percentage of imports is added to the recorded imports for 1965/6 only because it is assumed that imports in the previous years, i.e. 1961/2 to 1964/5, would have been fully recorded by then. However, it is possible in the pre-1960 period that some imports were never recorded. Therefore it is necessary to add a certain percentage to the total imports during that period.

Row 4: Payments for technical assistance

These are based on the actual payments made for particular projects which received credits from certain East European countries (see table 13). Other information available about payments for project-tied technical assistance suggests that the USSR charges more on this count than other East European countries. Moreover, during the fifties the USSR provided more technical personnel and know-how than in the sixties, because a number of Soviet technicians were engaged in exploration for crude oil and there was a very elaborate training scheme for Bhilai. In the case of the USSR therefore, total technical assistance payments were put at 20 per cent and 15 per cent of the gross development credits utilised for the periods 1956/7 to 1960/1 and 1961/2 to 1965/6 respectively. For the other East European countries, the corresponding figure is 10 per cent of the gross development credits utilised.

This figure for technical assistance payments includes payments for working drawings and project reports, as well as salaries of foreign technicians. The East European countries include payments for working drawings etc. in the import bill. Therefore, the item 'net current invisibles' does not include all payments for technical assistance.

Row 6: Transport, freight and insurance

The Reserve Bank of India does not give an itemised breakdown of current invisibles, only a net figure (table 24). This was broken down into technical assistance payments, interest, freight, and insurance. The official interest payments figures are available. Technical assistance payments have been estimated. The rest or most of it must, therefore, be due to payments/receipts on account of transport etc.

India has shipping agreements with three countries – the USSR, Poland, and Czechoslovakia – and an informal understanding with other countries, whereby the goods traded between the two countries are carried in each country's ships. The cargo is supposed to be equally divided. If the shipping agreements work as they should, therefore, there should be very little net receipts/payments. However, since imports are recorded c.i.f., this overestimate in payment has to be corrected by a corresponding receipt. It is also possible that India paid in advance for export/import shipments and was reimbursed later.

The sub-totals for the periods 1956/7 to 1960/1 and 1961/2 to 1965/6 respectively are Rs.+194 million and Rs.+22 million. As pointed out above, some of the payments included in this item are technical assistance payments (e.g. for salaries of technicians) and are estimated at slightly less than half of the total technical assistance payments. The amounts in each period are Rs.65 million and Rs.170 million respectively. The interest payments on development credits during both the periods are around Rs.20 million and Rs.170 million respectively.

Table 24   *Net current invisibles 1956/7 to 1960/1* (in Rs. million)

1956/7	+35	1961/2	+30
1957/8	+41	1962/3	+33
1958/9	+43	1963/4	−5
1959/60	+32	1964/5	−13
1960/1	+43	1965/6	−33

Source: (169).

The residual after these deductions represents the receipts for transport etc., viz. Rs.290 million and Rs.370 million during the two periods 1956/7 to 1965/6. This estimate is supported by the figures given in the IMF balance of payments which shows that India had a net credit on transport and insurance.

Since the total trade turnover during the two periods under

consideration was Rs.3,500 million and Rs. 14,000 million respectively, these figures are not unreasonable. Moreover, the amounts shown here are not entirely on account of transport and freight but include items such as embassy expenditure of these countries in India, on which, however, no information is available.

Appendix 3.1   *Reconciliation of trade statistics from the Reserve Bank of India and the Director General of Commercial Intelligence and Statistics*

A reconciliation of the trade statistics as published by the Director General of Commercial Intelligence and Statistics (DGCIS) and by the Exchange Control Division of the Reserve Bank of India (RBI) proved essential for the present study. This note explains the discrepancies and discusses the extent of reconciliation possible.[1]

Comparing the data available from any two Indian sources is a difficult task, but the discrepancies and deficiencies of the DGCIS and RBI present a special problem. The discrepancies were so widespread and persistent that the government formed an informal working party group to eliminate them as far as possible and also published a booklet explaining how DGCIS and RBI data are compiled and where the differences arise. Some people are very sceptical about the attempt at reconciliation and would regard any conclusion based on this data as of dubious validity. The objections to this procedure, however, lose some of their force when the Rupee Payment Area alone is being discussed, because many of the factors which give rise to discrepancies in the overall balance of payments statistics do not apply in this case – for instance, different territorial coverage is an important factor in producing discrepancies and this problem does not arise in the case of East European countries. Another example is the normal discrepancies which arise from the fact that payments may be made either before or after goods arrive. This factor creates discrepancies in the short run, but over a number of years it is not so important.

Before discussing the individual items which give rise to discrepancies, one general fact should be pointed out. The discrepancy between import figures from DGCIS and the RBI is much wider than the discrepancy between export figures, and this is particularly true of imports from the East European countries. The discrepancies

---

[1] The material for this section was gathered from the following sources:
  (1) *A Guide to Official Statistics of India, Shipping and Customs and Excise Revenue in India*, Department of Commercial Intelligence and Statistics (pp. 52–63 in particular).
  (2) *Report of the Informal Working Group on the Discrepancies between Customs and Exchange Control Data*, Ministry of Finance, 1964 (mimeographed).
  (3) *India's Balance of Payments 1948/9 to 1961/2*, RBI, mainly ch. 1 and 2.
  (4) Information directly collected from various official sources.
  I am very grateful to D. R. Khatkhate for explaining some technical points concerning the trade and balance of payments statistics.

are attributed to the differences in valuation, coverage and timing, methods of registration, and other factors.

Exports and imports are discussed separately: there are no serious difficulties in reconciling the export figures from the two sources, and the real bone of contention is imports.

EXPORTS

Method of registration and timing

The DGCIS and the RBI use the same raw data – the shipping bill submitted by an exporter. But the timing of the entry as well as the valuation differs. When an exporter submits a shipping bill, Customs authorities make adjustments for any unrealistic values and pass the original on to the RBI. The RBI accepts the values given by the exporter because it is interested in the actual inflow or outflow of funds. The Customs record imports not when goods are *physically* shipped from India, but on the date of passing the shipping bill. These figures are adjusted later for short and cancelled shipments, i.e. if the exporter exported less than originally declared or did not export anything, the figures are revised accordingly.

The RBI on the other hand used to record exports after the goods had actually been shipped. The exporter had to send a duplicate of the relevant documents to his bank after the goods had been shipped and the bank had to forward a duplicate to the RBI within 28 days of receipt. The RBI used to employ these duplicates to record exports as the expected receipts from shipped goods, but now uses the date on the original shipping bill.

The difference in the timing of registration does mean that at one point of time export figures from these two sources are not strictly comparable and that RBI figures probably understate exports. But DGCIS export figures are inaccurate to the extent that expected shipments do not materialise or that only a part of 'consignment' exports are actually accepted abroad.

Valuation

The Customs figures are for revenue collection and the RBI is only interested in the inflow and outflow of foreign exchange. So the RBI accepts the exporter's valuation, whereas Customs make any adjustments they think necessary. Since exchange control was strict in India, exporters were tempted to hold back a part of their earnings abroad by under-invoicing their exports. But this temptation would be greatest in freely convertible currency areas and least with respect to non-convertible currency. Therefore, this problem of under-invoicing does not arise in the East European countries.

The RBI and DGCIS follow different practices concerning incidental expenses.

(1) The RBI allows exporters to deduct discounts, commission and bank charges from the invoice, but Customs allow only the normal trade discount as stipulated in the contract.

(2) Customs exports are f.o.b. but the RBI data are based on returns from exporters, which may be f.o.b./f.o.r. or c.i.f. The RBI does make a general downward adjustment for any c.i.f. exports on a sampling basis. So the discrepancies arise only in the cases of individual commodities and not on an aggregate basis.

COVERAGE

The differences in coverage arise from exclusion/inclusion of territories and certain categories of items. For instance, parcel post export figures – around Rs.150 million a year – are included in the RBI data but were entirely excluded from Customs data until 1964. Trade between India and Nepal was excluded from the RBI figures because there is no exchange control between India and Nepal. But neither of these factors applies to the East European countries. There is very little, if any, parcel export to them and they are all in the rupee payments area. Hence all East European transactions are included in the RBI data.

IMPORTS

Recording

The Customs data should record imports on the basis of 'bill of entry' when the goods arrive. When goods are for home consumption the date of entry is the date of assessing duty. The RBI figures, on the other hand, relate to the timing of payment and if payments are made in advance, there will be some discrepancy between the two sets of figures.

A more serious problem regarding imports is the so-called 'Note Pass System'. Though each importer is supposed to fill in a form declaring the value of goods imported, the description of goods etc., government departments may clear the shipment before the full and detailed information is made available to the Customs. The departments give only an approximate value and a vague description of the goods. They are supposed to submit the documents as soon as possible, but it takes them some time to send the forms. Three to six months was the normal time lag but delays ranging from two and a half years to seven years have occurred in exceptional cases. This system, introduced during the Second World War, accounted for wide gaps in import statistics in the fifties. Government departments were being so difficult about reporting the correct value of imports or even reporting at all, that the Central Revenue Board consequently decided in 1958 that the concession of the Note Pass procedure should be withdrawn after giving notice of three months to various government departments. The concession would, however, continue to be available in respect of individual cases if there were exceptional circumstances justifying its application. It is, however, found in practice that the system exists to a considerable extent and many government departments are still enjoying the concession, thus accounting for large deficiencies in import statistics.[1]

The problem still exists that at any one point of time the Customs coverage of imports is incomplete. The severity of the problem depends upon the nature of goods imported. Imports like defence and railway stores and development projects are specifically mentioned among goods for which documents are not available when they arrive, so they get through Customs under the Note Pass procedure. However, due to the special efforts made to reduce delays, the coverage of imports in the sixties is much better than in the fifties. Moreover, though the DGCIS import coverage is incomplete at one time, this defect can be largely eliminated by adding a certain percentage to the figure of recorded imports. The allowance made for incomplete coverage is a matter of judgement and will be arbitrary to some extent.

Valuation

Differences in valuation arise from the same reasons as in the case of exports. Private importers have a special incentive to declare a false value of imports. Customs did not necessarily accept the valuation of the imports, but did not follow a uniform procedure. They accepted tariff values in a few cases and market prices in a few cases, whereas the RBI figures for imports are *debit* items, based on outflows of foreign exchange.

Different coverage

The differences in coverage arise from the lack of uniformity in the territorial and commodity coverage. The RBI figures did not include trade between India and Nepal while there was no exchange control between the two territories. The recording or not recording

---

[1] *A Guide to Official Statistics of Trade Shipping and Customs and Excise Revenue in India*, Department of Commercial Intelligence and Statistics, Calcutta, 1965.

of defence imports is the single most important factor accounting for the discrepancy in import statistics. DGCIS statistics include only non-combatant items of defence, whereas RBI accounts include by and large all defence imports. In the guide to the trade statistics, defence goods and fissionable materials are specifically mentioned as items excluded from trade statistics. Thus it says, 'Trade in the combatant items of defence equipment and in fissionable materials are not recorded as the relevant information is withheld from the Customs authorities for security reasons. Trade in non-combatant items is, however, recorded under a single omnibus head "Defence Stores, all kinds" ', whereas 'the exchange control statistics by and large include, however, all defence imports except those received by way of grant from friendly countries'.[1]

The size of defence imports in the fifties is not known. From the political events in India and the trend in defence expenditures in the 1950s it is clear that after the Chinese invasion there was a quick escalation in the domestic defence budget and defence imports increased substantially.

There are certain other differences in the coverage of commodities. For example:

(1) Personal gifts, samples and dutiable personal items are not included in RBI statistics, as they do not give rise to foreign exchange transactions.

(2) Oil companies in India have a special arrangement whereby they are allowed to unload oil/oil products and remove them straight-away after making sufficient deposits to cover payment of taxes. The imports are actually recorded only when the Customs complete the assessment and not at the time of the physical removal, and this time lag extends over years. But the imports are paid for much earlier.

(3) When foreign investors bring in machinery and equipment, it is recorded in DGCIS but not in RBI statistics, because it does not give rise to foreign exchange transactions.

(4) Imports of ships are excluded from the DGCIS statistics but not from the RBI.

The need for handling statistics carefully cannot be over-emphasised and it would be risky to offer as a general hypothesis that the otherwise unaccountable payments in import statistics are for defence imports. The special circumstances in connection with the trading partner, the commodity composition of trade and the other items in the balance of payments have to be taken into account. But if all other factors have been taken into account and it is known

[1] *A Guide to Official Statistics of Trade Shipping and Customs and Excise Revenue of India*, pp. 12 and 57–8.

that India imported defence equipment, it may be inferred that the otherwise unexplained gap, or most of it, must be due to defence imports.

Among the different factors mentioned above, the differences in territorial coverage are not applicable to the East European countries. The differences in the time of recording remain but this problem is much less important in discussing a period of years than a short period. The most important items which account for differences between the RBI and DGCIS series for the East European countries are the Note Pass system and the treatment of some technical assistance payments and the inclusion/exclusion of defence imports.

INCOMPLETE COVERAGE DUE TO THE NOTE PASS SYSTEM

Because the USSR is the biggest lender and the biggest exporter of 'development goods' the under-recording may be greater in their case than for other countries in Eastern Europe. Therefore, separate estimates should be made for the two. Similarly, the under-recording was a more serious problem in the fifties than in the sixties. It is possible that in the fifties some imports were never recorded at all, but in the sixties imports would have been recorded, even though with some time lag. Therefore, it is necessary to add a certain percentage to the annual recorded imports during the period 1956/7 to 1960/1. It is suggested that 20 and 10 per cent respectively of each years' annual imports from the USSR and other countries should be added to the figure of recorded imports (DGCIS). But during the period 1961/2 to 1965/6, it is assumed that the imports in the earlier years, until the end of 1964/5, would have been recorded in recorded imports of 1965/6. The coverage of imports in 1965/6 alone would be incomplete. Therefore, it is sufficient to add 20 and 10 per cent to the recorded imports (DGCIS) from the USSR and other East European countries in 1965/6.

TECHNICAL ASSISTANCE PAYMENTS

The RBI import figures are debit items and include some payments for technical services received with imports of complete plants, because the East European countries include these payments in their invoice for imports. However, these are not included in the DGCIS trade statistics. From a sample survey of projects financed with East European countries it seems that these payments amount to about 8 per cent of the development credits utilised.

After the DGCIS figure has been corrected by adding something for incomplete coverage and technical assistance payments, the residual, or most of it, must be due to the fact that combatant defence imports are not included in the DGCIS series.

Appendix 3.2 *Comparison between Indian and East European trade statistics*

Since the discussion of the size of India's trade deficit and of imports of defence equipment is based upon an interpretation of the trade data from different sources, it is worthwhile to check how trade figures from the national statistics of India and each East European country compare. Table 3.2.3 (pp. 118–19), shows each East European country's imports from and exports to India expressed in terms of their own national currencies. These figures are compiled from the reporting country's trade statistics published by the U.N. statistical office (*Yearbook of International Trade*). However, the figures of the USSR's exports to and imports from India are taken directly from the USSR trade publication *Vneshnyaya Torgovlya SSSR* (annual). Table 3.2.4 (p. 120), compares India's trade balance/deficit with each European country, as shown in the Indian and the partner country's trade statistics.

The following points should be noted before comparing the two series.

1. The exchange rates used are official exchange rates. This is consistent with the practice adopted by the East European countries in compiling their trade statistics. In the introductory section of the *Yearbook of International Trade Statistics 1965*, the explanatory note on trade statistics of the centrally planned economies reads, 'These countries have systems of official rates between their currencies and other currencies, all consistent with a rate of 0·90 new roubles to the United States dollar, and they generally use these rates when it is necessary to convert foreign into domestic currencies for the purpose of compiling external trade statistics.' The actual exchange rates used for converting various currencies into rupees were taken from Pick's *Currency Yearbooks*, 1960 and 1966.

2. *Definitions.* The U.N. yearbook explanatory note mentioned above points out that East European countries adopt somewhat different definitions from those adopted in other countries when referring to the same flow of goods and this gives rise to discrepancies between the trade returns from the centrally planned economies and other countries.

3. *Valuation.* Except for Hungary and Yugoslavia all other countries included in the group here value imports f.o.b. and not c.i.f. This is another source of discrepancy.

4. *Inclusion of payments for technical services.* The item 'complete equipment for industry', item 16 in the USSR's export statistics, for instance, includes payments for technical services rendered and Indian trade statistics do not.

Table 3.2.1   *India's trade with each East European country as shown in the reporting country's statistics, 1960–5* (in Rs. million)

Country	Reporting country: India			Reporting country: East European country concerned		
	Exports from	Imports into	Trade balance	Exports from	Imports into	Trade balance
Bulgaria	106·7	134·8	−28·1	131·1	119·3	+11·3
Czechoslovakia	681·2	930·6	−249·4	964·9	690·3	+274·3
East Germany	497·7	452·1	+45·3	491·7	479·2	+12·2
Hungary	324·1	290·0	+34·0	360·5	422·5	−62·0
Poland	459·3	565·9	−106·6	569·6	414·8	+154·4
Rumania	164·4	122·0	+42·4	157·5	199·3	−41·8
USSR	2,933·5	3,275·4	−341·9	4,283·2	2,744·8	+1,538·4
Yugoslavia	494·6	490·5	+4·6	510·2	496·3	+13·9
Trade balance (excluding USSR)			−262·9			+362·6
Trade balance adjusted for c.i.f.			−262·9			+192·6

Note: Bulgaria, Czechoslovakia, East Germany, Poland, Rumania, and the USSR record imports f.o.b.
Source: See Appendix 3.2, tables 3.2.3 and 3.2.4, and Appendix 3.3.

If a comparison is made between the trade statistics as recorded by India and by each partner country in Eastern Europe the following inferences can be drawn (see table 3.2.1).

Exports. The statistics of Indian exports and imports from the two sources are comparable except for the USSR and Hungary. The figures are not identical but the differences are insignificant enough to be attributed to errors and omissions.

Imports. India records imports c.i.f. but the East European countries record exports f.o.b. To make the two comparable, an amount of 10 per cent should be added to the f.o.b. value of exports from each country. After making this adjustment it seems that the earnings of East European countries from exports to India are higher than the value of imports into India. However, these differences can be explained by making allowance for the inclusion of some technical

5

assistance payments in the export statistics of the East European countries concerned. The discrepancies between the Indian and Hungarian and Indian and Soviet statistics are greater than in the case of other East European countries and require further examination.

In Hungary's case the figures for both Hungarian exports to and imports from India are greater by nearly 30 per cent than the corresponding Indian figures. There is no obvious explanation. Probably either the official exchange rate is wrong or Hungary records trade at prices different from those used by India.

INDIA AND THE SOVIET UNION

The discrepancies between Indian and Soviet Union statistics concerning Indian imports are much greater than those concerning Indian exports and imports and exports must be treated separately.

Exports. The USSR records imports on a f.o.b. basis. Indian exports are also on a f.o.b. basis and the two are therefore comparable. While the two figures are not exactly identical the differences are small enough to be attributed to errors and omissions (see 3.2.2, below) and to leads and lags.

Indian imports. The figures of Indian imports (c.i.f.) from the Soviet Union as recorded in the Indian statistics are much lower than the figures for Soviet exports as recorded in that country's statistics. It is suggested that this discrepancy arises from the Indian failure to publish imports of defence goods.

Table 3.2.2   *A comparison of Indo–Soviet trade statistics, 1960–5* (in Rs. million)

	Indian exports (f.o.b.)	Soviet imports (f.o.b.)	Indian imports (c.i.f.)	Soviet exports (f.o.b.)	Soviet exports (c.i.f. 10%)	Difference between Indian and Soviet figures (Indian imports)
1960	228·2	326·4	158·7	224·1	246·0	87·3
1961	322·1	319·0	399·4	455·2	510·0	110·6
1962	382·5	314·8	586·4	595·1	690·0	129·6
1963	521·0	452·0	684·6	1,058·4	1,216·0	531·4
1964	779·2	743·5	779·8	1,119·8	1,230·0	460·2
1965	928·7	897·8	825·2	1,025·5	1,150·0	324·8

When the Soviet export statistics have been corrected to include the cost of insurance and freight, the total Soviet exports in the years 1960–5 are greater by about Rs.1,430 million than Indian imports during the same period. The explanation lies in both the under-recording and non-recording of some commodities in the Indian import statistics and the inclusion of certain items as technical assistance payments and combatant defence equipment in the Soviet Union's export statistics, and errors and omissions.

In Appendix 3.1 it was estimated that 20 per cent of the imports in the year 1965/6 would not have been recorded in that year. As India's imports in 1965/6 were more than Rs.900 million, a sum of Rs.180 million should be added to the figure of Indian imports in that year. Then the difference between the two figures is about Rs.1,250 million.

India's imports of the item 'complete plants and machinery' amounted to Rs.2,000 million in the period 1961–5, according to the USSR's trade statistics – item 16. From a survey of technical service payments to the USSR for development aided projects it appears that the payments for documents etc. came to about 10 per cent of the amount of the credit. If it is assumed that about 10 per cent of the price of the complete plant was paid for technical services, then Rs.200 million out of this sum of Rs.2,000 million would not be included in India's imports.

But even after deducting payments for invisibles, the unexplained gap is Rs.1,050 million. Some of this can be attributed to errors and omissions, but most of it is due either to exports of defence equipment from the USSR or to differences in valuation. The latter explanation does not seem very likely, because the two country's returns concerning Indian exports to the USSR generally agree. Therefore, the unexplained gap of Rs.1,050 million, or most of it, must be due to the inclusion of some defence imports. This explanation seems more plausible when the annual import statistics are analysed. The difference between Indian and Soviet statistics is much greater from 1963 onwards than before. This is the time – after the Chinese invasion in 1962 – that India started importing defence equipment on a large scale.

It is interesting to note in this context that the size of combatant defence imports from all East European countries, as inferred by comparing the two Indian series – RBI and DGCIS – is approximately Rs.800 million, of which about Rs.750 million is attributable to the USSR. The Indian figure is lower than the Soviet figure partly because of leads, lags, errors and omissions, but also because the RBI statistics do not include imports of combatant defence equipment which are grants.

Table 3.2.3 *India's trade balance with East European countries, 1954–65* (from the foreign trade statistics of East European countries)

	1954	1955	1956	1957	1958	1959	1960	1961	1962	1963	1964	1965
Bulgaria (in millions of leva)												
Imports f.o.b.								0·8	1·3	7·3	10·9	9·1
Exports f.o.b.								2·1	1·3	10·8	8·5	9·6
Trade balance								+1·3	—	+3·5	-2·4	+0·5
Czechoslovakia (in millions of koruny)												
Imports f.o.b.				65	65	72	87	149	179	227	241	250
Exports f.o.b.				82	82	89	140	213	278	252	365	344
Trade balance				+17	+17	+17	+53	+64	+99	+25	+134	+94
East Germany (in millions of marks)												
Imports f.o.b.				7·1	6·0	9·8	14·9	11·8	87·4	102·1	99·6	122·6
Exports f.o.b.				6·6	8·4	11·4	12·2	17·3	104·1	105·9	90·5	116·5
Trade balance				-0·5	+2·4	+1·6	-2·7	+5·5	+16·7	+3·8	-9·1	-6·1
Hungary (in millions of florins)												
Imports c.i.f.				3·2	14·6	19·1	55·2	108·6	246·7	202·2	241·9	256·9
Exports f.o.b.				19·8	27·8	33·2	53·5	165·9	132·1	186·0	219·9	197·4
Trade balance				+16·6	+13·2	+14·1	-1·7	+57·3	-114·6	-16·2	-22·0	-59·5

Poland (in millions of zlotys)												
Imports f.o.b.				11·8	7·5	25·5	32·7	29·2	76·2	79·4	91·7	72·1
Exports f.o.b.				29·6	27·1	23·1	24·7	65·8	80·0	82·4	122·1	128·4
Trade balance				+17·8	+19·5	−2·4	−8·0	+36·6	+3·8	+3·0	+30·4	+56·3
Rumania (in millions of lei)												
Imports f.o.b.					6·6	23·7	20·4	28·0	44·9	33·2	40·4	52·9
Exports f.o.b.					9·2	30·3	69·3	23·9	36·0	31·1	36·0	40·5
Trade balance					+2·6	+6·6	+48·9	−4·1	−8·9	−2·1	−4·4	−12·4
USSR (in millions of roubles)												
Imports f.o.b.		17·6	73·2	167·8	203·7	242·1	61·6	60·2	64·5	85·3	140·3	169·4
Exports f.o.b.		29·3	161·6	338·6	520·0	272·1	42·3	85·9	112·3	199·7	211·3	193·5
Trade balance		+11·7	+88·4	+170·8	+316·3	+30·0	−19·3	+25·7	+47·8	+114·4	+71·0	+24·1
Yugoslavia (in millions of dinars)												
Special imports c.i.f.	14·47	109·26	264·89	896	672	1,532	2,543	2,628	6,769	7,734	6,430	7,851
Exports f.o.b.	61·51	76·22	1,144·66	1,292	3,163	3,132	2,263	4,939	5,557	4,440	8,457	8,900
Trade balance	47·04	−33·04	+879·77	+396	+2,491	+1,600	−280	+2,311	−1,212	−3,294	+2,027	+1,049

Note: U.N. Yearbook of International Trade does not derive data on the trade of the USSR, Rumania and Yugoslavia from the respective national statistics. Certain other countries supply the U.N. with trade figures which do not include India. Imports here are those of the partner country and exports those to India. All currencies are *devisa* units, viz. employed only for foreign transactions; a currency redenomination took place in the USSR series in 1960 and in the East German in 1962.

Source: U.N. Yearbook of International Trade, 1961, 1965.

Table 3.2.4 *India's trade balance with East European countries: comparison of Indian statistics with those of the partner* (in Rs. million)

	Total 1955–60	1955	1956	1957	1958	1959	1960	1961	1962	1963	1964	1965	1960–5
Bulgaria													
Indian statistics								−1·3	−6·7	−9·2	+6·6	−18·1	−28·6
Bulgarian statistics								+0·9	—	+1·4	−9·7	+2·0	+5·4
Czechoslovakia													
Indian statistics	−15·6		−40·1	−21·0	−17·6	+4·6	−14·6	−63·0	−81·6	−11·7	−29·9	−53·3	−239·5
Czechoslovak statistics				+11·2	+11·2	+11·2	+35·0	+42·0	+65·3	+16·5	+88·4	+62·0	+274·2
East Germany													
Indian statistics				+8·7	−8·3	+2·4	−0·2	−10·9	+6·7	+2·9	+40·0	+6·9	+45·6
East German statistics				−0·59	+2·85	+2·85	+3·21	6·54	+18·8	+4·29	−10·89	−6·89	+12·0
Hungary													
Indian statistics				−4·1	−5·3	−12·6	−6·5	−8·5	+34·6	−5·9	+13·5	−6·8	+26·9
Hungarian statistics				+6·6	+5·3	+5·6	−0·7	+22·9	−45·8	−6·5	−8·8	−23·8	−61·8
Poland													
Indian statistics				−20·9	−14·2	+8·3	−5·5	−46·5	+34·6	−9·4	−39·7	−45·6	−106·6
Polish statistics				+21·1	+23·3	−2·85	−9·95	+43·55	+4·52	+3·57	+36·17	+66·99	+154·5
Rumania													
Indian statistics					−1·0	+7·3	−35·6	−12·2	+7·7	+9·0	+14·2	+23·7	+42·2
Rumanian statistics					+2·05	+5·21	+38·6	−3·23	−7·09	−1·65	−3·47	−9·79	−25·0
USSR													
Indian statistics	+225·8	−29·5	−14·3	−78·6	+86·9	+131·9	+129·4	−77·3	−203·9	−163·6	−0·6	+103·5	−345·6
Soviet statistics	+596·2	+13·9	+69·4	+203·2	+376·3	+35·3	−101·9	+135·6	+257·1	+603·5	+374·8	+127·2	+1,498·2
Yugoslavia													
Indian statistics	−62·3	+0·4	−17·4	−22·7	−6·7	−4·0	−11·1	−12·8	+34·0	−16·2	+5·5	−6·3	+4·2
Yugoslav statistics	+165·2	+5·2	+13·9	+62·5	+39·43	+25·28	+44·2	+365·51	−19·14	−52·04	+32·0	+40·9	+38·0

+ Means that the reporting country had an excess of exports over imports.
Source: Tables 3.2.3 and 3.3.1.

In conclusion, it may be said that the trade statistics of India's trade with each East European country as reported by India and its partner country can be reconciled with relatively little effort. There are wide discrepancies between India's imports from the USSR as reported by the two countries. These discrepancies can be only accounted for by assuming that the USSR includes exports of combatant defence equipment whereas India does not.

Appendix 3.3   *India's trade balance with individual countries in Eastern Europe*

Table 3.3.1   *India's trade with the East European countries, 1950/1 to 1965/6* (in Rs. million) (*imports c.i.f.; exports f.o.b.*)

	1950/1	1951/2	1952/3	1953/4	1954/5	1955/6	1956/7	1957/8	1958/9	1959/60	1960/1	1961/2	1962/3	1963/4	1964/5	1965/6
Imports from and exports to:																
Soviet Union																
Imports	2·2	13·8	2·4	6·0	18·1	62·1	169·1	244·7	172·1	171·9	158·7	399·4	586·4	684·6	779·8	825·2
Exports	13·4	66·7	8·5	11·5	21·2	32·6	155·0	116·6	259·0	303·8	288·1	322·1	382·5	521·0	779·2	928·7
Bulgaria																
Imports	—	—	—	—	0·1	0·3	2·2	1·3	0·8	2·4	5·4	9·6	23·7	37·4	24·1	40·0
Exports	—	—	—	0·05	0·1	0·2	0·5	0·2	1·4	1·7	1·9	8·9	17·0	28·2	30·7	21·9
Czechoslovakia																
Imports	28·2	28·1	13·5	11·4	12·5	28·9	72·7	54·8	57·8	45·4	87·6	150·2	197·1	173·3	198·4	211·5
Exports	13·0	11·9	10·7	31·5	16·7	13·3	32·6	33·8	40·2	50·2	73·0	87·2	115·5	161·6	158·5	158·2

East Germany																
Imports	7·5	0·7	1·0	0·8	2·3	3·7	4·0	6·3	20·0	26·7	33·1	56·4	78·2	98·0	89·2	130·3
Exports	0·3	0·1	0·2	0·1	0·4	0·2	4·6	15·0	11·7	29·1	32·9	45·5	84·9	100·9	129·2	137·2
Hungary																
Imports	1·0	3·2	1·6	1·0	1·0	4·1	6·6	7·9	12·9	19·7	20·2	56·1	29·6	66·5	69·0	75·9
Exports	0·2	—	0·4	0·2	1·9	0·8	4·9	3·8	7·6	7·1	13·7	47·6	64·3	60·6	82·5	69·1
Poland																
Imports	3·0	3·4	2·6	1·6	4·2	4·3	44·4	30·0	23·0	41·9	44·2	91·6	81·3	105·4	150·9	136·7
Exports	0·9	1·1	0·4	1·6	4·6	3·3	12·4	9·2	8·8	49·3	38·7	45·1	115·9	96·0	111·2	91·1
Rumania																
Imports	—	—	—	—	2·8	3·2	1·9	6·3	5·4	16·4	49·5	38·3	26·1	18·5	17·7	21·4
Exports	0·2	—	0·3	—	0·4	—	2·2	5·6	4·4	23·7	13·9	26·1	33·8	27·5	31·9	45·1
Total above																
Imports	42·0	49·2	21·1	20·8	79·2	106·6	300·9	351·3	292·0	324·4	398·7	801·6	1,022·4	1,183·7	1,329·1	1,441·0
Exports	28·0	79·8	20·5	44·9	45·3	50·5	212·2	234·2	333·1	464·9	462·2	582·5	813·9	995·8	1,323·2	1,451·3
Yugoslavia																
Imports	1·2	1·4	0·9	0·7	1·6	2·0	20·0	30·6	16·0	29·8	44·4	74·6	78·9	108·9	109·5	118·5
Exports	0·9	2·6	1·1	0·1	0·2	2·4	2·6	7·9	9·3	25·8	33·3	61·8	112·9	92·7	115·0	112·2
Total including Yugoslavia																
Imports	43·2	50·6	22·0	21·5	80·8	108·6	320·9	381·9	308·0	354·2	443·1	876·2	1,101·3	1,292·6	1,438·6	1,559·9
Exports	28·9	82·4	21·6	45·0	45·5	52·9	214·8	242·1	342·4	490·7	495·5	644·3	926·8	1,088·5	1,438·2	1,563·6
World																
Imports	6,094·4	9,708·3	6,712·3	5,757·4	6,564·3	7,064·3	8,324·4	10,258·2	8,641·8	8,873·8	10,701·6	10,386·8	11,314·7	12,228·5	13,490·3	13,940·5
Exports	5,968·2	7,288·8	5,723·0	5,261·5	5,884·7	6,038·7	6,070·2	6,377·4	5,705·6	6,157·8	6,329·4	6,551·7	6,781·5	7,892·8	8,131·5	8,055·6

Sources: Indian Institute of Foreign Trade, *India's Trade with East Europe*, Delhi, 1966; *Monthly Statistics of Foreign Trade of India*.
Notes: (1) Years April to March. (2) A dash indicates less than Rs. 50,000. (3) Rs. 1 = 21 U.S. cents.

Table 3.3.2 *India's exports to and imports from and balance of trade with East European countries, 1966/7 to 1969/70 (in Rs. million)*

	1966/7			1967/8			1968/9			1969/70		
	Imports	Exports	Balance of trade	Imports	Exports	Balance of trade	Imports	Exports	Balance of trade	Imports	Exports	Balance of trade
Bulgaria	30·7	36·8	6·1	19·3	39·7	20·4	87·4	72·5	−14·9	87·8	66·4	−21·4
Czechoslovakia	25·35	23·19	−21·6	273·4	291·7	18·3	352·7	317·7	−35·0	229·7	300·7	71·0
East Germany	172·6	159·0	−13·6	215·6	203·1	−12·5	205·3	198·4	−6·9	243·1	200·1	−43·0
Hungary	101·2	81·1	−20·1	117·2	128·2	11·0	139·9	100·6	−39·3	171·6	94·0	−77·6
Poland	135·5	108·8	−26·7	237·5	220·1	−17·4	213·0	248·8	30·5	224·6	212·8	−11·8
Rumania	32·5	46·9	14·4	45·9	42·2	−3·7	62·8	55·8	−7·8	91·1	98·0	6·9
USSR	849·3	1,014·8	165·5	1,112·2	1,217·9	105·7	1,855·1	1,483·1	−372·0	1,703·9	1,762·4	58·5
Yugoslavia	187·5	151·1	−36·4	163·1	116·5	−46·6	88·9	189·0	100·1	61·7	339·7	287·0
Total East Europe	1,762·8	1,830·4	67·6	2,030·1	2,259·4	229·3	3,010·4	2,665·1	−345·3	2,814·0	3,074·4	260·4
Total World	17,950·0	11,565·0	−6,385·0	20,788·0	11,987·0	−8,801·0	19,086·2	13,600·0	−5,486·0	15,674·0	14,086·2	−1,587·8

Source: Table 3.3.1.

Appendix 3.4 *Estimated repayments of development and defence credits to the USSR* (in Rs. million)

	1967/8	1968/9	1969/70	1970/1	1971/2	1972/3	1973/4	1974/5
Bhilai^a	52·5	52·5	52·5					
Drugs^b	14·3	14·3	14·3	14·3	14·3	14·3		
Others^c (utilised till 1966)	183·3	183·3	183·3	183·3	183·3	183·3	183·3	183·3
Bokaro	4·1	24·9	66·5	83·1	83·1	83·1	83·1	83·1
Others:								
1966/7			19·1	19·1	19·1	19·1	19·1	19·1
1967/8								
1968/9			26·7	26·7	26·7	26·7	26·7	26·7
1969/70				31·7	31·7	31·7	31·7	31·7
1970/1					31·2	31·2	31·2	31·2
Principal	254·2	294·1	362·2	358·2	389·4	389·4	365·3	365·3
Interest	71·0	80·5	86·5	89·0	80·0	70·0	60·0	50·0
Principal:								
1967/8, Rs. 2,840 m.								
1968/9, Rs. 3,220 m.								
1969/70, Rs. 3,450 m.								
1970/1, Rs. 3,550 m.								
	325·3	374·6	444·9	434·8	469	459	425	415
Downpayment and repayment of commercial credit					200·0			
Defence repayments	330	330	330	330				
	66	66	52	46				

^a By the agreement of March 1966, Rs. 210·3 million of the Bhilai credit was to be paid back in 4 years (*External Assistance* 1965/6); assuming one-quarter was paid in 1965/6, the rest is divided among 3 years.

^b Assuming that Rs.10 million of the principal had been paid back by March 1966, the rest in 6 years.

^c The principal outstanding on March 1966 was Rs.2,200 million. As the credits were used up over a time span of 3–4 years, the repayment during the first two and last two years would be uneven. But once the credit is fully utilised and being repaid, the instalments in middle years will be equal, as these credits are paid back in equal annual instalments.

Note: The repayments of credits utilised since 1967/8 are based on expected utilisation of these credits and therefore these figures differ from official figures.

4

INDIA'S TRADE WITH THE EAST EUROPEAN COUNTRIES

India's trade with the East European countries is an essential part of its credit arrangements with them, because India repays the credits by exporting goods. To the East European countries the arrangement of repayment in kind is a guarantee of timely repayment of India's debts, since debt servicing is effectively the first claim on India's earnings from exports to the lender country. For India, the actual, or hoped for, advantages from this arrangement are a tied market for the exports needed to repay debts, and some additional outlets for India's exports over and above this certain minimum.

India's trade with the East European countries can be viewed either as purely commercial transactions or as a part of the trade and credits arrangement. The judgement in both cases about whether this trade was beneficial or not, depends upon the commodity composition of trade, the terms of trade, and whether India's exports to these markets were additional to exports elsewhere or not. The conclusions, however, may not be the same, because the weights attached to these considerations are different in each case. For example, if India was paying higher prices for imports and a significant part of its exports to these countries was diversionary then this additional trade by itself might not be worthwhile. As part of a trade and credit relationship, however, it may have to be accepted if, for instance, an East European country gave a credit for purchasing equipment which India could not have bought without a credit, and for which no other donors would have given a credit. Since the answers to the questions about the real worth of such trade as a strictly commercial transaction and as a supplement to the trade and credit arrangements may be different, these two questions should be clearly distinguished.

The long-term value of this trade depends upon whether (i) India's exports to the East European countries are additional to its exports elsewhere, (ii) these additional markets have provided a long-term stimulus to India's exports at satisfactory prices, (iii) exports to these countries have resulted in diversifying India's exports in accordance with the trade agreements and (iv) India has received high priority goods at competitive prices in return for its current exports or commitments to future exports.

The possible costs, or modifications of the hoped-for advantages, associated with bilateral trade are (i) that India's exports to the East European countries may result in trade diversion, not trade creation, and (ii) that the import purchasing power of India's exports to the East European countries may be lower than the import purchasing power of exports elsewhere. It is, however, possible that, even though the East European countries themselves may pay a lower price than other countries for commodities which are diverted from other markets, the unit prices in other markets may rise due to low price elasticity. Therefore India's total foreign exchange receipts may actually increase, even though the volume of its exports to other markets may be reduced.

While discussing the question of the burden of repayment, it should be made clear that repayment to the East European countries is less burdensome than repayment of credits in convertible currency only in a relative sense and only if it is assumed that India has difficulty in finding markets for her exportable surpluses elsewhere. Repayment in kind is not less burdensome in the sense that the East European countries accept goods which have no opportunity cost in India or that the quality of a particular good exported to an East European country is worse than that exported to other markets.

The problems involved are considered as follows. There is first a discussion of Indian state trading and then a consideration of possible diversion of exports and related problems of commodity composition and prices of imports. This leads to the question of resales of Indian exports to third parties and then to that of the tying of India's imports under the trade and aid agreements. The chapter goes on to analyse terms of trade: in a bilateral agreement the prices of imports and exports are not generally made explicit, but what really matters is the import purchasing power of exports. Treating the prices of either in isolation may be misleading, because the effect of receiving higher or lower prices for exports than are obtainable in other markets may be cancelled by offsetting differences in prices paid for imports. However, the prices of exports may indirectly affect exports to other markets. For example, abnormally high prices paid for India's exports by the East European countries may cause a shift in India's supply to the rest of the world, either because of supply inelasticity or unwillingness of the Indian exporters to sell in other markets at prices lower than the prices received in East European countries. The chapter ends with some tentative conclusions.

STATE TRADING

In understanding trade relations with centrally planned economies the institutional arrangements are very important, because superior marketing arrangements with the East European countries may be an important factor contributing to diversion. Exports may have grown faster to these countries than to others because East Europe pays higher prices than the others, but among institutional factors it is possible that the Government of India's export incentive schemes may have favoured these markets, and that its State Trading Corporation acts to ensure that the annual targets for exports to East Europe are fulfilled.

Established by the government in 1956, the State Trading Corporation (STC) has the tasks of promoting exports of difficult goods and making barter arrangements for imports of essential commodities. While its activities are by no means confined to trade with the East European countries, it has been a very useful instrument for fulfilling export quotas under the agreements with them because of the flexibility regarding prices, as well as the fact that the East European countries welcomed an institutional agreement of this type.

Under the trade agreements with the East European countries the annual commodity quotas are only indicative targets. Although the purchasing country is not committed to buying a certain quantity, it can insist on the quotas being met by the exporting country. The STC can act as the government's agency for purchasing and exporting the commodity concerned, should the private exporters be unwilling to do so. Generally speaking, East European countries make their purchases in the open market, and the STC steps in if the agents of East European countries have any difficulties in buying the required quantities. Therefore, the direct exports handled by the STC are only a small percentage of India's total exports to the East European countries. But this is a poor indicator of the role played by the STC. Its contribution has been in bringing the buyer and the purchaser together, and since the East European countries also conduct trade through state agencies, the STC is admirably suited for this purpose. The STC has been directly responsible for handling iron ore, manganese ore, unmanufactured tobacco, leather shoes, and woollen garments, though occasionally it has also exported commodities such as raw jute, bananas, raw wool, spices, coffee, mica, jute goods, and groundnuts.

During the period 1956/7 to 1965/6 the STC's aggregate export earnings amounted to Rs.640 million, of which Rs.460 million was earned in the period after 1960. About 60 to 66 per cent of STC's exports go to East European countries. Since India's total exports to the East European countries during this period were more than Rs.7,000 million, the STC's direct exports were only around 5 per cent of India's total exports to the East European countries. However, the STC also acted as a broker in identifying market opportunities for Indian businessmen. From the available evidence it appears that the problem in promoting exports has been a lack of aggressive salesmanship rather than the product itself. Not being organised to compete in Western markets, Indian exporters welcomed an agency which found willing buyers for their products.

The presence of the STC may have influenced the direction of exports in another way. Since one of the criteria used by the STC (and later by the Mineral Trading Corporation) to measure its success was the opening of new markets, it may have given preference to the East European countries over other potential buyers. Their willingness to deal with the STC and to enter into long-term contracts produced the same result as did the reluctance of some Western countries to deal with the STC. Dr R. K. Singh quotes an economic intelligence report on manganese ore which concluded that the STC's operations were a contributory factor to India's unsatisfactory export performance in the U.S.A.[1] Another example is iron ore. West Germany's reluctance to enter into a contract with the STC may be one reason why India's exports of iron ore to West Germany declined in the 1960s.

The STC does not publish the prices obtained for exports. When necessary, it can export at a loss, i.e. below the market price. This temporary loss is justified on the ground that new markets are opened up. The STC's willingness to sell at a loss is also a great help in exporting certain items to the East European countries when the Indian sellers want a higher price than the East European buyers are willing to pay.

On the import side, the STC's operations have not meant any additional interference with an individual importer's choice, because all imports have been regulated by import licences. If the STC imports a particular commodity, instead of a private importer, it only means that in reselling it the STC gets the profit, rather than a private individual. There has been such a shortage of most raw materials and commodities in India that the question of making losses on resale of imports does not arise. On the contrary, the STC probably covers its losses on exports by reselling imports. On the other hand, the export incentive schemes have been neutral between markets.

India's export incentives scheme[2] fell under three headings: concessions on local taxes, import entitlement against export earnings, and direct subsidies for exports. These schemes were not biased, since every exporter was entitled to the benefits regardless of the destination of exports. Tax concessions were merely an exemption from local taxes, and the rates varied from 2 to 5 per cent. The exporter could only claim a reimbursement after exporting the goods. This tax concession was not very effective because the amounts involved were small and, owing to administrative delays and inefficiency, it was difficult to get any reimbursement.

Import entitlement schemes were very effective because the exporter was entitled to an import licence to the value of a certain percentage of the export earnings. Since the choice of

---

[1] R. K. Singh (76, p. 12).
[2] This description is valid only for the pre-devaluation period.

goods is much wider in the freely convertible currency markets than in the East European countries, import entitlement schemes resulted in making hard currency markets more attractive.

EXPORT DIVERSION AND COMMODITY COMPOSITION

Before analysing the element of diversion in India's exports to the East European countries the different situations in which diversion can arise have to be distinguished.

(i) If India can sell a particular commodity in the convertible currency areas without lowering the prices of her exports in these countries, but such price-inelastic supplies are redirected to the East European markets instead, this is diversion. Even a lowering of export price in the other markets may be acceptable if this price is more favourable than that obtained bilaterally from the East European countries. This type of diversion arises because domestic production is inadequate to take advantage of the opportunities in all markets, and supplies are switched by Indian exporters to the East European countries.

(ii) If it can be shown that the East European countries re-export the commodities imported from India, the existence of this practice would indicate that India could have sold the commodities in question itself in the markets concerned. They may re-export the commodities for two possible reasons: (1) because they have little use for the goods imported from India and they need foreign exchange, so they 'dump' them in the 'convertible currency' markets; (2) because the products they re-export are in great demand in the convertible currency areas and hence re-exporting these goods is an additional way of earning free foreign exchange.

To establish the first type of diversion it is necessary to show both that India was losing other markets and that this loss was attributable to the increased exports to Eastern Europe. The link between India's loss in other markets and increased exports to the East European countries can only be established by an analysis of external demand for each of the commodities in the other markets, India's competitive position in these markets, and the domestic supply situation. In the analysis of external demand the crucial thing is to establish how far the emergence of the East European countries as important markets affects India's export performance elsewhere, and to isolate this effect from what would have happened independently of the trade with the East European countries.

Until 1960 India's exports (or exports of most individual commodities) to the East European countries were not a significant percentage of her total exports. Therefore, it is reasonable to say that India's export performance in the fifties was independent of her trade with the East European countries. By comparing the rate of growth of India's exports to other markets (E_I) and the rate of growth of demand for those commodities in other markets (M_W) in the two periods 1954–9 and 1960–5, the influence of East European countries on India's export performance can be isolated. In other words, if the increase in India's exports of these selected commodities to the other markets kept pace with the growth of demand for imports of those commodities in these markets, then it can be argued that all India's export trade with the East European countries was of an additional character and did not constitute a diversion of exports from the traditional markets to new outlets.

As the commodities exported by India are not necessarily the same as those imported from other competing countries in the traditional markets, there is a case for a slightly different basic assumption. Instead of defining diversion as a deviation between India's export growth and the development of less traditional markets in the sixties, it may be assumed that any change in market shares which occurred during the 1950s, before trade with the East European countries became significant, was the result of this lack of homogeneity and would therefore continue in the 1960s. Figure 1 shows India's annual exports, E_I, to other markets and their total imports, M_W. The appropriate measure of diversion would be against an extrapolation of the change in the market shares that occurred in the 1950s. If India's relative share in the other markets declined at the same rate in the 1960s as in the 1950s, it can be argued that it was only a continuation of the trend of the 1950s. However, if India's relative share declined much faster in the 1960s than in the 1950s, increased exports to the East European countries may be at least partially responsible.

'Diversion' is here described as switching supplies to the East European countries by neglecting market opportunities elsewhere. This question can be approached from two angles. First, had the Government of India adopted a different attitude towards exports and followed the appropriate domestic policies to encourage exports, what would have been its export performance? Second, given the set of policies followed by the Government of India and the domestic supply and external demand in the important markets, could India have exported more to the other markets than she did in the absence of East European trade? The answer to the first question would be very interesting but irrelevant, because the purpose of this enquiry is not to recommend what export policies should have been adopted to encourage exports elsewhere but to find out what India could actually have sold in the other markets during the period under consideration. It is, therefore, more appropriate to take certain factors (that is, India's export policies, domestic supply and external demand) as given and then to decide whether, within this framework, India could have exported more to other markets.

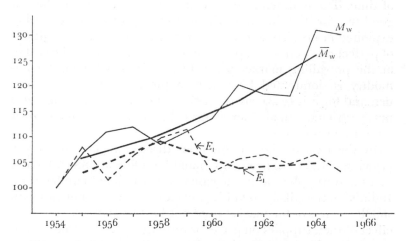

Figure 1   India's exports (E_I) and imports (M_W) into other markets.

The two questions asked in discussing diversion are whether the rate of decline of India's relative share in other markets was faster in the sixties than in the fifties and, if so, how much of this decline is attributable to the increased exports to East European countries and how much is explained by other factors, such as lack of competitiveness and the restrictive trade policies of importing countries.

Three chief reasons, usually put forward, for sluggish growth or stagnation of the total value of exports of a commodity are: (i) low price and income elasticities of demand for the commodity concerned; (ii) inelastic supply in the exporting country; (iii) large market share of the exporting country, so that its offerings affect the price (e.g. Brazilian coffee). While the first reason (i) would affect only the rate of growth of value of exports, the other two reasons (ii) and (iii) would affect the market share of the country concerned as well. It is obvious that if an exporting country has an inelastic supply curve, it will lose ground to other exporting countries with more elastic supplies. It is also clear that the larger the market share, the more the country has to worry about the effect of its increased supplies on prices. The importance of being an unimportant supplier in this situation is well known. Countries having large market shares are likely to find their shares eroded purely as a function of time. The maintenance of relative share is not, therefore, a good test for deciding whether market opportunities are being exploited or not. To take an obvious example, under conditions of perfect competition, a producer can sell as much as he wishes at the prevailing market price. Or, if the market for a commodity is dominated by a few major producers, the world demand for it is relatively inelastic and entry into the market is not restricted, small newcomers have an advantage over established producers.

In the case of the commodities discussed here the slowly growing market has been dominated by a few suppliers. Hence, as a major supplier, as in the case of tea and jute manufactures, India's share is likely to fall in any case, because countries with smaller shares of the market need not bother as much about the effect of their supplies on prices or retaliatory action from major exporters. If the countries with smaller shares are newly emerging suppliers, have more up-to-date techniques, and are lower cost suppliers, that would be an additional reason for India to lose its share. The point is that even if a large market-share country is equally efficient it will still find that its share is gradually eroded. On the other hand, if India were (i) a minor supplier itself, and (ii) a more efficient producer than the established suppliers, it might even be able to increase its market share. Therefore, by using 'the relative share constant' criterion, India's market opportunities may be underestimated in commodities where it has been a minor supplier, and over-estimated where it has been a major supplier.

Instead of using the usual 'the relative rate constant' criterion therefore, the yardstick adopted here for measuring possible loss in the other markets is constant rate of decline.

Exports to the East European countries can only be called diversionary if exports were competitive in terms of price and quality, were not restricted by quotas or tariffs imposed by importing countries and there was a domestic supply constraint.

There may be several objections to the procedure adopted here. It may be argued that the period involved is too short to identify a trend. However, it is not possible to extend the coverage to the years before 1954. After the Second World War the supplies of many commodities were disrupted and the Korean War aggravated the situation further. If these years are included in the exercise to estimate India's average share in world markets, the picture that emerges may be misleading.

There is also a positive argument for using only the fifties to establish a trend. There was no special effort to promote exports on the part of the government. In fact government policy regarding duties and quotas probably hindered exports. India's performance in the fifties was in a sense the minimum that the exporters could do without any help from the government and it is reasonable to assume that what exporters could manage without any official support in the fifties could have been managed in the sixties when the government was deliberately trying to promote exports.

Another objection that might be raised concerns the assumptions about the domestic supply situation. The question of diversion does not arise if domestic production can respond quickly to demand. There are two claims on domestic production: consumption and exports. If elasticity of supply is low in both the short and long run, the problem is to decide the optimum level of domestic consumption. This is a tricky question and can only be discussed with reference to a particular commodity. It may be argued that exportable surplus is an administrator's concept; but in a market economy the government's ability to restrict consumption by means of fiscal and other means may be limited.

It is assumed here that with the rate of growth of income and of population, domestic consumption of the commodities discussed would have increased. The yardstick used is whether exports of a commodity kept pace with domestic production or not. When domestic production has increased much less rapidly than exports, one is on stronger ground in arguing that there was a shortage of supply, as in the cases of raw wool, black pepper and coffee. When domestic production and exports have both risen fast and exports are not a significant proportion of total production it is more difficult to assess whether the government could have curbed domestic consumption. In the short run, however, it is argued here that if the exportable surplus were limited, for whatever reason, new markets could only be cultivated at the expense of the traditional markets.

Another objection may be against assuming that India's position was competitive if supplies were available at the going market price. The actual market price is only one point on a country's supply curve. Without knowing the shape and the position of India's supply curve, it is not possible to say what effect East European trade had on it. The questions to be answered in determining competitiveness or non-competitiveness are: what was the impact, if any, of India's exports to the East European countries on the world price of the commodity concerned and were Indian exports still competitive at this hypothetical price? In answering these questions one would have to take into account not only the price and income elasticity of demand for the commodity in question and the existence of close substitutes but the reactions of other suppliers to any price fixed. No such exercise has been attempted here because, apart from the conceptual and statistical difficulties involved, there is a factual consideration. The additional amounts of each commodity sold to the East European countries were not big enough to affect the world supply situation significantly. In many cases India was not a price setter and it seems that the quantities in question would not have affected the world market price. Therefore, as a working hypothesis, it is accepted here that at the given price India was in the same position as under perfect competition.

There is another consideration. Indian exports to East Europe may have affected India's supply position *vis-à-vis* the rest of the world. The presence of East European countries in the market did help to stabilise the local market prices from time to time. However, as discussed later, the East European countries used the world prices of commodities as a guide in fixing the prices of Indian exports. The differential does not appear to have been wide enough over a period of time to affect India's supply situation elsewhere. Higher prices have been paid for commodities in short supply and this resulted in trade diversion, but again this by itself was not enough to influence India's export prices elsewhere.

To measure the loss in the other markets, weighted annual index numbers of India's exports to (E_I) and imports from the other markets (M_W) were worked out for the whole period 1954–65. The averages for the periods 1954–9 and 1960–5 are shown in columns 1 and 2 of table 25. The loss is not, however, measured as the difference between actual E_I and M_W in the period 1960–5 but against a hypothetical number $E_I 1$ which shows what India's exports would have been if the rate of decline had been no faster in the sixties than in the fifties. The loss $M_W - E_I 1$ is shown in column 3, table 25.

The estimate of the loss in other markets has been made for India's total exports as well as for each commodity. To establish diversion, a study of separate commodities is necessary. The procedure followed in the case of each commodity is similar. The starting point is to check whether the relative rate of decline of India's export share to other markets was faster in the sixties than in the fifties and if so how much of this acceleration can be explained by other factors, such as increasing competition from other sources, higher relative export prices, and bad quality etc. If none of these factors can explain India's export performance in the other markets and there is a supply constraint, the inference is that the further decline in India's relative share is attributable to increased exports to the East European countries.

Table 25 summarises the world demand and supply position as well as India's exports to the other countries, the role of prices in India's export performance and the resultant diversion.

Table 25 *Estimated diversion of important exports*

Commodity	Growth of demand in other countries (M_W) (1)	India's exports to others countries E_I (2)	Loss of share in other markets (%) (3)	India's position as a supplier (4)	Competition from other sources (5)	India's export prices (relative) (6)	Domestic supply situation		Estimated diversion annually (9)
							Production (7)	Exports (8)	
Total exports of 9 commodities									
1954–9	108·40	106·35	15 (Rs.400 m.)						
1960–5	122·15	105·05							
Tea									
1954–9	100·5	97·70	13 (Rs.160 m.)	Major exporter.	The share of East African exporters increased in the sixties at India's expense. India's loss would amount to Rs.75–80 million (1954 prices).	Relative prices were in line with those of other competition.	107·0	100·0	Rs.55 m.
1959–65	101·35	85·45					123·1	98·0	
							Supply of superior tea which is exported to Eastern Europe is limited.		
Jute manufactures									
1954–9	114·6	106·9	12 (Rs.140 m.)	Major exporter.	As a result of increased competition from Pakistan India would have lost about Rs.60 million	Effective export prices were in line with Pakistan from 1960–1 onwards.	103·6	108·0	Rs.100 m.
1960–5	125·4	105·9					113·4	118·0	
							Availability of good quality raw jute was a constraint.		
Tobacco manufactures									
1954–9	101·0	116·9	6·5 (Rs.7 m.)	Minor exporter.	U.K.'s suppliers had an agreement with S. Rhodesia.	India is not a price setter.	Fluctuating.		Rs.7 m.
1960–5	104·4	113·2							

Commodity / period			Export target	India's position	Market competition	Prices / quality			Supply	Revenue
Black pepper										
1954–9	92·3	99·9	14 (Rs.14 m.)	Important but not a major supplier.	Indonesia was a major supplier but its supplies fluctuated widely.	Indian pepper, though more expensive, is of superior quality and preferred in the U.S. market.	102·5	116·5	Very tight.	Rs.14 m.
1960–5	96·2	119·2					102·0	157·6		
Coffee										
1954–9	132·4	304·9	10 (Rs.4 m.)	Minor exporter.		Prices regulated by Coffee Agreement in 1960s.	141·65	350·4		Rs.4 m.
1960–5	205·8	450·0					161·15	937·0		
Cashew nuts										
1954–9	101·3	119·6		India provides more than 90% of world's exports.	India sets the price.		144·75	128·1		
1960–5	101·6	139·6					210·60	179·9		
Raw wool										
1954–9	104·6	144·2	28 (Rs.24 m.)	Minor supplier.	Indian wool enjoys good demand for carpet backing.	Competitive in U.S. and U.K.	101·7	163·75	Supply position.	Rs.28 m.
1960–5	81·5	72·5					104·7	127·30		
Raw skins and hides										
1954–6	108·4	85·5		Important supplier.	Main competition was from synthetic materials but Indian skins enjoy good demand.	Prices not a problem.			Production of hides remained stagnant and good skins increased but not much.	Rs.60 m.
1956–9	132·8	70·9	40 (Rs.25 m.)							
1960–5	121·2	44·3	60 (Rs.40 m.)							
Iron ore										
1954–9	154·0	105·05	40 (Rs.20 m.)	Important supplier.					There was a supply constraint because auxiliary facilities had not been developed.	Rs.20 m.
1960–5	521·2	328·0								
Groundnut cakes and meal										
1959–60	91·05	95·5	22 (Rs.28 m.)	Important supplier.	Main competitor was Nigeria.				The supply constraint was the availability of raw material – groundnuts.	Rs.28 m.
1960–5	88·70									

Loss of share in the other markets in the fifties is not worked out as the difference between columns 1 and 2 but by computing an additional index which shows what India's exports would have been had the rate of decline in the 1960s been no faster than in the 1950s.

Source: Appendixes 4.1 and 4.3.

The commodities grouped here vary as regards (i) their importance in India's total exports, (ii) their competitiveness, in terms of both price and quality, *vis-à-vis* other suppliers. The estimate of diversion depends upon all these factors and therefore the special factors relevant to each commodity are discussed separately below. The only common characteristic shared by these commodities is that, compared to India's performance in the other markets in the fifties, the rate of decline of India's relative share in the sixties was much faster (except for cashew nuts).

In the case of tea, it is a commonly held view that the deteriorating quality of teas produced and increased competition for common teas from Ceylon and East Africa (reflected in relatively higher export prices of Indian tea) accounted for India's export performance in the other markets. A closer look at India's exports shows that, in fact, India was exporting only very high quality tea to the East European countries. This tea enjoyed good demand elsewhere in the world even in the sixties and the supplies were limited because the quality of domestically produced teas was deteriorating. Only about 40 per cent of India's total tea production was high grade tea[1] and whatever India supplied to the East European countries had to come out of this limited supply.

There is some evidence that the relatively higher prices of Indian teas contributed to India's export performance in the fifties. Manmohan Singh concludes that, while the pricing policies of the exporting countries would not have had much effect on the growth of demand in the importing countries, India could have exported more than she actually did. Indian exporters were at a disadvantage *vis-à-vis* the Ceylonese because the Indian businessmen had to pay export and excise duties which accounted for 10–15 per cent of the export price of tea in the fifties.[2]

On the basis of least square regression of logarithmic values for five commodities and assuming that the commodities exported by two competitors – tea from Ceylon and India – have equal income elasticities of demand and cross price elasticities of demand for all other commodities, Benjamin Cohen argues

---

[1] Roy (70, p. 120).
[2] Manmohan Singh (75, pp. 66–8).

that the correlation co-efficient between relative export prices and export market share is significant (0·90) for U.K. imports of tea from India[1] (the period considered is 1950–61). As table 26 shows, India's prices were in line with those of her competitors and relative prices changed little after 1960.

Table 26   *Average unit prices of tea: India, Ceylon and Kenya* (per 100 lb in U.S. $)

	1960	1961	1962	1963	1964	1965
India	59·20	57·50	55·63	55·53	56·53	55·71
Ceylon	56·13	54·94	53·30	52·42	52·62	51·32
Kenya	51·48	51·21	48·99	48·14	46·42	48·55

Source: IMF International Finance Statistics.

Since Indian prices were generally in line with those of its competitors the further loss of India's relative market share in the sixties is not explained by the movement of relative prices. It is possible, however, that even though the relative prices did not change further, supplies from East African countries increased and in a relatively stagnant market, rather than engage in a price war, India accepted a loss of her market share. The exports of East African countries affected India more than Ceylon, because the East African countries export common teas which constitute the bulk of India's production and exports. India was losing to East African countries in the fifties and this trend continued in the sixties as the (domestic) production in East African countries increased.

To quantify this loss it is assumed here that any increase in the annual share of East African countries over and above what was achieved in the period 1958–60 was at India's expense. The share of East African countries in total world imports increased from around 5·3 per cent in 1959–60 to an average of 6·8 per cent in the period 1960–5. In volume terms this increase amounts to about 16/17 million kg. per year and, converted into the unit price of Indian tea during the base period, the

[1] Cohen (17, pp. 610–11).

maximum loss caused by the increasing exports of the East African countries is Rs.75 million to Rs.80 million annually.

In conclusion, the faster rate of decline of India's exports to Western Europe in the sixties was not caused by the relatively stagnant world demand or by the relative prices. The increased competition from East African countries was certainly a factor, accounting for the loss of about Rs.80 million annually. The other factors responsible were increase in domestic consumption and increased exports to Eastern Europe, which account for a loss of another Rs.80 million. The domestic consumption of high quality tea could not have increased by more than Rs.25 million annually; so the increase in India's exports to Eastern Europe in the sixties (Rs.55 million) must be responsible for this loss and must be considered diversionary.

India's poor export performance in jute manufactures is generally explained as a result of increased competition from Pakistan in a relatively stagnant market, and the competition from synthetic substitutes. The analysis below shows that even though the demand for jute manufactures was not growing very fast and India suffered from Pakistan's competition, this is not the whole story. India could have exported more hessian cloth to other countries, but there was a shortage of good quality raw jute. Since Pakistan offered relatively less competition in hessian cloth and hessian cloth enjoyed a good demand in other markets, exports of hessian cloth to the East European countries were diversionary. Moreover, in 1964 and 1965 Pakistan had domestic supply problems and Pakistan's exports to the world remained stagnant, but India could not take advantage of this situation because she was exporting to Eastern Europe.

The impact of Pakistan in the early fifties was not serious because it was a small and inefficient producer. However, the situation changed in the late fifties when Pakistan adopted an aggressive export promotion policy. It imposed a duty on the exports of raw jute and took steps to remove the price differences between Pakistani and Indian products. R. K. Singh points out that Pakistan in effect gave an export subsidy to exporters of jute manufactures. He explains that its advantages included 'supply of abundant, cheap and better quality jute, relatively low wages and, by far the most important, the Export Bonus Scheme which alone gives the industry a cost advantage of

Rs.140 per ton'.[1] He also quotes G. M. Adamjee, an ex-President of the Pakistan Jute Mills Association, commenting on the fact that in a single year after the introduction of the Bonus Scheme in January 1959 exports increased by 62 per cent. As the authorities in India decided not to retaliate by giving similar incentives to their exporters, India was bound to lose some ground to Pakistan. Since 1959–60, however, relative prices have changed very little (see table 27). Therefore after the initial loss up to 1960, India should not have lost any further ground to Pakistan.

Table 27   *Average prices of jute manufactures in India and Pakistan*

	India		Pakistan	
	40 in. × 10 oz. hessian Rs. per 100 yards	Sacking B-twills (2¼ lb) Rs. per 100 bags	45 in. × 11 oz. hessian[a] Rs. per 100 yards	Sacking B-twills Rs. per 100 bags
1958/9	41·26	94·95	50·69	109·88
1959/60	42·76	112·76	43·19	113·00
1960/1	55·48	168·04	55·53	167·76
1961/2	54·08	134·97	53·69	134·88
1962/3	52·47	116·96	52·32	116·21
1963/4	46·61	112·55	47·58[b]	112·22[b]
1964/5	51·33	152·84	51·46	152·74

[a] 40 in. × 10 oz. from 1959/60 onwards.
[b] July–January only.
Source: *Commonwealth Industrial Fibres* No. 16, 1966, p. 191.

Since India was bound to lose her relative market share to Pakistan in 1959, regardless of her exports to the East European countries, the base period should be changed to take into account Pakistan's new position. The question is whether India's relative share in the other markets declined at a faster rate than in 1959/60. Even if India's exports to the other markets declined at the same rate in the period 1960–5 as they did between 1959 and 1960, further loss in her relative share due to Pakistani competition would have been 5 per cent of the average annual exports to these markets in the base period (1954–6), which

[1] R. K. Singh (76, p. 154).

amounts to Rs.60 million. Therefore Rs.80 million annually is the maximum loss that could have been caused by increasing exports to the East European countries. However, this loss can only be attributed to the increased exports to the East European markets if it can be demonstrated that a supply constraint existed and India had to choose between markets.

Considering next the domestic supply situation, table 28 shows that exports of jute manufactures kept pace with domestic production. Since the needs of Indian industry for packaging requirements were growing fast, it may be argued that there was a supply constraint; that is to say that India could not have released significant additional quantities for export. However, in the case of jute manufactures this comparison is not conclusive, because the table does not tell us whether or not the mills were working at full capacity or whether installed capacity could have been increased to expand production. The Indian Jute Mills Association publishes an annual report on the industry which for the period 1960–5 admits that, except in 1963, the mills did not operate at full capacity[1] and that production had to be partly curtailed, not because of the lack of demand, but to keep the prices of raw jute under control.

Since more than 50 per cent of the cost of production is the cost of raw jute, the prices of manufactured jute goods are closely linked to the price of the raw material. The demand for jute goods is not very responsive to price reductions, but on the other hand a price rise has an adverse effect on demand because it encourages the use of other synthetic materials. Therefore when there has been a shortage of raw jute, the Indian jute mills have responded by accepting a voluntary cut in production and rationing the quota of raw material among themselves. It would be incorrect to infer from the fact that the mills were not producing at full capacity that there was no demand for jute manufactures. It reflects the mills' inability to provide sufficient quantities without raising the price.

Another aspect of the domestic supply situation is the quality of raw material produced. The production of raw jute in India depends mainly upon two factors; the weather and the price of raw jute at the time of sowing the crop. Therefore, a year of acute shortages might be followed by a bumper crop because

[1] See IJMA Annual Reports (131, 1960–5).

Table 28 *Production, stocks and exports of raw jute and jute manufactures* (thousand tons)

	Raw jute			Hessian			Sacking			Total		
	Domestic production[a]	Imports	Total availability	Production	Stock	Export	Production	Stock	Export	Production	Stock	Export
Average, 1956-60	786	139	925	416·2	32		537	56		1,082	98	845
1961/2	961	195	1,056	408	24	432·6	500	39	343·3	1,006	180	345
1962/3	965	164	1,129	507	32	477·5	523	47	380·1	1,219	226	858
1963/4	1,096	139	1,235	525	45	500·2	488	45	372·4	1,281	269	890
1964/5	1,067	128	1,195	518	41	548·7	565	50	492·0	1,354	273	1,047
1965/6	795	126	921	480	44	466·5	539	50	387·0	1,258	282	940

[a] Year: July–June.

Sources: Domestic Production and Stocks of Jute Manufactures, Indian Jute Mills Association, *Annual Report, 1960, 1966 and 1967. Exports of Jute Manufactures*, Commonwealth Economic Committee, *Industrial Fibres*, 1960, 1963 and 1966. Imports of raw jute, *Monthly Statistics of Foreign Trade*. Production of raw jute, *Annual Production: Yield and Acreage of, Under Principal Crops.*

Notes: (1) The year for agricultural production begins in June. The trade year is April–March. (2) The production for jute manufactures relates to IJMA members only. Exports are all India. (3) Exports of jute manufactures include carpet backing. Therefore these figures differ from table 4.3, which refers to jute bags and hessian cloth only.

many farmers switch to jute. However, although in such circumstances the total production is increased, the supply of good quality raw jute is relatively inelastic, as output from many of these additional lands is of very inferior quality. In the long run the problem can be solved by increasing the yield per acre and improving the quality of raw jute produced. During the period under consideration, however, the supply of high quality raw jute was limited. As high quality jute is necessary for producing both carpet backing and hessian, the output of these items was affected more than that of sacking bags. In discussing possible diversion therefore, the commodity composition of jute manufactures should be carefully examined.

Table 29 *India's exports of jute manufactures to East European countries* (in Rs. million)

	1961/2	1962/3	1963/4	1964/5	1965/6
Hessian cloth	42·2	46·3	57·6	64·5	82·0
Sacking bags	60·9	58·0	92·0	158·5	231·7

Source: DGCI, *Monthly Statistics of Foreign Trade.*

As table 29 shows, in the sixties India was exporting hessian cloth worth Rs.58 million annually to the East European countries. Since hessian cloth was in good demand in other markets and the availability of good quality raw jute imposed a limit on production, these exports were also diversionary.

India's average annual exports of sacking bags to the East European countries were around Rs.100 million per annum in the period 1960–5 (see table 29). As explained previously, India would have lost about Rs.60 million to Pakistan anyway. Since Pakistan's exports were mostly sacking bags, it seems reasonable to say that India's exports of gunny bags to the East European countries were largely additional. However, India's exports to Eastern Europe were stepped up after 1962/3, precisely at the time that India had crop failures and experienced shortages of raw materials. Moreover, during this period Pakistan also had troubles. A strike in Pakistan interrupted production for eight weeks in 1964 and the resulting loss in production amounted to 42,000 tons or approximately one-third of India's exports of jute manufactures to the USSR in 1964/5. Pakistan's exports of jute manufactures – mainly sacking bags – remained stagnant at 230,000 tons a year but, because of increased exports to Eastern Europe, India could not take advantage of this situation. In view of the factors mentioned above, it appears that, of the total exports of sacking bags of Rs.100 million annually to Eastern Europe, exports worth Rs.60 million were additional, but the rest, or most of it, was diversionary.

It may be argued that since India needed other markets, this diversion of about Rs.100 million annually, was justified as a necessary investment for building up future markets. The East European countries were, however, re-exporting some of these commodities themselves.[1] Therefore India was not building up new markets to the extent indicated by the increasing exports to Eastern Europe.

In the case of tobacco, the amount involved is quite small, about 5 per cent of India's average earnings from this commodity, and it can be argued that if India had had the supplies she would have had no difficulty in selling them. It is true that Indian tobacco is of inferior quality but this is reflected in the lower unit price.

India's exports of black pepper increased much faster than domestic production (see table 25) but exports to Eastern Europe grew much faster than those to the rest of the world. This increase is diversionary because the world supply situation was such that India could have gained the other markets at Indonesia's expense by establishing her reputation as a reliable supplier. As table 30, below, shows, Indonesia's exports dropped significantly from the high level reached in 1959 and only reached that level again in 1963.

Although Indian pepper is considerably more expensive than Indonesian pepper, it is of a superior quality and is preferred in the United States. Since no definite estimate of cross elasticity of substitution between different qualities of black pepper has been made, it is difficult to establish the role of prices in India's exports of black pepper. However, India could not have benefited from the fluctuation in Indonesia's exports because her

---

[1] See the section on re-exports, pp. 157–63.

exportable surplus was limited and she had commitments to export a certain amount to the East European countries under trade agreements. The East European countries paid higher prices to purchase black pepper in the open market and that probably explains why supplies were diverted to them. In fact the NCAER report on exports of black pepper points out that large-scale purchases by the USSR may have led to an artificial rise in price in the domestic market, making producers unwilling to export to other markets.[1] Exports of coffee conformed to the normal pattern in that India was losing ground in the other markets. If India had maintained the relative share in the other markets which she had in the fifties, her average export earnings would have been higher by 10 per cent during the period 1960–5 than during the period 1954–6.

Table 30   *Indonesia's exports of black pepper* (in thousand metric tons)

1959	1960	1961	1962	1963	1964	1965
28	13	19	11	28	23	12

Source: BAPPENAS (Planning Organisation of Indonesia).

India's production of coffee was not even adequate to meet domestic demand and therefore in the fifties coffee exports were regulated by a quota. This policy was revised in 1957 and subsequently India's exports increased much faster than domestic production. Indian coffee has a special aroma and its own market. Since even after curbing domestic consumption India's exports had to be rationed, India could only have increased exports to the East European countries by restricting exports elsewhere. A study made by the Indian Institute of Foreign Trade argues that the effective constraint on India's exports after 1962 was the quotas imposed by the International Coffee Agreement rather than domestic supply.[2] Technically this may

[1] NCAER (51, p. 84).
[2] Indian Institute of Foreign Trade (113, p. 32).

be correct but it involves an assumption that quotas are 'fixed' and cannot be revised. This assumption is not justified.

It is true that, except in one year (1963/4), India has practically fulfilled her quota to the export markets. But in 1963/4 she could not fulfil her quota. Therefore her initial quota in 1964/5 was reduced by 4,000 tons. By the Coffee Agreement,[1] each country is assigned a quota at the beginning of the year. This quota is fixed in the light of the country's past export performance and expectations of crop yield. If India had exported more to the markets other than the East European countries after 1957, when the export policy was revised, her initial annual export quota would have been higher. Moreover, the initial quota is only provisional. Had India fulfilled her quota in the first six months of the year, she could have requested a revision of the initial quota (as has been done by many countries). This she could not do because of the limited availability of domestic supply and the increasing exports to East European countries. Moreover, as the East European countries re-exported Indian coffee, her exports to the East European countries did not entirely constitute a net increase in these markets either.

In the case of cashew nuts, India more than maintained her relative share in the other markets. There was no diversion in the sense in which the term has been used here, but this does not mean that India did not neglect market opportunities elsewhere. Since India was practically the only supplier, it is only natural that imports in important markets grew in line with Indian exports. The really interesting question is whether there was unfulfilled demand, i.e. whether India could have exported additional quantities to these markets if supplies had been available. R. K. Singh[2] points out that India's direct exports to the European Common Market (EEC) exceeded her exports to the United Kingdom in 1962/3 and that they were additional

---

[1] The International Coffee Agreement was signed by the major producing countries in 1962 with a view to regulating the exports to and stabilising the prices of coffee in the important coffee-importing countries. The markets are divided into quota and non-quota markets. Prices in the quota markets tend to be higher than elsewhere. So even non-signatories have found it profitable to export coffee to quota countries. The author has relied for the description of the International Coffee Agreement and its history on a study on the same subject under preparation in the World Bank.   [2] R. K. Singh (76, p. 197).

to the quantities re-exported by Britain. From the market indications available regarding consumer tastes, Manmohan
Singh concluded that doubling exports of cashews in the sixties
from the level reached in the fifties would have been possible if
adequate supplies of raw materials had been available.[1]

Table 31   *India's exports of cashew nut kernels to selected markets* (in
Rs. million)

Years	Total	U.K.	U.S.A.	Austra-lia	Canada	EEC	USSR	Total Eastern Europe
1958	152·1	9·4	109·4	4·1	5·5	3·5	20·0	20·3
1959	160·0	7·8	106·0	2·7	5·5	4·3	18·2	20·4
1960/1	189·1	13·4	125·3	5·9	6·8	5·4	22·5	25·1
1961/2	181·7	12·5	105·5	6·5	7·4	6·0	27·8	35·7
1962/3	192·7	9·4	108·7	6·8	6·0	10·5	21·3	44·1
1963/4	214·3	10·7	119·3	7·2	6·9	9·6	42·5	52·1
1964/5	290·3	17·5	146·8	10·7	9·5	9·2	77·0	86·2
1965/6	274·0	12·3	147·5	8·2	9·0	9·0	69·1	78·1

Source: DGCIS, *Monthly Bulletin of India's Foreign Trade.*

India's total exports of cashews did increase very rapidly in
the sixties (see table 31) but the geographical distribution shows
a rapid rise in the share to East European countries. As the table
shows, India's exports to the U.K., Canada, Australia and the
EEC countries were smaller than her exports to the East
European countries in the period 1960/1 to 1965/6. Judging by
per capita income and consumption, it is hard to believe that the
other countries listed here could not have absorbed at least the
amounts imported by the East European countries. As discussed later, the East European countries have re-exported
large quantities of cashew nuts themselves. If the East European
countries could sell cashews in the Western markets, India could
have done the same. India's exports to the East European
countries in the period 1962/3 to 1965/6 amounted to Rs.260
million, and it would appear that East European countries were
primarily interested in buying cashew nuts because of their resale value in the hard currency areas and as such exports to the
East European countries did not represent net gains to India.

[1] Manmohan Singh (75, p. 213).

Cashew nuts are a luxury item and it may be argued that India should have curbed domestic consumption to increase exportable supplies. This may have increased the exportable supply marginally, but the main problem was the availability of raw cashews. Table 32 in itself is not very useful because, although it shows that the domestic production of cashews increased sharply from 1961/2 to 1962/3, the increase after 1962/3 is mostly statistical and not a real increase in production. Moreover, as the table shows, imports did not increase very fast after 1962/3. Therefore the total supplies did not increase much although India's exports did. India did not produce enough cashews to meet the demand from all sources.

Table 32   *Total availability of raw cashews in India* (thousand tons)

Period	Imports	Domestic production	Total
1955/6	62	80	142
1956/7	51	81	132
1957/8	101	95	196
1958/9	122	103	231
1959/60	97	113	210
1960/1	112	122	240
1961/2	102	129	231
1962/3	155	157[a]	312
1963/4	157	161	318
1964/5	192	171	363
1965/6	162	135	336

[a] From 1962/3 onwards the figures are not comparable with figures for earlier years because the coverage increased in that year.
Sources: DGCIS, *Monthly Statistics of Foreign Trade.* Ministry of Agriculture, *Production Area Yield and Production of Principal Crops.*

India exports a special type of raw wool which is used in making carpets etc. As a minor supplier, India was a price taker and had no difficulty in exporting wool. The main constraint was the fact that the raw wool supply was not growing very fast. After 1962, due to increased defence requirements, the restrictions on imports of raw wool meant that the supplies available for exports were rather limited and India increased her exports to the East European countries only by losing her share in other markets.

Raw skins and hides, like raw wool, are another commodity the main constraint on the exports of which is domestic supply. As table 25 shows, India started losing her relative share in the other markets in the late fifties, and this trend continued in the sixties. This loss is diversionary because, though India has one of the largest cattle populations in the world, the supply of skins and hides cannot be significantly increased in response to changed demand conditions. Because of the widespread prejudice against animal slaughter in India and the anti-cow-slaughter legislation passed by many state governments, India has to rely on the natural death rate for hides. There is no inhibition regarding the slaughter of goats and the goat population in India did increase during the fifties. But the *per capita* availability of animals in India is lower than in many other countries of the world, and *per capita* consumption is very low. With increasing income and urbanisation, domestic demand is bound to grow and thus affect the size of the exportable surplus.

As Indian hides and skins are smaller and free of fat, there is a special market for them among the manufacturers of shoes and handbags. India had no quality problems, but is not a price setter in the world markets and would have had to accept the prevailing market price. The East European countries, especially the USSR, paid a higher price for raw skins and hides (see table 33) to attract supplies from other markets. The interesting thing is that in the sixties the price differential was much narrower than in the fifties. It would appear that once the USSR had established its position as a buyer, it did not feel it necessary to pay a higher price.

India lost its share of iron ore in the other markets as a result of a combination of circumstances. Although India had considerable supply potential, actual output was not adequate to meet all external demand and the marketing arrangements favoured East European countries. There is no inherent supply constraint in iron ore. India has vast deposits, estimated at about 22,000 million tons, approximately a quarter of the world's reserves. This is high grade iron ore (comprising 63 per cent iron and above).[1] But since the related mining and transport

[1] R. K. Singh (76, pp. 222-3).

facilities have not been developed, there has been a short-term supply limitation. The output of iron ore from the public sector enterprises did not reach the targets set during the sixties. A good example is provided by the Kiriburu mine where the arrangement was that the ore produced would be exported to Japan. Japan had agreed to import a certain quantity every year. In 1964/5, there was a shortfall of one million tons in the output from this mine, but Japan was not provided with alternative supplies from other mines.

Out of whatever output was available, the commitments to the East European countries have received first priority because the STC has been in charge of exporting iron ore since 1956,[1] and there is a bias in favour of countries which enter into long-term contracts and prefer to deal with the STC. That may be one explanation of the fact that India's exports to Japan increased in the sixties, but not those to Italy and West Germany.

Groundnut cake and meal is one of the newer exports which had a good market in the West European countries, but the output of the expeller and extractor industries in India has been limited by the availability of the raw material – groundnuts. The production of groundnuts was below the level reached in 1958/9 in all years except 1964/5, while the volume of groundnut cake exports more than doubled. India has not been able to meet the internal demand as well as the requirements of all export markets.

It is argued that India could not have exported groundnut cakes and meal to other countries because of increased competition from Nigeria. Nigerian transport costs are much lower than Indian because of its greater proximity to European markets. But, Indian transport costs would have been similar whatever the destination in Europe: India was not saving much on transport by exporting to the East European countries rather than to Western Europe. Moreover, if groundnut cakes and meal were uncompetitive, they would have received special assistance. India introduced special export incentives in 1962/3, but groundnut cakes and meal were not given any special assistance, except a 2 per cent exemption from local taxes. The Ministry of Commerce and Industry Report on trade and

[1] The exports of minerals were transferred to the Mineral Trading Corporation, another state trading agency, in 1962–3.

industry lists groundnut cake and meal as one of the commodities with internal prices similar to those prevailing inter-
nationally, and therefore competitive. So the argument that
groundnut cake and meal were being priced out of other
markets is not tenable.

The other important commodities are mica, lac, manganese
ore, raw jute, groundnuts, woollen manufactures and castor oil,
which together account for about 10 per cent of total exports
to the East European countries. It is not necessary to compare
India's relative market share in these commodities in the two
periods because the purpose of this exercise is to find out how
much of the loss is attributable to the East European markets.
India lost its share in these markets because of other factors, as
described below.[1]

In the fifties India was one of the main exporters of castor oil
to world markets and the principal markets were the U.K. and
the U.S.A. India's share was well maintained in the early fifties
but it started losing ground later in the decade to Brazil.
Brazilian oil is of a superior quality and the price was lower
than the Indian price. In addition, the United States probably
preferred to rely on Brazil rather than India because it was a
nearer source of supply. Throughout the sixties Brazil increased
the volume of its exports. As India was not in a position to
compete, the question of diversion does not arise.

India is very rich in resources of manganese ore and there is
no supply constraint on exports. If domestic output has not
grown rapidly, it is because the output is governed by the export
demand prospects. India's exports of manganese ore have
fluctuated widely in the fifties and sixties due to the following
factors:

(1) The preferences of buyers for particular sources of supply.
For example, the U.S. companies were encouraged to invest in
the Brazilian mines and hence have a vested interest in Brazil's
exports.

(2) The emergence of the USSR as a serious competitor after
1955. Previously its exports were disrupted following the
Second World War.

---

[1] For the discussion of exports of castor oil and manganese ore the author has
drawn upon Manmohan Singh, R. K. Singh (75, 76) and two publications by the
Indian Chamber of Commerce (145, 146).

(3) India's pricing policy may have been partly responsible for the loss because India imposed an export levy on manganese ore.

Under these circumstances, the East European countries were a welcome addition to India's export markets. The only reservation here is that if the USSR, for example, was using Indian manganese ore to satisfy domestic consumption and increasing its own exports to the hard currency areas, it was in effect re-exporting Indian manganese ore.

India's total exports of raw jute and groundnuts in the sixties amounted to Rs.35 million and to Rs.25 million respectively.

These two commodities are examples of undesirable exports. Because of the shortage of supplies at home and the policy of exporting processed products as far as possible, India banned exports of raw jute throughout most of the fifties. Exports of groundnuts have been governed by the size of the crop and the internal demand. The shortage of domestic supply continued into the sixties and it was a mistake to export these commodities at all, unless the raw jute exported was of such inferior quality that there was little internal demand for it. The quantities involved in both cases are small. It is quite possible that India was forced to export these commodities to make good the shortfalls in other commodities and meet the annual trade targets.

Indian exports of mica fluctuated in the fifties and the sixties.[1] The only change in the sixties was that the share of the East European countries in India's total exports increased from 20 to 40 per cent. This increase probably did not constitute diversion. India would have lost in the U.S.A. anyway, because the demand for mica in the U.S.A. was not rising very fast and there was competition from the substitution of inferior scrap mica. Moreover, the U.S. authorities deliberately encouraged the production of mica in Brazil by raising the price paid by 25 cents in 1955. As a consequence of all these factors, exports to the U.S.A. were not increasing very quickly in the fifties and were expected to suffer a further setback in the sixties, because the U.S. government had earlier bought mica valued at Rs.20

[1] For the discussion of mica exports, the author has relied upon the used sources in the case of castor oil and manganese ore, and NCAER Report (53).

million every year under defence contract for stockpiling, but this contract was not renewed in the sixties.

Both woollen manufactures and leather footwear have become promising export items in very recent years. The East European countries are becoming important markets for both of them. India could have exported these to Western markets but has had both quality and cost problems. Indian businessmen did not pay enough attention to consumer preferences. The production cost of the Indian products in question is still high, so India should welcome the additional markets. There is, however, the danger that, because the markets are assured, Indian products will continue being high cost, low quality, and non-competitive in other markets.

The commodities discussed so far cover the bulk of India's exports to the East European countries up to 1965/6. Table 25 and the preceding discussion show that the estimated diversion amounts to Rs.285 million per annum in base year prices or nearly Rs.340 million in terms of 1965/6 prices. Diversion, therefore, amounts to about 21 per cent of total exports to the East European countries in 1965/6. In addition, India's exports of manganese ore and cashew nuts may not have been entirely beneficial.

Although exports of cashew nuts to the East European countries cannot be called diversion, India did suffer a loss in the other potential markets because of the increase in these exports. India could have earned Rs.50 million more per annum, or about 5 per cent of its exports to the East European countries, from hard currency markets. Similarly India might have been able to export more manganese ore to the hard currency areas. But without figures of domestic consumption, production and exports of manganese ore from the USSR, this cost cannot be quantified. Other non-quantifiable costs, such as undesirable exports and the possible encouragement of inefficient, high cost production, have been discussed with reference to specific commodities.

The above discussion of diversion shows how much more India could have exported. If the East European countries had consumed everything they imported from India, then the 21 per cent diversion might be treated as a necessary cost for opening new markets, but in fact the East European countries re-exported some of the commodities imported from India. To the extent that India was not establishing a foothold in the new markets, this is an additional cost.

RESALE OF INDIAN EXPORTS BY TRADING PARTNERS

So far only one kind of diversion – Indian exporters exporting to the East European countries rather than to the other markets – has been discussed. The more general interpretation of diversion is the re-export of Indian goods by East European countries. While it is well known that most East European countries have engaged in re-exporting Indian goods, there are both conceptual and statistical difficulties in quantifying this. On a narrow interpretation of the concept, the question is: how can it be shown that the East European countries were re-exporting *Indian* goods. When the product is of unmistakable origin, for example, Indian cashews, one's task is easy. By examining a country's trade statistics alone it can be demonstrated that country X was exporting cashews which it did not produce. Most cases, however, fall within a category of goods which are domestically produced and traded. If Hungary were both to import black pepper from India and to export it, trade statistics will not answer the question of re-exports. On a narrow interpretation, one has to show that the importing country concerned produces little of the good in question and that it re-exports Indian goods rather than goods imported from some other country.

If the total export of any of these commodities exceeds the total domestic production in the re-exporting country and the main source of supply for that commodity is India, it is a reasonable inference that the re-exported goods are Indian, but there are very few cases like this.

A broader interpretation of re-exports, however, includes the case of where the importer of an Indian commodity exports domestically produced goods. It can be argued that, if an increase, say, in the USSR's imports of tea from India did not result in a corresponding increase in domestic consumption, but enabled the USSR to increase her exports of tea, in effect, this constitutes a re-export of Indian tea. To the extent that the USSR was using imports from India to increase her exports and not domestic consumption, the effect on Indian exports was the same as if the Indian imports were being re-exported.

The statistical difficulties are that trade statistics are either not available or ambiguous (see table 33). For example, if Czechoslovakia and East Germany export coffee, or Poland and Rumania black pepper or tea, it may be argued that the goods were not of Indian origin, and hence it may not be possible to enforce an agreement prohibiting resale.

The checking can be done from the statistics of either the re-exporting or the receiving country. In the re-exporting country one may run into any or all of the following problems. The country may use commodity groups which are too broad. For example, 'edible nuts' is too broad a category to be useful in deciding whether the country was re-exporting Indian cashews or not. Secondly, the re-exporting country may be a producer itself. For example, the USSR produces and exports raw skins and hides, manganese ore and tea and it is difficult to prove in these cases that the USSR was re-exporting Indian goods. Even if the country is exporting its own goods, what may have happened is this: during the time in which the USSR increased its imports from India, domestic consumption remained con-stant and imports from India were used to increase the ex-portable surplus. This in effect constitutes re-export of Indian goods. To arrive at this sort of conclusion, however, one needs not only figures concerning trade and domestic production, but also independent estimates of domestic consumption. Since these are not always available, this question concerning real re-exports cannot be answered satisfactorily.

If one approaches the problem by examining the trade statistics of the importing country the difficulty is that, unless an East European country is an important exporter of the com-modity concerned, the importing country may not list these imports separately. An examination of the United Kingdom's imports of commodities by country of origin for the period 1957–65 produced very meagre results (see table 34). There were other cases in which the United Kingdom was importing substantial quantities of a commodity from a particular East European country, but where the particular country was a producer and exporter of the commodity concerned.

Table 33   *Western Europe's imports of certain selected commodities from Eastern Europe* (in dollars)

	1965	1966
	$	$
Fresh fruit; nuts, fresh, dry	25,570	22,980
Bulgaria	7,990	3,760
Czechoslovakia	1,100	1,920
East Germany	20	—
Hungary	9,670	8,440
Poland	2,510	4,310
Rumania	3,890	3,690
USSR	270	650
Coffee		
Hungary	20	—
Poland	830	1,390
Tea		
Bulgaria	10	1,390
Spices		
Bulgaria	580	630
Czechoslovakia	100	10
Hungary	2,270	2,430
Poland	310	340
Rumania	250	230
Hides and skins, undressed		
Bulgaria	5,490	5,940
Czechoslovakia	60	70
East Germany	170	50
Hungary	70	70
Poland	200	450
Rumania	3,850	4,330
USSR	10	10
Tobacco		
All East European countries	24,630	29,570
Jute fibres		
All East European countries	480	250
Iron ore		
Poland	13,860	17,670
USSR	200	170

Source: U.N. Economic Bulletin for Europe, vol. 19, No. 1, November 1967, Geneva, table B.

The difficulties in interpreting trade statistics are further increased because many goods are often re-exported through third countries. If Hungary, for instance, sends tea or cotton to Britain via Finland or the Netherlands, the exports will be recorded as Finnish or Dutch exports of tea to the U.K. If the Netherlands only shows imports and exports of tea and not re-exports it is not possible to relate imports of Indian tea from Hungary and re-exports to Britain thereof. To identify all the links in the chain would involve a full-scale study in itself. However, the point can be illustrated with a few examples.

Table 34 *Imports of some commodities into the U.K. from East European countries*

	1961	1962	1963	1964	1965
Castor oil					
Rumania (000 cwt.)	26	33·1			
Raw wool					
East Germany[a]					
Rumania (000 lb.)	7·75	83·9			
Black tea					
Poland (000 lb.)				109	
Coffee					
Poland (000 cwt.)					19·6

[a] In 1959 and 1960 East Germany exported 52,000 lb. of raw wool.
Source: U.K. Customs and Excise, *Annual Statement of the Trade of the U.K.*, vol. 2, table 1.

The imports of tea into the United Kingdom from the Netherlands did show an increase in 1963/4. They went up from 2·35 million lb. in 1962/3 to 4·75 million lb. in 1963/4, a doubling in one year.[1] It was during these years that India was losing ground in the U.K. and it was reported in the newspapers that Indian tea was being re-exported to Britain.

Goldman has described how cashews are re-exported. He says the nuts are placed on board a ship destined for Eastern Europe

[1] Indian Chamber of Commerce (145).

via Port Said or some other intermediate port. Midway in transit these goods are rerouted to Rotterdam or sent directly to New York, where they are sold at a 5 per cent discount on the world price. The American importer then opens a credit in dollars for the East European country, which in turn opens a non-dollar credit in favour of the Indian shipper. Naturally, India has strongly protested against such practices, which are a violation of its trade agreements with the East European countries. According to Indian Customs officials, the Rumanians at least have agreed to split any commission they make on such re-exports with the Indians.[1] However, because of all the difficulties mentioned in identifying goods of Indian origin there is no effective check against resale. The question of resale has been investigated by the Indian authorities. It is accepted in official circles that there is diversion, and the range suggested for commodities like tea, coffee, spices, jute goods and grey cotton cloth is between 5 to 10 per cent of India's exports to the East European countries.[2]

The question of resale was recently raised in the Estimates Committee by a non-official organisation, which alleged that 'there have been cases where the goods exported to East European countries under the barter agreements have been re-exported by them to other countries'. When the representative of the Ministry was asked about this, he admitted it, but pointed out that there is no concrete evidence except in a few cases. He said, 'We have found some cases of this type. We have investigated into them as far as possible. We have put in one stipulation in our agreement with these countries that the goods are intended for use in their country ... Whenever we found that there was any diversion, we have analysed the statistics of West European countries to find out whether any Indian origin goods have been finding their way to Western Europe. There is no direct and concrete evidence of this, excepting a few stray cases. We take due notice of it and those governments have made amends also.'[3]

In a subsequent communication to the Committee, the government representative has given more details. 'Cases of

---

[1] Goldman (28, pp. 110–11).
[2] Personal discussions in New Delhi.
[3] Ministry of Finance (114, pp. 223–34).

diversion and resale of Indian goods at and through Hamburg, Antwerp, Rijeka etc. have come to our notice from time to time through indirect sources. The items involved are cashew nuts, hides and skins, groundnuts, spices, tanned skins, coffee, tea, mica, jute goods etc. These diversion resales were stated to have been resorted to by almost all the East European countries ... The only exception is the USSR about whom very few complaints have come to our notice. All these cases ... have been investigated in detail by us through our Consulates General and other Indian missions, but we could not get any concrete proof of resale although it is felt from evidences collected that some East European countries have indulged in this practice.'[1]

The government also admits that there is not much it can do to prevent this sort of diversion. It has stated, 'as a remedial measure we tried to enforce a system of production of "Landing Certificate" from the ultimate consignee. But it could not be put into effect as it has no *de jure* force and because it would amount to open discrimination, rendering the whole operation as an action of doubtful efficacy. We are therefore depending on the operation of our trade and payments agreements understanding by exchange of confidential letters that neither party will indulge in re-exports.'[2]

Other studies, such as those by the Institute of Foreign Trade[3] and by Surendra Dave,[4] state that there is some evidence of resale of oil cakes and coffee respectively. The Estimates Committee report goes much further. The list given therein includes commodities which India had to divert to the East European countries because of the limitation of domestic supply, such as cashew nuts, de-oiled cakes, goat skins, and coffee.

The East European countries, however, have also re-exported commodities for which demand was not so favourable, for example, tea and grey cotton. Since they offer a discount, other countries prefer to buy from the East European countries and India loses her share in the market, even though she has enough supplies to meet the demand in all markets. If the quantities are large enough, the East European countries may even succeed in forcing the price downward. When the demand for the com-

---

[1] Ministry of Finance (114, pp. 222–34).   [2] *Ibid.*
[3] Institute of Foreign Trade (113).   [4] Dave (20).

modity is not price elastic, India does not gain anything by lowering her price.

THE TYING OF IMPORTS

Since by the trade agreements India is committed to utilising its export earnings to purchase goods and services from the partner country, the partner's ability to provide goods is at least as important a consideration in evaluating this expansion of trade as its willingness to import goods from India. The relevant questions are (i) whether the partner countries provided goods unobtainable from other sources and the variety of goods provided, and (ii) the prices and quality of goods available compared to other sources of supply. The first question discussed regarding imports is the amount of choice India actually had in placing orders for goods. The trade agreements include a wide variety of goods but none of these are special in the sense that only East European countries could have provided them. Table 35 shows that the commodity composition of imports from the East European countries has been similar to that of imports from the rest of the world. There is no evidence that India was importing these commodities only to use up its export earnings. The share of machinery is quite high – 50 per cent of total imports from the East European countries in the sixties – but that is to be expected because all the credits utilised up to 1965/6 were for imports of machinery. Moreover countries like Czechoslovakia and the USSR specialise in exports of complete plants.

A definitive general conclusion – either that India had free choice or that it was forced to buy low priority goods – is not possible. On the one hand, since India's imports were regulated by import licensing, it is possible to argue that if the government granted a licence the import was necessary. On the other hand, it is possible that the government would have preferred to give a licence for something else, but given the partner country's willingness to provide certain goods it had no choice. Only the negotiators who discussed the commodity composition of imports can throw any light on this question. The fact that the choice of goods was limited even among those for which licences were issued is brought out by the fact that import licences issued

Table 35 *Composition of India's major imports from East European rupee payment agreement countries (in Rs. million)*

	1959/60	1960/1	1961/2	1962/3	1963/4	1964/5	1965/6
Base metals	151·3	138·2	208·9	174·3	155·3	218·1	256·6
Manufactures of metals	17·3	15·4	19·3	52·5	21·0	27·6	25·0
Machinery	81·3	158·8	372·4	547·1	655·8	897·3	855·2
Chemical elements and compounds	18·9	20·5	33·1	53·2	52·1	46·3	73·7
Paper and paper manufactures	33·2	16·7	19·8	21·4	19·0	20·4	31·7
Transport equipment	19·9	9·6	21·8	25·9	37·2	27·9	43·5
Dyeing, tanning and colouring materials	12·2	3·4	6·3	7·4	5·4	5·8	4·5
Medicinal and pharmaceutical products	2·0	6·1	6·2	8·1	11·2	9·9	14·8
Fertilisers manufactured	3·2	16·5	23·9	40·6	34·7	13·5	33·7
Professional, scientific and controlling instruments	9·0	14·4	21·7	30·0	28·9	28·2	32·1
Petroleum products	—	3·2	24·5	58·4	89·2	64·9	115·4
Total imports (including others)	354·2	443·1	876·2	1,101·3	1,292·6	1,449·9	1,566·8

Source: DGCIS, *Monthly Statistics of Foreign Trade.*

Note: Until 1959/60, India's imports from the East European countries were less than 5 per cent of her total imports and their share in total imports of most commodities is small – less than 10 per cent. Therefore a detailed breakdown by commodities has not been given for earlier years.

were not fully utilised for many items, i.e. contracts had not been placed for these goods even six months or a year after the licences were issued.[1]

The difficulties in finding the goods are to some extent unavoidable, because the East European countries have a different economic and political system. Since foreign trade is a part of the plan they can plan their purchases in advance, but domestic production cannot be expanded in response to changed demand conditions abroad. If orders can be placed while the plans are being formulated, these can be incorporated in the production targets. But in India both private firms and government organisations can import from the East European countries. Apart from a few suppliers' credits, most of the private sector imports were not credit financed. Private firms in India do not plan their purchases in advance and this is a major source of difficulty in obtaining current imports from the East European countries.

Import licences are issued against the annual target fixed for imports. As no commodity quotas are agreed upon, the licences are issued for the commodities included in trade agreements. The country concerned is not consulted about its ability to supply these goods within the specified time limit. This is another reason why actual imports are not equal to the value of licences issued. Another problem regarding current imports is that the East European countries cater for large-scale production. Small producers find it difficult to find something to meet their requirements.

A special difficulty in arranging imports from the Soviet Union is their inexperience in trading. Since the revolution in 1917, one of the principal aims of Soviet policy has been to achieve self-sufficiency and there is no effective apparatus to handle trade with developing countries. The USSR does not have any marketing organisation in India. While Hungary and Czechoslovakia are active in establishing contacts with Indian importers, the USSR has made no effort to promote its exports. Sometimes Indian importers are not even aware of what the Russians have to offer. Since an import licence is given for the rupee payment area as a whole, importers try other East

---

[1] The data concerning countrywise licences for importing goods and the actual imports against these licences are still not available. But the author was told in personal interviews that the private importers had difficulties in getting the items for which the licences had been issued.

European countries first. All this is very time consuming and involves long negotiations. Both the public sector and private importers have suffered from long delivery dates.

In this connection it is worth mentioning that India has not been the only country facing difficulties in obtaining imports from the East European countries resulting in either accumulation of credits by the developing country concerned or a settlement in convertible currency. Thus R. L. Allen points out, 'In 1955, the Soviet Union imported $92 million more than it exported. In 1956, imports were $112 million more than exports and this disparity increased to $139 million by 1957. Some of the purchases were covered by convertible currency payments, as in the case of Cuban sugar. Many countries, however, are tied to the Soviet Union by trade and payments agreements which specify bilateral balancing of trade (except for Soviet credit) and hence some of the export surplus of developing countries is in fact short-term credit granted unwillingly by them to the Soviet Union. Argentina felt this most acutely when in early 1958 a delegation toured the Soviet Union and Eastern Europe to try to buy enough goods to settle accounts.'[1] India also had difficulties in the late fifties in obtaining goods from the USSR, which resulted in India giving short-term credits to the USSR (as discussed in chapter 3).

As a result of all the difficulties mentioned in importing, the lag between ordering and actually receiving equipment is long. Projects which receive East European credits take a long time in construction and in some cases at least the major cause has been delay in the arrival of equipment – for example, oil refineries and heavy machine building plant. There have been complaints from private investors as well. The Estimates Committee inquiring into import licences tied to particular countries gives some instances, for example: 'In the first case, where the import licence has been tied to Czechoslovakia, the Indian company has been obliged to wait two and a half years for delivery and even then has been offered less than half the original order.' Similar difficulties arose in a second case where the import licence was tied to the USSR and where the actual user in India had only received delivery of one model of the original order.[2]

[1] Allen (3).   [2] Ministry of Finance (114, pp. 223–8).

Any discussion about the quality of imports must be inconclusive because the most important imports from the East European countries have been machinery and equipment. Unless the goods provided are identical or even similar in all important respects to goods from other sources, it is not possible to make meaningful comparisons. The USSR and Czechoslovakia find it difficult to promote exports of machinery and equipment to Western markets and so it appears that their products are not good enough to compete with Western products. In private discussions, government officials seemed to accept this as natural. They argue that unless the East European countries have some equipment they cannot sell in the convertible currency markets, they will not find the arrangement of repayment in kind convenient. The East European countries look upon credit agreements as a measure to promote exports. When discussing the matter before the Estimates Committee, the Indian government representative said, 'About quality one can only compare like with like. As India imported specialised machinery and equipment from the East European countries it is not possible to compare it with imports from other countries.'[1]

TERMS OF TRADE

In discussing India's terms of trade with the East European countries, it is important to distinguish between and discuss separately: (a) whether the prices India pays for its imports and receives for its exports from trade partners are comparable to those it would have paid to and received from other countries; and (b) whether the import purchasing power of exports is comparable in both cases.

It is possible, for example, that though India pays 15 per cent more for its imports from the East European countries than it would elsewhere, the export prices it receives there are 15 per cent higher than those elsewhere in the world. If so, the 'import purchasing power of its exports' is comparable in both cases even though the prices are different from world market prices; and India's terms of trade with the East European countries are comparable to the terms of trade with the rest of the world. However, the export prices India receives from the East

[1] Ministry of Finance (114, pp. 222–3).

European countries are important in themselves, because higher prices paid by the East European countries than India receives elsewhere may result in the domestic prices being raised and, therefore, making other markets less attractive to the exporters. Of course, the effect on prices depends upon the share of East European markets in India's total exports of a commodity, the supply situation in India and the method of purchase. Because the East European countries buy many commodities in open markets and in large quantities at a time, prices can shoot up in local markets. This artificial rise in local prices, if it persists, has two disadvantages. Firstly, higher prices may be used to divert limited supplies from other markets to the East European countries. Secondly, because the East European countries are willing to pay a higher price, India may lose in other markets even if there is no supply constraint, because the exporters prefer to sell in the domestic markets. India may be priced out of the market in commodities where competition is very tough, but if it is in a monopoly position it may be able to benefit by restricting exports to other countries.

When both export and import prices are higher, India may lose both ways: firstly, because of possible trade diversion, and secondly, because it pays higher prices for imports. The centrally planned economies lose nothing in the bargain because if they pay higher prices for their imports, they receive higher prices for their exports. Because external trade is handled by the central authorities, they fix the prices arbitrarily. Prices do not play the same role in fixing the direction of trade in the centrally planned economies as in India. On the other hand, except for the exports handled by the STC, India's export trade is in the hands of private exporters who are guided by the profit criterion. Therefore, the prices received for its exports from the East European countries may influence the prices of its exports elsewhere.

It may be argued that if the redistribution of exports brings India a higher unit price, India should export to the East European countries, because it is maximising its profits by so doing. In the short run, of course, this may mean that India loses its share in other markets because other suppliers have replaced it. Whether India would lose in other markets in the long run depends upon India's supply elasticity, the supply elasticity of its competitors and the rate of growth of demand in the important markets. If India is only one of many suppliers of a commodity and the import demand for that commodity is not growing very fast, it is very risky to let other exporters get a foothold in a highly competitive market because it may be difficult to recapture a share. Private exporters may not be willing to accept a lower price in the other markets. Therefore, in order to ensure that higher prices in the East European markets do not affect India's supply in the long run elsewhere, the government will have to equalise the realised unit export receipts from all markets to private exporters. If the domestic supply of a commodity is completely inelastic in both the short and the long run and India expects the East European countries to continue paying higher unit prices, it makes sense to switch supplies. Otherwise India may be a net loser in the bargain. If a policy decision had been made to re-orient its trade pattern, then again switching supplies to the East European countries would be correct. However, if India wants to maintain its exports to other markets, it is vital that its exports are not priced out.

The questions regarding India's export prices can be answered only by comparing the unit value of India's exports to the East European countries with the unit value of exports to the other markets. There are many difficulties in doing this, because of quality differences and some other inadequacies of trade statistics discussed later. However, it is still possible to get some idea of the overall picture. Tables 36 and 37 show the unit values of important export commodities to the East European countries as a group and to other markets, and the unit values of India's exports to the USSR and other important markets. Table 37 shows that the East European countries paid consistently higher prices for raw wool and coffee and paid higher prices in all but one or two years for black pepper, tea, raw skins and hides, and jute manufactures. They paid lower prices for cashew nut kernels and iron ore in some years.

Though the average price paid by East European countries may not have been significantly higher than that which India received from other countries, the method and timing of purchases may have affected domestic, and thereby export, prices. This effect may be either beneficial or harmful. For

Table 36   *Unit values of some important exports to East Europe and other markets*

	1953/4	1954/5	1955/6	1957	1958	1959	1960/1	1961/2	1962/3	1963/4	1964/5	1965/6
Raw wool												
East European countries	6·31	5·19	6·39	7·69	5·80	5·79	6·07	5·91	6·16	6·53	6·55	6·25
Others				6·26	5·64	5·39	5·34	5·71	5·51	6·06	6·31	5·54
Raw skins and hides												
East European countries	7·00	5·46	5·80	9·10	6·62	9·28	8·82	7·25	7·50	8·59	6·56	8·60
Others	5·89	6·09	7·54	4·06	5·32	5·96	5·63	6·81	7·42	7·78	9·33	9·91
Tobacco unmanufactured												
East European countries	3·46	3·07	2·65	1·52	1·29	1·77	1·59	1·40	1·98	2·50	2·36	2·56
Others				3·53	3·20	3·64	2·54	3·68	3·99	4·11	3·94	4·19
Cashew nut kernels												
East European countries	4·05	3·08	4·11	3·66	3·90	3·92	5·22	4·41	3·90	4·12	5·10	5·20
Others				4·19	3·75	3·95	3·26	4·33	3·99	4·22	5·27	5·39

Tea												
East European countries	4·90	7·16		7·54	7·65	7·47	5·69	7·12	6·97	6·32	6·40	6·72
Others			6·02	5·87	5·85	5·43	6·60	5·86	5·73	5·82	5·80	6·27
Jute manufactures												
East European countries	161·3	145·9		129·6	148·2	86·2	195·3	198·4	173·2	168·2	170·0	200·0
Others			137·8	148·0	123·0	116·2	157·1	180·1	174·6	166·7	178·3	204·7
Iron ore												
East European countries	479·3	412·2	477·2	202·0	533·4	495·2	666·4	495·0	488·7	438·3	442·6	417·3
Others	433·9	427·5	457·3	320·9	524·3	522·4	474·2	296·2	376·5	351·4	331·0	328·2
Coffee												
East European countries	6·55	7·39		6·55	5·56	5·89	4·76	3·03	3·85	3·67	4·39	5·20
Others			5·30	5·04	4·70	3·45	3·28	3·04	3·24	3·47	4·25	4·30
Black pepper												
East European countries	9·9	9·16	3·52	2·04	2·12	1·96	5·09	3·57	3·20	3·23	3·94	4·27
Others	9·83	4·14	3·64	1·36	1·76	3·22	4·33	3·67	3·11	2·38	3·85	4·17

Source: Computed from the volume and value figures.
Note: Blanks indicate that India's exports during these years were negligible.

Table 37   *A comparison of unit values of selected commodities to major markets* (Rs. per kg.)

	1958	1959	1960/1	1961/2	1962/3	1963/4	1964/5	1965/6
Tea								
U.K.	5·9	5·9	6·2	6·1	5·8	6·3	5·9	5·3
U.S.A.	6·1	5·7	6·1	6·3	5·7	5·7	5·5	6·0
USSR	7·2	7·3	7·2	8·6	7·5	6·6	6·3	6·8
World	5·9	5·8	6·2	5·9	5·8	5·8	5·8	6·4
Coffee								
U.K.	4·7	4·9	4·1	3·2	3·80	3·78	4·47	3·55
U.S.A.	3·92	3·92	3·60	3·04	2·33	3·19	4·20	3·8
USSR	4·9	4·4	4·34	3·7	5·5	4·2	4·5	5·6
East Germany	6·2	4·4	4·8	2·1	3·3	3·3	7·3	5·2
World	4·98	4·16	3·66	3·04	3·73	3·58	4·32	4·93
Tobacco unmanufactured								
U.K.	4·92	5·35	4·52	5·78	5·76	5·90	5·79	5·22
USSR	1·61	1·62	1·89	1·06	1·94	2·54	2·34	2·51
World	2·99	3·45	3·32	3·62	2·87	3·31	3·15	3·57
Goat skins undressed								
U.S.A.	4·3	6·0	6·9	6·3	6·5	8·1	9·0	8·2
USSR	7·3	8·9	7·8	5·9	6·7	8·3	9·4	7·6
World		8·0				7·7	6·8	8·0
Black pepper								
U.S.A.	2·12	3·04	3·70	3·66	3·10	3·00	4·36	4·11
USSR	2·00	2·72	4·88	3·77	3·20	3·17	4·08	4·26
World	1·49	1·42	4·93	3·73	3·15	3·11	3·26	4·23
Raw wool								
U.S.A.	6·2	5·8	5·7	5·5	5·5	6·0	7·0	9·0
USSR	5·7	5·8	6·0	5·9	6·1	6·7	6·5	6·1
U.K.	5·1	5·3	5·2	5·0	5·8	6·1	6·5	neg.
World	3·8	5·7	6·0	5·9	6·1	6·7	6·5	6·1
Cashew nut kernels								
U.S.A.	3·9	4·0	4·1	4·3	4·2	3·6	5·3	5·8
U.K.	3·4	3·5	4·4	4·0	3·9	4·1	4·9	5·7
West Germany	3·7	3·0	4·4	4·3	4·0	4·1	4·8	6·0
Canada	4·2	4·3	5·3	4·8	4·2	4·6	5·5	6·0
East Germany		3·3	3·9	3·8	3·5	3·7	4·1	5·0
USSR	3·9	4·0	5·4	4·6	4·1	4·3	5·4	5·9
World	3·5	4·1	4·3	4·3	3·9	4·2	5·2	5·7
Castor oil								
U.K.	14·0	13·3	18·8	15·3	13·4	12·7	13·9	20·0
U.S.A.	9·8	13·3	13·0		10·0		20·0	20·0
USSR	15·3	14·6	15·8	16·1	14·2	13·4	18·5	17·1
World			14·3	16·0		13·5	16·3	17·3
Groundnut meal								
U.K.				3·59	3·66	3·75	4·16	4·06
Czechoslovakia				3·37	3·96	3·72	4·37	4·11
Hungary			3·25	3·69	3·70	4·40	4·20	4·34
Poland			3·33	3·89	3·86	4·38	4·24	4·24
East Germany			3·33	3·83	3·69	4·49	4·28	4·28

Sources: Computed from volume and quantity figures.

example, if the East European countries purchase at a time when the new crop is just on the market, and, due to a large carryover from last year and a good new crop, the supply exceeds demand and too many exporters are making the situation worse by undercutting each other, the purchases of the East European countries may be a stabilising influence. It is argued in official circles that in the late fifties bulk purchases from the USSR helped to stabilise the price of tea and particular varieties of unmanufactured tobacco. But the pressure of East European demand can be a harmful influence as well. When India is a price taker in the world market and the export prices of the other competitors are steady, the rise in price resulting from the purchases made by the East European countries may possibly result in making the Indian product too expensive in the other markets. This situation may not last very long, depending upon the supply elasticity. The NCAER report on black pepper points out that, 'When large-scale purchases are made by the USSR and the other countries in that region, price in India goes up. This is an important reason for higher prices on exports to the USSR and for the wide fluctuations in the domestic prices. When the USSR is in the Indian market, sometimes the Indian price becomes non-competitive in the other markets.'[1] Similarly the domestic supplies of raw wool were limited in the sixties while the demand was increasing. The higher price from the USSR helped in both increasing the domestic prices of raw wool and diverting supplies from other markets.

Other authors on the subject maintain that exports to the East European countries were responsible for an artificial increase in domestic prices of the goods concerned. Ahuja, discussing India's trade with the East European countries in the fifties, says that this trade 'has been largely responsible for an artificial raising of prices. This is especially so in the case of tea, coffee, as well as hides and skins.'[2] She goes on to suggest that higher prices were used to divert limited supplies. 'Even though prices are generally higher in East Europe, the divergence is not uniform for all commodities. This is highly significant, for it will be seen that for commodities where supplies are limited the price divergence is wide and for commodities for which supply conditions were easier, the gap is narrow.'[3]

[1] NCAER (51, p. 84).   [2] Ahuja (2, pp. 361–5).   [3] *Ibid.*

However, as pointed out above, the East European countries have been buying better quality tea and coffee, so the comparison is not valid. Moreover, the influence on price depends on the quantities bought. Their share in the exports of raw skins and hides was high and the prices they paid for these goods were also high compared to prices elsewhere. Therefore Dave's conclusion that the artificial rise in prices and the consequent diversion of supplies occurred only for raw skins appears more reasonable.[1] There may have been individual instances where artificial rises in price rendered Indian exports non-competitive elsewhere, but this has not been a serious problem. In some cases, higher unit prices may have been used to divert supplies to the East European countries, as discussed before.

A comparison of unit values of certain important exports to the United Kingdom, the U.S.A., and the USSR shows that the unit values of exports to the USSR are higher than those to the U.K. or the U.S. for tea, coffee, and raw wool and higher in all years except one for black pepper, goat skins (undressed), groundnut meal, and castor oil. The USSR paid consistently lower prices for unmanufactured tobacco and lower prices for cashew nuts in some years. The comparison of average unit values of India's exports to the East European countries and other markets shows that the former are higher in most cases than the latter. The notable exceptions are tobacco (unmanufactured) and cashew nuts. But before concluding that the East European countries paid higher prices, the following qualifications should be made:

(1) As Dave points out, India exported better qualities of tea and coffee to the East European countries.[2] It is probably true of black pepper, raw wool, and raw skins and hides as well that the average price is influenced by the share of each quality.

(2) The unit value is also dependent on how broad the commodity group is. For example, the category of 'jute manufactures' is too broad, and the average unit value would depend on the share of individual items. The East European countries paid a higher price for gunny bags but not for hessian cloth. However, since they imported more gunny bags than hessian cloth, the average unit value of exports of jute manufactures

[1] Dave (21).   [2] Dave (20, pp. 479–88).

to the East European countries is higher than to other markets.

(3) Depending upon what time of the year they buy, since they buy in large quantities and pay rupees, the East European countries may have to pay higher prices to purchase goods in the open market. But when the STC is responsible for exporting certain items, they may in fact pay lower prices. For example, the STC is responsible for exporting unmanufactured tobacco.

(4) An important reason why unit values of exports to the other markets appear lower may be that Indian exporters under-invoice their exports. Indian exporters have preferred to keep a part of their export proceeds abroad and therefore the export proceeds have been understated. There has been no incentive to understate export earnings to the East European countries because these holdings cannot be transferred elsewhere. The under-invoicing may mean that for some commodities at least the unit prices realised in the other markets may be higher than those recorded in the trade statistics.

(5) Fifty per cent of India's exports are required to be shipped in Indian vessels, i.e. India is responsible for arranging the transport. The East European countries may have paid a higher price in the market but may not have paid anything extra for transport.

Broadly speaking, it is probably true to say that India obtained slightly higher prices for her exports to the East European countries for some commodities, but because of the quality difference it is not possible to say whether these prices are really significantly higher than elsewhere, except for raw skins and hides and possibly iron ore and groundnut cake and meal.

While a comparison between unit values of exports to different markets is difficult, a similar comparison concerning imports is even more so. Several attempts to compare India's imports from Eastern Europe and other countries have been made. Thus Surendra Dave says, 'A study of about a hundred unit values of imports of chemicals, fertilizers, newsprint and iron and steel products from these countries for the three years 1957–9 suggests that no higher prices were charged.' But he goes on to say 'the commodities for which the prices are higher, according to the information provided by some traders, consist largely of re-exports of West European goods' and 'capital goods are not taken into account because of the obvious difficulties involved'.[1]

A study of India's trade with Eastern Europe conducted by the Institute of Foreign Trade arrives at a similar conclusion, namely, that for the items compared there is no evidence that the USSR charged higher prices than other countries.[2] The author is careful to point out that the goods imported from various countries are not identical and that a comparison of unit prices should be supplemented by detailed investigation of individual commodity prices. But even with all the qualifications, the only items compared are base metals, chemicals, raw materials, metals and metal manufactures, and newsprint. These items accounted for between 20 to 25 per cent of India's imports from the East European countries during the period 1961/2 to 1965/6 (see table 38).

There is little information available on the prices of machinery and equipment, which constituted 60 per cent of India's imports from these countries. Even government officials admit that the prices of machinery and equipment have sometimes been higher by 10 to 30 per cent, compared to the cheapest source of supply. But it is not possible to say whether these imports were more expensive than other credit financed imports. As a significant proportion of the imports of machinery and equipment from the East European countries has been financed by tied credits, it is not fair to compare these prices with the prices offered by the cheapest supplier. There is no conclusive evidence that the East European countries charged higher prices than other suppliers in the case of imports tied to the country of origin.

To summarise the discussion: as far as merchandise trade is concerned, the East European countries have paid higher prices for some of India's exports but in some cases the prices for exports were lower. Generally the prices of current imports from Eastern European countries have not been higher. However, this description applies only to 25–30 per cent of India's total imports from these countries. India's net barter terms of trade with the East European countries are probably comparable to

[1] Dave (20, pp. 479–88).
[2] The Indian Institute of Foreign Trade, (113) *Unit Values of Selected Imports from USSR, Czechoslovakia, U.K., U.S.A. and West Germany, 1960–61 to 1965–66*, pp. 26–7 table 7, and pp. 69–76.

Table 38 *Import items included in the Institute's study of foreign trade for a comparison of unit values as a percentage of India's total imports from the East European countries*

	Base metals	Manufacture of metals	Paper and paper manufactures	Total of (1)+(2)+(3)	Total imports from East European countries	(4) as % of (5)
	(1)	(2)	(3)	(4)	(5)	(6)
1959/60	151·2	17·3	15·8	184·5	354·2	35·4
1960/1	138·2	15·4	16·7	170·3	443·1	38·4
1961/2	208·9	19·3	19·8	248·0	876·2	28·3
1962/3	174·3	62·5	21·4	258·2	1,101·3	23·4
1963/4	155·3	24·0	19·0	198·7	1,292·6	15·4
1964/5	218·1	27·6	20·4	266·1	1,449·9	18·4
1965/6	256·6	25·0	31·7	313·3	1,566·8	20·0

Sources: DGCIS, *Monthly Statistics of Foreign Trade*, and the Office of the Economic Adviser to the Government of India.

Table 39   *Unit values of some export commodities to the East European countries and others (1961–2 to 1965–6)*

	1961/2			1962/3			1963/4			1964/5			1965/6		
	Quantity	Value	Unit value	Quantity	Value	Unit value	Quantity	Value	Unit value	Quantity	Value	Unit value	Quantity	Value	Unit value
Tea (per kg.)															
East European countries	13	92.6	7.1	16	115.5	7.2	20	126.5	6.4	27	173.0	6.4	26	174.8	6.7
Others	193	1,131.4	5.8	205	1,176.4	5.7	190	1,107.3	5.8	185	1,073.5	5.8	171	1,073.6	6.2
Jute manufactures (per ton)															
East European countries (000 tons)	52	103.2	198.4	62	107.4	173.2	92	154.8	168.2	149	253.4	170.0	170	340.2	200.1
Others	746	1,344.7	180.2	830	1,449.2	174.6	838	1,397.5	166.7	801	1,428.8	178.3	727	1,488.2	204.7
Hides and skins, raw (per kg.)															
East European countries	62	45.0	7.25	95	71.3	7.5	69	59.3	8.5	91	59.7	6.56	75	58.8	7.8
Others	55	37.2	6.76	50	37.1	7.4	47	36.6	7.7	33	30.8	9.33	37	36.7	9.9
Iron ore (per ton)															
East European countries (000 tons)	1,404	69.5	495.0	1,946	95.1	368.4	1,978	86.7	438.3	1,972	87.3	442.6	2,075	86.6	477.3
Others	8,396	284.7	339.9	6,854	258.1	376.5	7,890	277.3	351.4	8,602	284.8	331.0	1,019	334.4	328.1

7

Oilseeds (per ton)															
East European countries	14	14·8	105·7	12	11·9	99·1	23·0	24·3	105·6	9	10·5	116·6	—	—	—
Others	27	31·4	116·2	32	31·3	97·8	18·0	18·7	103·9	8	9·6	120·0	—	2	2·3
Oil cakes (per ton)															
East European countries	118	39·2	332·2	31·4	119·5	380·5	420	158·7	377·8	65·4	237·1	362·5	446	195·9	439·2
Others	388	134·0	345·3	52·1	191·5	367·5	516	195·1	378·1	60·9	160·5	263·5	382	150·5	393·9
Cashew kernels (per kg.)															
East European countries	8·1	35·8	4·4	11·3	44·1	3·9	12·6	52·0	4·1	16·9	86·2	5·1	15·0	78·1	5·2
Others	33·7	145·9	4·3	37·2	148·6	3·9	38·4	162·3	4·2	38·7	204·1	5·2	36·3	195·9	5·3
Coffee (per kg.)															
East European countries	9·5	29·0	3·0	15·5	59·9	3·8	10·4	38·3	3·6	17·4	76·8	4·4	16·9	88·6	5·2
Others	20·1	61·3	3·0	4·9	16·2	3·3	12·9	44·8	3·4	13·5	57·4	4·2	9·5	40·8	4·2
Tobacco (per kg.)															
East European countries	10·1	14·2	1·4	30·0	6·0	2·0	32·9	82·4	25·0	42·2	99·9	2·3	25·8	66·3	2·5
Others	34·3	126·3	3·6	30·2	119·9	3·9	31·0	128·5	4·1	35·8	141·4	3·9	30·9	129·5	4·1
Pepper (per kg.)															
East European countries	6·3	24·5	3·9	7·2	23·1	3·2	9·8	31·7	3·2	9·4	37·1	3·9	12·9	55·1	4·2
Others	15·4	56·6	3·7	13·7	42·7	3·1	9·1	27·2	3·2	8·0	30·8	3·8	13·4	55·9	4·1
Wool, raw (per kg.)															
East European countries	6·8	40·8	6·0	5·3	32·7	6·1	2·5	17·0	6·8	5·6	36·7	6·5	6·5	40·4	6·1
Others	7·6	43·4	5·7	4·3	23·7	5·5	7·3	44·3	6·0	6·3	39·8	6·3	4·5	24·5	5·3

Source: Office of the Economic Adviser to the Government of India.

or at least not significantly worse than its terms of trade with other countries. But this description may not apply if the imports of machinery and equipment are taken into account. In many cases the machinery imported from East European countries was of a special kind and it is therefore not possible to show whether these prices were reasonable.

The discussion of net gains from India's exports to Eastern Europe would be incomplete without a consideration of the possible effect of this trade on the price of particular commodities in other markets. Even supposing the East European countries themselves paid a lower price for a commodity, the withdrawal of these supplies from other markets may have pushed up the price in these markets. Therefore, even though some exports to the East European countries may have resulted in diversion and in India obtaining a lower unit price, these disadvantages may to some extent have been compensated for by the higher unit price realised in the other markets.

However, the effect on the world market prices depends upon the Indian share in the world markets, the quantities withdrawn, the short-term supply elasticities elsewhere, the price elasticity of the commodity in question and the availability or otherwise of close substitutes. Among the commodities discussed here, India was in a position to influence the prices of only tea, jute manufactures, black pepper and cashew nuts. In the case of the first two commodities the quantities involved were not in themselves big enough to create a pressure on supply elsewhere. India's exports of tea and jute manufactures to Eastern Europe rose rapidly in the sixties but were still not more than 15 per cent of India's total exports to the world, or about 5–6 per cent of total world exports. Even if India had maintained her relative share in other markets, she could not have sold more than half of this – 2–3 per cent of total world exports. These quantities might have influenced the price but it is not possible to argue either way. What is more likely, however, is that, rather than lower the export prices, Indian business men would have sold the goods at home. Moreover, the price of both these commodities depends more on the production of and the stocks held by other producers. Therefore the world market prices of tea and jute manufactures are more closely related to the world supply position than to India's exports to Eastern Europe. The same is true of black pepper. Total world supplies and the unit price of black pepper fluctuated with Indonesian supplies. India's exports of black pepper to Eastern Europe would not by themselves have exerted a pressure on world supplies.

It should be pointed out that the manner and timing of purchases of tea by the East European countries may have temporarily stabilised the prices of tea in the Calcutta auction. Again the prices in the auction at any particular time depend upon stocks and new supplies and move closely with London auction prices. When there are only a few buyers on the market, speculators may force the price down excessively and in such circumstances the purchases of East European countries have helped, because they represent additional demand. It is not possible, however, to isolate the speculative price movements from the real and thereby to establish how far these purchases may have influenced the world market prices of tea.

India has practically a monopoly position in exports of cashew nut kernels, and in the sixties India's exports to the East European countries were big enough to affect the world supply of cashew nuts. Therefore it is reasonable to say that, even though East European countries did not pay a higher price for cashew nuts, the unit price of cashews realised elsewhere was influenced by the withdrawal of large quantities from these markets. However, this was not the only factor influencing prices. Cashews became very popular with Western European countries in the sixties. This popularity and the relative shortage created by exporting large quantities to the East European countries and the low supply elasticity in the short run all exerted pressure on prices.

Briefly, it may be said that increasing exports to the East European countries was one of the contributing factors influencing Indian export prices of some commodities at particular times, but it is doubtful whether the influence was strong enough to influence world market prices. When the USSR buys the entire crop of, say, cotton from the UAR or cocoa from Ghana, the effect on market prices in the other markets is immediate and unambiguous. There are no such cases in Indo–East European trade. Moreover, to influence the prices in other markets the East European countries must absorb internally the quantities they import. If they re-export these commodities, then the effect on prices, if any, will be only temporary.

CONCLUSIONS

At the beginning of this chapter two questions were raised regarding the real worth of Eastern European trade to India and the burden of repayment. A commoditywise study of India's exports to the East European countries shows that between 20 and 25 per cent of India's exports to them were diversionary, in the sense that they could have been exported to the hard currency areas. This diversion, by itself, is a cost because it reduces the amount of free foreign exchange available. Since proceeds from exports to East European countries cannot be used for importing goods and services from any other country or to settle debt payments, these earnings may be relatively less useful than export receipts in hard currency.

The evidence available shows that the East European countries offered higher prices for some exports but lower prices for others and, as far as imports of raw materials are concerned, the prices from East European countries and others were comparable. Therefore, it would appear that for merchandise trade alone, India's net barter terms of trade were probably comparable, or at least not significantly worse than it obtained from the rest of the world. However, this comparison excludes imports of machinery and equipment. From the case studies presented in chapter 5 and other evidence, such as complaints from private investors, it appears that the prices of machinery and equipment from the East European countries were higher than prices offered by other countries. Imports of machinery constituted at least 50 per cent of India's total imports from East European countries. Therefore, taking into account all imports and exports, India's net terms of trade were probably worse with the East European countries than with the rest of the world.

The third possible cost benefit is the impact of Indo–East European trade on Indian trade with other countries. As discussed earlier, the share of East European countries in India's total exports was not enough for any commodity to influence Indian export prices or world market prices for that commodity. So this impact was not very important.

On the positive side, the East European countries did provide additional outlets for India's traditional exports and, because they purchased in large quantities, their purchases did, on certain occasions, help to stabilise the domestic prices of certain commodities, such as tea.

Since India's exports to Eastern Europe were largely additional to, rather than instead of, exports elsewhere, and on the whole it managed to secure high priority goods from these countries at satisfactory prices, it may be concluded that this trade has been beneficial during the period 1953/4 to 1965/6. However, it is difficult to say whether solid foundations for the future development of this trade have been laid or whether the limit of useful exchange has been reached. There are two sources of uncertainty. The first is India's weak bargaining position, for, while India depends upon these countries for essential supplies, she is not an indispensable supplier of any commodity. The second source of uncertainty is that India has replaced communist China as a supplier, and if Sino–East European relations improve, India may not be needed any more.

The conclusion regarding trade is that so far the East European countries have played a useful role in India's development, but the future depends upon many 'ifs', including the trade policy of East European countries.

The second question raised concerned the burden of repayment in kind. Since exports to the East European countries by and large have been additional to exports elsewhere, and the terms of trade not significantly worse than India had obtained elsewhere, it may be concluded that the burden of repaying in kind has probably not been higher than the burden of repaying in convertible currency. But taking into account other indirect costs, such as undesirable exports and the need to give technical credits, it is not clear that repayment in kind has been significantly less burdensome than repayment in hard currency. Moreover, India had repaid only a part of its credits up to 1965/6. Since devaluation of the rupee in June 1966, the real burden of repayment has increased because India's terms of trade with the East European countries deteriorated somewhat. The future costs of repaying these credits should be assessed in the light of Indo–East European trade since June 1966 and its future prospects. These questions are considered in the next chapter.

Appendix 4.1 *Weighted foreign demand for Indian exports by major commodities (M_W) and Indian exports to countries outside Eastern Europe (E_I), in volume terms (index, 1954 = 100)*

		1954	1955	1956	1957	1958	1959	1960	1961	1962	1963	1964	1965	Weight %
Jute manufactures	M_W	100·0	120·6	115·9	116·2	109·5	125·2	120·5	129·0	122·5	117·9	132·7	130·1	41·46
	E_I	100·0	109·2	109·8	101·1	106·5	114·9	103·7	100·5	111·9	112·9	108·0	98·0	
Coffee	M_W	100·0	126·8	133·8	133·9	140·4	159·4	172·9	190·3	200·3	212·8	227·4	231·7	0·55
	E_I	100·0	366·3	100·0	475·1	462·7	325·2	540·7	714·1	177·0	456·7	478·7	339·9	
Iron ore	M_W	100·0	116·4	163·9	192·9	156·9	193·8	313·3	416·5	430·6	492·5	756·9	719·8	2·19
	E_I	100·0	95·1	153·3	275·7	180·9	236·9	286·9	1,094·2	893·3	1,028·2	1,121·0	1,318·1	
Excluding Goa									(338·9)	(143·4)	(273·7)	(364·9)	(560·4)	
Cashew nuts	M_W	100·0	108·2	92·7	96·7	108·3	101·9	104·5	97·9	105·0	79·7	114·6	108·3	4·16
	E_I	100·0	127·7	115·7	119·9	132·1	122·5	143·2	124·4	137·3	141·6	142·8	133·9	
Black pepper	M_W	100·0	98·8	96·5	95·9	104·5	103·6	109·7	100·7	112·0	123·1	132·9	138·9	4·67
	E_I	100·0	111·7	75·8	109·2	76·7	80·8	80·8	128·3	114·2	75·8	66·6	111·7	
Unmanufactured tobacco	M_W	100·0	105·1	100·4	100·8	100·7	99·1	110·5	106·5	93·9	104·6	106·1	105·3	3·83
	E_I	100·0	123·1	128·6	100·3	142·7	107·0	137·6	110·2	96·5	100·3	105·1	99·4	
Raw hides and skins	M_W	100·0	111·1	114·2	126·1	124·3	148·1	129·9	120·2	112·7	105·4	142·1	117·0	2·29
	E_I	100·0	77·6	69·9	78·6	74·8	59·2	50·5	53·4	48·5	45·6	32·0	35·9	

Raw wool	M_W	100·0	107·0	104·6	101·1	95·4	120·5	82·0	85·7	94·3	86·1	66·5	71·9	2·22
	E_I	100·0	149·5	163·4	155·9	122·6	174·2	109·7	82·8	47·3	75·6	68·8	49·5	
Tea	M_W	100·0	92·0	107·8	107·6	104·7	92·0	96·4	101·6	102·5	104·7	99·2	104·0	38·43
	E_I	100·0	98·6	86·6	96·3	104·7	98·5	83·9	92·6	98·4	91·1	88·8	82·0	
Total commodities listed (excluding Goa iron ore)	M_W	100·0	106·9	111·4	112·2	108·3	111·5	113·5	120·4	118·8	118·7	131·0	130·5	100·0
(excluding Goa iron ore)	E_I	100·0	107·8	101·4	107·2	110·0	111·7	103·2	122·5	121·4	123·6	121·7	120·2	
Annual percentage change	M_W		+6·9	+4·2	+0·7	-5·6	+3·0	+1·8	(106·0) +6·1	(105·0) -1·3	(107·1) -0·1	(105·5) +10·4	(103·7) -0·4	
	E_I		+7·8	-5·9	+5·7	+3·6	+1·3	-7·6	+18·7 (+2·7)	-1·1	+2·3	-1·9	-1·5	

Sources: Other countries M_W:

Black pepper, tobacco unmanufactured, raw wool and tea: FAO Commodity Yearbooks, 1956, 1958, 1960 and 1966.

Jute manufactures: The figures for the years 1954 to 1963 are taken from *Commonwealth Economic Committee Industrial Fibres No. 16*, 1966. For 1964 and 1965, the figures had to be collected from national trade statistics of the countries concerned, HMSO, *Annual Statement of the Trade of the U.K.*, vol. II, and U.S. Bureau of Census, *U.S. Imports of Merchandise for Consumption Annual Reports*, supplemented by the U.N. *Yearbook of International Trade*, 1965.

Cashew nuts and raw skins and hides: From the national trade statistics of the U.K. and U.S.

Iron ore: Statistical Office of the U.N., *Yearbook of International Trade Statistics*; from the STC Commodity table for the countries concerned.

Indian exports E_I

The figures for Indian exports are taken from the foreign trade statistics published annually by the Directorate General of Commercial Intelligence and Statistics, *Monthly Statistics of Foreign Trade*, vol. I, 'Exports', and the data supplied by the Economic Adviser to India, *India's Trade with Rupee Payment Countries of Eastern Europe*.

Notes: (1) For other countries, the figures refer to calendar years. For India the data are on a fiscal year basis, April–March, except for 1957, 1958 and 1959. For these years the data are available on a calendar year. (2) The base year for Indian exports is 1953/4. (3) The Indian figures refer to fiscal years 1953/4 to 1955/6, and then from 1957 onwards to 1965/6. It was necessary to do this because since 1957 the coverage was changed to calendar years and it was not possible to obtain volume figures for either fiscal or calendar year 1956.

Appendix 4.2 *Index numbers of domestic production and India's total exports of selected commodities, in volume terms* (index, 1954 = 100)

	1954	1955	1956	1957	1958	1959	1960	1961	1962	1963	1964	1965
Tea												
Production	100·0	99·9	109·1	107·1	111·2	114·3	112·6	124·2	121·8	121·4	130·5	128·0
Exports	100·0	97·8	85·8	99·0	109·2	108·3	94·7	98·0	105·1	99·9	100·9	93·7
Jute manufactures												
Production	100·0	109·8	99·5	102·5	101·0	108·5	101·7	106·4	121·3	124·4	126·1	100·6
Exports	100·0	109·2	109·8	102·4	108·6	117·9	106·9	107·4	120·2	125·3	128·0	120·1
Raw wool												
Production	100·0	101·3	101·3	101·3	101·3	104·0	104·0	104·0	104·0	104·0	104·0	104·0
Exports	100·0	151·0	165·2	185·9	167·4	207·6	140·2	158·7	105·4	107·6	130·0	121·7
Coffee												
Production	100·0	134·5	134·6	151·5	158·6	171·0	162·4	151·9	156·8	165·0		
Exports	100·0	366·3	100·0	527·6	528·3	510·6	698·6	1,052·8	723·7	1,170·1	1,097·1	886·4
Tobacco												
Production	100·0	118·8	119·6	80·0	124·3	114·5	120·4	132·9	143·5	140·4	135·7	107·4
Exports	100·0	123·0	128·6	111·9	155·6	121·2	152·4	142·8	193·6	206·1	250·8	182·3
Black pepper												
Production	100·0	107·7	103·8	103·8	100·0	100·0	107·7	107·7	100·0	96·1	92·3	88·5
Exports	100·0	107·6	102·3	150·8	119·2	119·2	140·0	163·0	160·7	145·4	133·8	203·0
Cashews												
Production	100·0	130·2	133·8	156·5	166·7	182·4	196·8	204·8	215·8	220·0	225·4	
Exports	100·0	127·7	115·8	132·1	141·3	141·7	160·9	154·2	179·0	188·1	205·2	189·2

Source: Indian exports: Same as Appendix 4.1. Directorate of Economics and Statistics, *Estimates of Area and Production of Principal Crops in India, 1965–66*, for agricultural production.

Note: The figures of production refer to agricultural years (year ending June).

Appendix 4.3 India's exports of selected commodities to Eastern European countries and others (in volume terms)

	1953/4	1954/5	1955/6	1957	1958	1959	1960/61	1961/62	1962/63	1963/64	1964/65	1965/66
Cashew nut kernels (mfg.)	27·1	34·6	31·4	35·8	41·0	38·4	43·6	41·8	48·5	51·0	55·6	51·3
Others	27·1	34·6	31·4	32·5	35·8	33·2	38·8	33·7	37·2	38·4	38·7	36·3
Eastern Europe	—	—	—	3·3	5·2	5·2	4·8	8·1	11·3	12·6	16·9	15·0
Coffee	28·2	103·3	28·2	148·8	149·0	144·0	197·0	296·9	204·1	330·0	309·4	265·0
Others	28·2	103·3	28·2	134·0	130·5	91·7	152·5	201·4	155·1	104·2	174·4	95·0
Eastern Europe	—	—	—	14·8	18·5	52·3	44·5	95·5	49·1	225·8	135·0	170·0
Tea (mfg.)	210·2	205·5	180·4	208·0	229·7	227·7	199·0	206·0	221·0	210·0	212·0	197·0
Others	208·4	205·5	180·4	200·7	218·3	215·3	174·8	193·0	205·0	190·0	185·0	185·0
Eastern Europe	1·8	—	—	7·3	11·4	12·4	24·2	13·0	16·0	20·0	27·0	12·0
Black pepper	13·0	14·0	13·3	19·6	15·5	15·5	18·2	21·7	20·9	18·9	17·4	26·3
Others	12·0	13·4	9·1	13·1	9·2	9·7	9·7	15·4	13·7	9·1	8·0	13·4
Eastern Europe	1·0	0·6	4·2	6·5	6·3	5·8	8·5	6·3	7·2	9·8	9·4	12·9
Tobacco unmanufactured	31·1	38·3	40·0	34·8	48·1	37·7	47·4	44·4	60·2	64·1	78·0	56·7
Others	31·1	38·3	40·0	31·2	44·4	33·3	42·8	34·3	30·0	32·9	35·8	30·9
Eastern Europe	—	—	—	3·6	3·7	4·4	4·6	10·1	30·2	31·2	42·2	25·8
Raw hides and skins	10·5	10·8	9·8	12·0	12·0	13·1	12·0	11·7	14·5	11·6	12·4	11·2
Others	10·3	8·0	7·2	8·1	7·7	6·1	5·2	5·5	5·0	4·7	3·3	3·7
Eastern Europe	0·2	2·8	2·6	3·9	4·3	7·0	6·8	6·2	9·5	6·9	9·1	7·5
Raw wool	9·3	13·9	15·2	17·1	15·4	19·1	12·9	14·6	9·7	9·9	12·0	11·2
Others	9·3	13·9	15·2	14·5	11·4	16·2	10·2	7·7	4·4	7·3	6·4	4·6
Eastern Europe	—	—	—	2·6	4·0	2·9	2·7	6·9	5·3	2·6	5·6	6·6
Jute manufactures	742·0	810·3	814·8	759·9	806·0	875·0	793·0	798·0	892·0	930·0	950·0	897·0
Others	742·0	810·3	814·8	750·1	790·0	853·2	769·5	746·0	830·0	838·0	801·0	727·0
Eastern Europe	—	—	—	9·8	16·0	21·8	23·5	52·0	62·0	92·0	149·0	170·0
Iron ore	1,261·9	1,008·8	1,362·9	2,251·9	1,896·3	2,511·1	3,190·5	9,800·0	8,800·0	9,868·0	10,574·0	12,769·0
Others	767·3	729·8	1,176·4	2,117·7	1,388·3	1,818·3	2,201·4	8,396·0	6,854·0	7,890·0	8,602·0	10,694·0
Eastern Europe	494·6	279·0	186·5	134·2	508·0	692·8	989·1	1,404·0	1,946·0	1,978·0	1,972·0	2,075·0

Iron ore (excluding Goa iron ore):

	1961/62	1962/63	1963/64	1964/65	1965/66
Iron ore	(3,800·0)	(2,800·0)	(3,860·0)	(4,574·0)	(6,189·0)
Others	(2,600·0)	1,700·0	2,100·0	2,800·0	4,300·0
Eastern Europe	1,200·0	1,100·0	1,768·0	1,774·0	1,889·0

Source: Same as Appendix 4.1.

Appendix 4.4 *India's exports of selected commodities to Eastern Europe* (in Rs. million)

	1953/4	1954/5	1955/6	1957	1958	1959	1960/1	1961/2	1962/3	1963/4	1964/5	1965/6
Jute manufactures	neg.	neg.	neg.	12·7	24·9	18·8	45·9	103·2	107·4	154·8	253·4	340·0
Coffee	neg.	neg.	neg.	9·7	10·3	30·8	21·2	29·0	59·9	38·3	76·7	82·6
Iron ore	24·6	11·5	8·9	39·5	27·1	34·3	65·9	69·5	95·1	86·7	87·3	86·6
Cashew nuts	neg.	neg.	neg.	11·0	20·3	20·4	25·1	35·8	44·1	52·0	86·2	78·1
Black pepper	9·9	5·5	14·8	13·3	13·4	11·4	43·3	22·5	23·1	31·7	37·1	55·1
Unmanufactured tobacco	—	—	0·4	5·5	14·8	7·8	7·3	24·2	60·0	82·4	99·9	66·3
Raw skins and hides	1·4	15·3	15·1	35·5	27·2	65·0	60·0	45·0	71·3	59·3	59·7	62·3
Raw wool	neg.	neg.	neg.	20·0	23·2	16·8	16·4	40·8	32·7	17·0	36·7	41·3
Tea	—	—	—	55·1	87·3	92·7	80·9	92·6	115·5	126·5	173·0	174·8

Source: DGCIS, *Monthly Bulletin of Statistics*, and Economic Adviser to the Government of India, *India's Trade with East European Countries*.

Appendix 4.5 *Unit values of selected imports from the East European countries, 1965/6 to 1968/9 (all values in thousands of rupees)*

Commodities	Unit	1965/6		April–May 1966		June 1966 to March 1967	
		Quantity	Value	Quantity	Value	Quantity	Value
Chemical elements and compounds	Value	—	737	—	133	—	658
Fertilisers, manufactured	000 tonne	126	337	38	114	190	804
Medicinal and pharmaceutical products	Value	—	148	—	51	—	248
Chemical materials and products n.e.s.	Value	—	59	—	9	—	107
Iron and steel	000 tonne	267	2,212	37	373	118	2,174
Zinc	per kg.	166	179	23	36	127	315
Machinery other than electrical	Value	—	7,365	—	1,082	—	6,683
Electrical machinery, apparatus and appliances	Value	—	1,185	—	213	—	744
Transport equipment	Value	—	435	—	47	—	385
Copper	per kg.	1	12	2	16	6	106
Professional, scientific and controlling instruments, photographic and optical goods etc.	Value	—	321	—	51	—	397
Dyeing, tanning and colouring materials	Value	—	44	—	12	—	50

APPENDIX 4

Appendix 4.5 (contd.)

Commodities	Unit	1967/8 Quantity	1967/8 Value	1968/9 Quantity	1968/9 Value
Explosives and pyrotechnic products	Value	—	75	—	61
Plastic materials, regenerated cellulose and artificial resins	Value	—	36	—	48
Paper, paper board and manufactures thereof	Value	—	317	—	615
Manufactures of metal	Value	—	249	—	339
Petroleum products	Value	—	1,153	—	863
Wheat	ooo tonne	142	670	139	726
Pulp and waste paper	per kg.	50	61	103	117
Asbestos, crude, washed or ground	per kg.	80	89	82	119
Lead	per kg.	78	194	62	156
Special transactions not classified according to kind	Value	—	63	—	1,284

Commodities	Unit	1967/8 Quantity	1967/8 Value	1968/9 Quantity	1968/9 Value
Chemical elements and compounds	Value	—	119,620	—	135,000
Fertilisers, manufactured	ooo tonne	343·3	156,550	431	206,200
Medicinal and pharmaceutical products	Value	—	23,350	—	36,600
Chemical materials and products, n.e.s.	Value	—	12,770	—	6,100
Iron and steel	ooo tonne	117·4	226,970	111	135,400

Zinc	per kg.	94·3	22,610	85	19,700
Machinery other than electrical	Value	—	883,380	—	1,197,700
Electrical machinery, apparatus and appliances	Value	—	90,840	—	151,800
Transport equipment	Value	—	68,600	—	82,300
Copper	per kg.	5·3	5,970	12	900
Professional, scientific and controlling instruments, photographic and optical goods etc.	Value	—	48,070	—	41,800
Dyeing, tanning and colouring materials	Value	—	5,420	—	12,400
Explosives and pyrotechnic products	Value	—	3,910	—	3,800
Plastic materials, regenerated cellulose and artificial resins	Value	—	12,770	—	8,500
Paper, paper board and manufactures thereof	Value	—	37,920	—	72,000
Manufactures of metal	Value	—	21,110	—	21,000
Petroleum products	Value	—	49,930	—	65,200
Wheat	000 tonne	62·0	33,150	—	—
Pulp and waste paper	per kg.	35·7	4,100	67	6,700
Asbestos, crude, washed or ground	per kg.	75·6	14,280	203	4,570
Lead	per kg.	2·3	640	3	..
Special transactions not classified according to kind	Value	—	112,780	—	..
Sulphur	per kg.	354·4	20,150	204	12,560
Milk and cream	Value	—	6,720	..	850
Yarn and thread of synthetic fibres	per kg.	5·5	8,360	1	320
Iron and steel scrap	000 tonne	4·1	6,470	1	420
Aluminium	per kg.	8·8	4,720	1	..
Non-ferrous metal scrap	per kg.	15·5	5,070	16	..

Appendix 4.6 *A comparison of unit values of India's major export commodities to East European countries and other markets*

	1953/4	1954/5	1955/6	1957	1958	1959	1960/1	1961/2	1962/3	1963/4	1964/5	1965/6
Tea												
Eastern Europe												
Quantity[a]	neg.	neg.	neg.	7·3	11·4	12·4	14·2	13·0	16·0	20·0	27·0	26·0
Value[b]				55·1	87·3	92·7	80·9	92·6	115·5	126·5	173·0	174·8
Unit price[c]				7·54	7·65	7·47	5·69	7·12	6·97	6·32	6·4	6·72
Others												
Quantity	208·4	205·5	180·4	200·7	218·3	215·3	174·8	193·0	205·0	190·0	185·0	171·0
Value	1,021·9	1,472·1	1,086·2	1,178·9	1,278·1	1,171·2	1,154·1	1,131·4	1,176·4	1,107·3	1,073·5	1,073·6
Unit price	4·90	7·16	6·02	5·87	5·85	5·43	6·60	5·86	5·73	5·82	5·80	6·27
Jute manufactures												
Eastern Europe												
Quantity (000 tons)				9·8	16·8	21·8	23·5	52·0	62·0	92·0	149·0	170·0
Value				12·7	24·9	18·8	45·9	103·2	107·4	154·8	253·4	340·0
Unit price (per ton)				129·6	148·2	86·2	195·3	198·4	173·2	168·2	170·0	200·0
Others												
Quantity	742·0	810·3	814·8	750·1	790·1	853·1	769·5	746·5	830·0	838·0	801·1	727·0
Value	1,196·9	1,182·5	1,123·2	1,110·5	976·0	995·8	1,209·5	1,344·7	1,449·2	1,397·5	1,428·8	1,488·2
Unit price	161·3	145·9	137·8	148·0	123·5	116·2	157·1	180·1	174·6	166·7	178·3	204·7

Iron ore												
Eastern Europe												
Quantity	494·6	279·0	186·5	134·2	508·0	692·8	989·1	1,404·0	1,946·0	1,978·0	1,972·0	2,075·0
Value	24·6	11·5	8·9	39·5	27·1	34·3	65·9	69·5	95·1	86·7	87·3	86·6
Unit price	479·3	412·2	477·2	202·0	533·4	495·2	666·2	495·0	488·7	438·3	442·6	417·3
Others												
Quantity	767·3	729·8	1,176·4	2,115·7	1,388·3	1,818·3	2,201·4	8,396·0	6,854·0	7,890·0	8,602·0	10,190·0
Value	33·3	31·2	53·8	67·9	72·8	95·0	104·4	248·7	258·1	277·3	284·8	334·4
Unit price	433·9	427·5	457·3	320·9	524·3	522·4	474·2	296·2	376·5	351·4	331·0	328·2
Coffee												
Eastern Europe												
Quantity				1·48	1·85	5·23	4·45	9·55	15·52	10·42	17·44	17·0
Value				9·7	10·3	30·8	21·2	29·0	59·9	38·3	76·7	88·5
Unit price				6·55	5·56	5·89	4·76	3·03	3·85	3·67	4·39	5·20
Others												
Quantity	28·2	103·3	28·2	134·0	130·5	91·7	152·5	20·14	4·99	12·88	135·0	95·0
Value	14·6	76·4	149·5	67·6	61·4	31·7	50·0	61·3	16·2	44·8	57·4	40·9
Unit price	6·55	7·39	5·30	5·04	4·70	3·45	3·28	3·04	3·24	3·47	4·25	4·30
Black pepper												
Eastern Europe												
Quantity	1·0	0·6	4·2	6·5	6·3	5·8	8·5	6·3	7·2	9·8	9·4	12·9
Value	9·9	5·5	14·8	13·3	13·4	11·4	43·3	22·5	23·1	31·7	37·1	55·1
Unit price	9·9	9·16	3·52	2·04	2·12	1·96	5·09	3·57	3·20	3·23	3·94	4·27
Others												
Quantity	12·0	13·4	9·1	13·1	9·2	9·7	9·7	15·4	13·7	9·1	8·0	13·4
Value	178·0	64·3	33·2	17·9	16·4	31·3	42·0	56·6	42·7	21·7	30·8	55·9
Unit price	9·83	4·64	3·64	1·36	1·76	3·22	4·32	3·67	3·11	2·38	3·85	4·17

Appendix 4.6   (contd.)

	1953/4	1954/5	1955/6	1957	1958	1959	1960/1	1961/2	1962/3	1963/4	1964/5	1965/6
Raw wool												
Eastern Europe												
Quantity				2·6	4·0	2·9	2·7	6·9	5·3	2·6	5·6	6·6
Value				20·0	23·2	16·8	16·4	40·8	32·7	17·0	36·7	41·3
Unit price				7·69	5·80	5·79	6·07	5·91	6·16	6·53	6·55	6·25
Others												
Quantity	9·3	13·9	15·2	14·5	11·4	16·2	10·2	7·6	4·3	7·3	6·3	4·5
Value	58·7	80·5	97·2	90·9	64·3	37·4	54·5	43·4	23·7	44·3	39·8	24·5
Unit price	6·31	5·19	6·39	6·26	5·64	5·39	5·34	5·71	5·51	6·06	6·31	5·44
Cashew nuts												
Eastern Europe												
Quantity				3·3	5·2	5·2	4·8	8·1	11·3	12·6	16·9	15·0
Value				11·0	20·3	20·4	25·1	35·8	44·1	52·0	86·2	78·1
Unit price				3·66	3·90	3·92	5·22	4·41	3·90	4·12	5·10	5·20
Others												
Quantity	27·1	34·6	31·4	32·5	35·8	33·2	38·8	33·7	37·2	38·4	38·7	36·3
Value	109·9	106·9	129·2	136·3	134·4	131·4	126·7	145·9	148·6	162·3	204·1	195·9
Unit price	4·05	3·08	4·11	4·19	3·75	3·95	3·26	4·33	3·99	4·22	5·27	5·39

Tobacco unmanufactured

Eastern Europe												
Quantity				3·6	3·7	4·4	4·6	10·1	30·2	32·9	42·2	25·8
Value				5·5	4·8	7·8	7·3	14·2	60·0	82·4	99·9	66·3
Unit price				1·52	1·29	1·77	1·59	1·40	1·98	2·50	2·36	2·56
Others												
Quantity	31·8	38·3	40·0	31·2	44·4	33·3	42·8	34·3	30·0	31·2	35·8	30·9
Value	110·2	117·6	106·0	110·4	142·2	121·4	108·8	126·3	119·9	128·5	141·4	129·5
Unit price	3·46	3·07	2·65	3·53	3·20	3·64	2·54	3·68	3·99	4·11	3·94	4·19

Raw skins and hides

Eastern Europe												
Quantity	0·2	2·8	2·6	3·9	4·3	7·0	6·8	6·2	9·5	6·9	9·1	7·5
Value	1·4	15·3	15·1	35·5	27·2	65·0	60·0	45·0	71·3	59·3	59·7	62·3
Unit price	7·0	5·46	5·80	9·10	6·62	9·28	8·82	7·25	7·50	8·59	6·56	8·60
Others												
Quantity	10·3	8·0	7·2	8·1	7·7	6·1	5·2	5·5	5·0	4·7	3·3	3·7
Value	60·7	43·0	54·3	32·9	41·2	36·4	34·4	37·5	37·1	36·6	30·8	36·7
Unit price	5·89	6·09	7·54	4·06	5·32	5·96	5·63	6·81	7·42	7·78	9·33	9·91

[a] All quantities in millions of kg, unless otherwise stated.

[b] All values in millions of Rs. unless otherwise stated.

[c] All unit prices are in Rs. per kg. unless otherwise stated.

Appendix 4.7   *India's exports of selected commodities to East Europe and to other countries*

	1966/7			1967/8			1968/9		
	Quantity	Value	Price	Quantity	Value	Price	Quantity	Value	Price
Tea (m. kg.)									
East Europe	22·5	205·9	9·15	23·66	230·95	9·76	24·6	230·0	9·35
Others	167·5	1,378·9	7·25	187·44	1,571·05	8·38	176·4	1,335·0	7·56
Total	190·0	158·4		203·0	1,802·0		201·0	1,565·0	
Coffee (m. kg.)									
East Europe	16·9	87·4	5·17	18·74	105·26	5·61	20·0	133·1	6·65
Others	9·1	70·6	7·75	15·26	76·74	5·02	9·0	44·9	4·98
Total	26·1	158·0		34·0	182·0		29·0	180·0	
Cashews (m. kg.)									
East Europe	19·25	176·3	9·16	13·95	111·4	7·98	22·6	211·8	9·37
Others	30·75	278·7	9·06	37·05	318·6	8·60	41·4	397·2	9·59
Total	50·0	45·55		51·0	430·0		64·0	609·0	
Tobacco (m. kg.)									
East Europe	7·7	31·1	4·03	10·0	52·9	5·29	8·0	46·9	5·86
Others	31·3	193·9	6·194	47·0	303·4	6·44	46·0	291·1	6·32
Total	39·0	225·0		57·0	356·0		54·0	338·0	

Jute manufactures (000 tonne)									
East Europe	190·5	467·7	245·51	147·4	427·0	289·7	133·0	367·0	275·93
Others	545·5	2,027·3	371·6	605·6	1,917·0	316·5	420·0	1,813·0	431·66
Total	736·0	2,495·0		753·0	2,341·0		653·0	2,180·0	
Oil cakes (000 tonne)									
East Europe	410·7	167·8	408·57	539·0	336·66	624·60	575·0	349·2	607·3
Others	411·3	333·22	810·49	207·0	118·34	571·69	257·0	145·8	567·0
Total	822·0	500·0		746·0	455·30		832·0	495·0	
Footwear (m. pairs)									
East Europe	1·9	41·6	20·8	1·24	41·85	33·75	1·1	31·2	28·36
Others	10·1	44·9	4·69	10·76	50·15	4·66	11·0	60·8	5·10
Total	12·0	88·0		11·0	92·0		13·0	92·0	
Iron ore (m. tonne)									
East Europe	1·67	97·2	582·9	2·1	127·2	606·2	2·2	137·7	625·9
Others	11·33	604·8	533·8	11·9	620·8	521·68	13·8	746·3	540·59
Total	13·00	702·0		14·0	748·0		16·0	884·0	
Black pepper (m. kg.)									
East Europe	10·0	50·7	5·7	13·5	74·7	5·53	10·4	60·6	5·80
Others	12·0	69·3	5·70	11·5	56·3	4·89	3·9	36·14	
Total	22·0	127·0		25·0	131·0		19·0	9·7	

5

THE COSTS OF TIED CREDITS

In assessing the real worth of credit financed imports the relative priority of projects in the development programme is just as important as the prices paid for equipment. Since the credits from East European countries were tied to projects in the public sector there is a further question: whether these credits resulted in the misallocation of public resources, misallocation in the sense that private firms would have done the job more efficiently.

The contribution of East European credits can be judged from the fact that they were financing the foreign exchange component of 23 out of the 39 public sector industrial projects during the Second and the Third Plans and the total investment made possible by the East European loans was about Rs.10,000 million (see table 40). These investments include the Bokaro steel plant, in which total investment is expected to be Rs.6,200 million, with a foreign exchange component of Rs.1,058 million.

The East European credits have been concentrated in the field of heavy industry, i.e. steel, metallurgy, heavy engineering, coal, oil exploration, refineries, and electricity. About fifty enterprises with East European collaboration were at various stages of preparation and construction in 1968. The USSR is providing assistance for more than forty projects, which, when completed, will turn out annually 4.5 million tons of steel, 6 million tons of oil products and 140,000 tons of modern mechanical equipment for India's machine building, metallurgical, coal and power industries.

RELATIVE PRIORITY OF PROJECTS FINANCED

Two questions should be distinguished in discussing the relative priority of projects. First, whether or not the sectors or industries for which East European credits were available had high priority in India's development programme. Second, whether the choice of a specific project – the design, layout, size, and

Table 40   *Statement showing the amounts of loans for, the total costs and the annual capacity of important industrial public sector undertakings* (in Rs. million)

Name of project	Amount of loan	Total costs	Final capacity
Bhilai steel	647·8	2,023·4	1 million tons of steel, ingot expansion to 2·5 million tons
Expansion of Bhilai	576·1	954·0	
Heavy machine building plant	225·6	577·5	80,000 tons of heavy machinery items
Coal mining machinery	112·5	293·0	45,000 tons of coal mining machinery
Ophthalmic glass	11·8	50·3	300 tons of ophthalmic glass
Drugs	95·2	393·0	Rs.350 million of drugs, antibiotics and surgical instruments
Barauni oil refinery	256·6	434·5	3 million tons
Heavy electrical (2 plants)	686·0	1,197·9	Rs.370 million worth of steam turbines, hydroturbines etc.
Koyali oil refinery	88·9	307·0	3 million tons
Refractories plant	1·6	30·0	24,000 tons of refractories
Precision instruments, Kerala	60·0	80·0	Not available
Compressor and pumps project	100·0	187·0	Not available
Bokaro	1,058·2	7,011·6	1·7 million tons of steel
Foundry forge Ranchi	185·5	1,133·9	146,000 tons of castings, pressing and rolled products
Heavy machine tools (Ranchi)	33·2	244·6	10,000 tons of various machine tools
Nunmati (Gauhati)	64·3	159·8	0·78 million tons of oil

Notes: (1) Amount of loan generally covers the total foreign exchange costs. The figures here refer to the amounts earmarked for each project. (2) The figures for total costs are taken from *Draft Fourth Five-Year Plan*, pp. 283–8, wherever available. These figures for individual projects may not compare with those in table 35 because these refer to earlier years. No attempt was made to reconcile these because it was not clear whether the revision was due to an expansion of capacity or to devaluation. The figures for total costs refer to total expected expenditure not actual expenditure incurred. (3) These are projects financed with credits granted till March 1966.

Source: Planning Commission Development, *Draft Fourth Five-Year Plan*, pp. 283–8.

product mix – was determined by what India wanted or by the availability of external finance.

In general terms the answer to the first question is in the affirmative. The East European credits were being used for the development of heavy industries in the public sector, and while the thinking of Indian planners themselves was probably influenced by the experience of the centrally planned economies, they had definitely opted for a development process in which the development of heavy industry in the public sector played a key role.

In this context, it is further desirable to ask whether these sectors should have been given this high priority. The justification for the relative priority given to the heavy industries is dependent upon the objective function which the plans were meant to maximise. Unfortunately, while the successive plans list objectives such as reaching a state of 'self-sustained' growth at the earliest stage, creating a socialist pattern of society, maximising the rate of growth of income and eliminating unemployment, these were not ranked.[1] Without the benefit of relative weights attached to the objectives, any investment decision can only be justified conditionally. If, for example, the objective of reaching self-sustained growth at the earliest possible time was given high priority, and it is assumed that the possibility for increasing export earnings was limited and dependent upon external factors, growth in the long run could only be maximised by producing machinery at home.

While there were different views on the role of foreign aid, the Second and Third Plans not only talk about self-sustained growth but a target date was fixed for the termination of foreign aid – by the end of the Fourth or the Fifth Plan, i.e. by 1975. The Indian Government itself may have shifted its position regarding the role of foreign aid. While the Second Plan was being formulated the international climate was such that the planners could not assume that external finance would be available or acceptable on the scale that materialised during the Third Plan. The predominant view was that India should achieve economic as well as political independence. During the Third Plan aid became more acceptable as a means to end

[1] See the chapters on objectives of planning in the Second and Third Plans.

dependence on aid, but the strategy of substitution did not change.[1]

Did reducing the dependence on 'aid' imply assigning a secondary place to foreign trade? This assumption appears to be unduly restrictive. Before going into the merits and demerits of the question, it is worth making one point here. Since the early fifties, the economic and political setting in India and abroad has changed enormously and the planners could not have foreseen these changes. The only fair question to ask, therefore, is whether in the light of the evidence available to planners at the time (i.e. in the early fifties) they made a rational choice.

The question is whether the decision to develop heavy industry domestically was taken after fully exploring the possibilities of 'exchanging' goods through foreign trade. The Mahalanobis two-sector model is a model of a closed economy. Mahalanobis justifies the decision to give investment industries high priority in the following way. He and his colleagues studied the experience of different countries in regard to investment and their studies showed that the larger the share of capital goods industries in total investment, the larger would be the increase in national income over a long period of time (of the order of 15, 20 or 30 years) and the smaller would be the immediate rise.[2] Mahalanobis discussed two important problems in planning: first, the most efficient way of feeding the additional population, and second, how to maximise capital accumulation.

He began from the proposition that a nutrition programme had four alternatives: to import food; to import fertilisers; to import machinery to produce fertilisers at home; and to import machinery to manufacture machinery and equipment for the production of fertilisers. Mahalanobis argued that 'in order to feed the population increasing at the rate of 5 million persons per year, it would be necessary to provide an additional quantity of 700,000 tons of foodgrains every year which would require Rs.4,500 million of foreign exchange over a period of five years. The cost could be reduced to Rs.1,350 million in a five-year period if an additional quantity of 350,000 tons of aluminium sulphate were ordered from abroad every year, at

---

[1] The change in the Government of India's position has been discussed in chapter 1. [2] Mahalanobis (46, p. 29).

least two years in advance of the crop season and further reduced to Rs.1,000 million (out of which the foreign exchange component would be Rs.600 million) over a five-year period if a new fertiliser factory of 350,000 ton capacity were started every year. This would call for a decision four or five years ahead of the crop season concerned. The apportioned cost of a heavy machine building factory which would manufacture machinery in India every year for producing a new fertiliser factory of 350,000 ton capacity would be, however, as small as Rs.120 million or Rs.150 million with a foreign exchange component of Rs.60 million. Such a decision would have to be made only once but 8 or 10 years in advance of the season for which fertiliser would be used.'[1] The other example he gave was that of setting up a heavy machine building factory – the foreign exchange cost of which could be recovered by the time three steel plants had been set up. If it was known, therefore, that three steel plants would be set up in India after the heavy machine building plant was ready, it was a worthwhile investment.

From his speeches, articles and the discussions of the frame of the Plan, however, it appears that foreign trade played a very secondary role in Mahalanobis' thinking. He did not himself discuss the basis on which it was concluded that the world demand for India's traditional exports was stagnant and import substitution was more efficient. Bhagwati and Chakravarty also make the point that the Second Plan did not explicitly state the rationale of the shift to heavy industries in terms of foreign trade constraints, so that later justification of this strategy by alluding to 'stagnant world demand' for Indian exports was somewhat of an *ex post facto* rationalisation. They point out that such a crucial assumption, if made, should have been thoroughly examined, whereas in fact the Second Plan only makes cursory references to the problem.[2]

It is worth emphasising at this stage that perhaps the reason why India's long-term export prospects or the costs of alternative strategies were not discussed in the Second Plan was that a 'stagnant world demand for traditional exports of primary producers' was a part of the accepted orthodoxy, not only

---

[1] Mahalanobis (47, pp. 71–2).
[2] Bhagwati and Chakravarty (9, p. 7).

in India but among development economists in the West also.[1]

A serious shortcoming of the Mahalanobis model is that it does not provide sufficient basis for allocating either a certain proportion of total investment to investment goods industries or the distribution of investment between various industries in the investment goods sector. Due to lack of experience in industrial planning or an inadequate appreciation of the interdependence among industries, the programme for industrial development was not well conceived. The Second Plan fixes output targets for various industries but does not rank industries or industry groups according to well defined criteria. Similarly, the Industrial Policy Resolution provides a list of strategic industries, but is more concerned with defining the respective roles of public and private sectors than in ranking output sectors. As a result of the failure to define priorities in industrial development, the choice of individual projects might have been arbitrary, and the availability or non-availability of credit was one of the factors in the investment decision. However, the availability or non-availability of external finance did not determine the *basic strategy* of developing heavy industry in the public sector. It may have influenced the *timing* of certain investments, because of the foreign exchange constraint. To illustrate this point one case study is discussed here.

This is the case of the heavy machine building plant and the other two related plants in Ranchi. The planners were very keen that a heavy machine building industry should be established in India, so that as soon as possible India could fabricate machinery for the production of steel (or cement or capital goods) to the value of, say, Rs.400 to Rs.500 million per year.[2] Mahalanobis calculated that the total cost of a machine building plant would be of the order of Rs.2,000 million (of which Rs.1,000 is foreign exchange cost). To develop a heavy machine building industry was accepted as an essential and indeed indispensable part of the strategy for self-sustained growth. Mahalanobis went as far as to say that even if some targets had

---

[1] Nurkse in his famous lecture (59) in Stockholm argued that unlike the nineteenth century, trade was not the engine of growth in the twentieth century. Prebisch (68) supported the view that export prospects of primary products were not very good.   [2] Mahalanobis (46, p. 27).

to be sacrificed, heavy machine building deserved very high priority. In one of his lectures he pointed out that China had given highest priority to developing those basic industries which would enable it to manufacture domestically the essential capital goods required for the future, and that China had set out on the way to industrialisation using its own resources.[1]

If reaching a state of 'self-sustained' growth as quickly as possible was indeed a serious objective, the decision to set up a heavy machine building plant at an early stage was a step in the desired direction. According to the calculations made by Mahalanobis, the foreign exchange savings from the new plant would be so great that if the machine building plant produced three steel plants, its foreign exchange cost would be recovered. It was therefore concluded that if it were known that at least three, new, million-ton steel plants would be installed after the establishment of the heavy machine building industry, then there would be no risk in the decision to establish such an industry.[2] But the timing of the decision is significant. The Heavy Engineering Corporation, Ranchi – the public sector agency in charge of implementing this project – was incorporated in 1958, about the time the Second Plan had to be cut down and tailored to available foreign exchange resources.[3] In undertaking an investment of this order – an estimated Rs.1,500 to Rs.2,000 million – availability of credit was bound to have some weight. The Indian Government considered alternative proposals and chose the Soviet.

Originally a team of British engineers, headed by S. E. Coates, was invited to advise the Government of India on the further heavy engineering capacity required and its most efficient division among the new manufacturing units and extensions of existing units. The team recommended four different plants to produce structured steel, heavy plates and vessels, and medium and heavy machine tool plants with capacities varying between 10,000 and 40,000 tons. About the same time, a Soviet team was also asked to discuss the possibility of producing equipment for a steel plant indigenously. The Soviet proposal was to produce 80,000 tons of equipment per year for a steel plant as well as coal mining equipment, a heavy machine building plant and a foundry forge. This plan was certainly more

---

[1] Mahalanobis (47).   [2] Mahalanobis (46, p. 28).   [3] See chapter 1.

ambitious than the British proposals. The heavy machine building plant was to be built in two stages, but would ultimately
have the capacity to supply the estimated requirements of the
entire Indian economy for steel mill equipment, as well as
heavy machinery required for other industries. A Loksabha
Committee under the chairmanship of Mr Feroz Gandhi, a
Congress member of Parliament, in fact preferred the British
proposal, because it covered a wider range of products and met
the needs of more industries. However, the Government
ultimately decided to accept the Soviet proposal, and according to the Gandhi Committee 'the primary consideration in
deciding on the collaboration has been the availability of
credit'.[1] Even the size of the project was dependent upon the
credit. The original planned capacity of the plant was 45,000
tons, as this was considered adequate to meet the demand in the
country. The first detailed project report was prepared on that
basis. But in 1959, the USSR offered a second credit and a
part of this was earmarked for the plant. Therefore, the capacity
was revised to 80,000 tons and two stages were going to be built
simultaneously. This meant that a revision of the project report
was necessary and the plans for the foundry forge had to be
revised as well, because the latter was meant to supply castings
and forgings for the heavy machine building plant.

Two key considerations in deciding whether this investment
was justified were the timing and the technical and economic
feasibility of the project. If indeed the heavy machine building
plant could meet the entire needs of the steel industry, no
foreign credits would be utilised for this particular industry.
One possible objection to the plant is precisely that it reduces
dependence on such imports as are eligible for credit financing.
Given the imperfections of the official capital market, the choice
may be to forgo a credit or leave domestic capacity unutilised.
This dilemma has already been faced in the case of the heavy
machine building plant.

Actual production started in the plant in 1965/6 and since
that time three steel plants have been expanded in the public
sector alone and a new steel plant has been started. The proposed expansion of the three steel plants was: Rourkela from
1 to 1·8 million tons, Bhilai from 1 to 2·5 million tons, and

[1] EC (110).

Durgapur from 1 to 1·6 million tons at an estimated cost of
Rs.3,860 million.[1] The plant was not in a position to meet all
these demands – it still is not. The latest estimates are that it
will reach its rated full capacity by 1975/6.[2] The fact is that
even in the initial years, the heavy machine building plant has
been suffering from under-utilisation of capacity, because the
foreign exchange cost of the steel project was being financed
from loans from external funds. These loans were available only
for imported equipment, not for purchasing local goods. Bhilai
was the only public sector plant using some equipment from
the heavy machine building plant. The British were approached
and had no objection to using equipment produced by the plant,
but would not have given a credit.

If donors were indifferent about the end use of credits, import
substitution in the field of machinery and equipment would
create no problems, in the sense that to supplement domestic
resources – real and financial – the borrowing country could
import raw materials or consumer goods. But credits are treated
as an export promotion device by all donors, and the principal
donor countries have built up industries capable of meeting the
requirements of other countries. In fact, as early as 1943, Rosenstein-Rodan was arguing that South-Eastern European and
East European countries should choose a pattern of industrialisation based on substantial international investment and lending.
One of the reasons he advanced for preferring light industries in
overpopulated areas was that 'even for the purposes of an expanding world economy, the existing heavy industries in Great
Britain, Germany, France and Switzerland could certainly
supply all the needs of the international depressed areas'.[3] Since
these West European countries have a vested interest in exporting machinery and equipment, any country trying to follow a
strategy of import substitution and using foreign aid to supplement domestic resources is bound to face this dilemma, which
becomes more widespread as industrialisation proceeds.

The crucial question is: by the time domestic capacity to
produce certain goods is created, will the country be in a
position to purchase these goods? Unless the investible surplus

---

[1] *Annual Report of Public Sector Undertakings, 1967/8* (101, pp. 17–19).
[2] *Annual Report, 1968/9*. See chapter on enterprises under construction, section
on the heavy machine building plant.   [3] See Rosenstein-Rodan in 1, p. 245.

is big enough, the physical capacity to produce may not be very relevant. In a centrally planned economy, where the government is in complete control of production and investment decisions, it is justifiable to equate the availability of investment goods with the ability to invest. In a mixed economy, the question of financial means has to be asked independently. Would the rate of savings be high enough or, more accurately, would the government be in a position to mobilise sufficient domestic savings?

It appears that in the Mahalanobis model, savings were not considered as an independent variable.[1] Perhaps this is an example of lack of co-ordination between physical and financial planning. The commodity balances worked out within the framework of a perspective plan may have shown that the internal demand for steel in period $t+n$ would justify the setting up of a steel machinery producing plant in period t. But the ability to *produce* investment goods does not by itself guarantee the ability to *finance* this investment in period $t+n$, at least in a mixed economy. In the Mahalanobis model the propensity to save is given by the capacity of investment goods created in the initial period. However, the identity of savings and investment is only an accounting concept and not a behavioural relationship.

If the Indian planners' problem was one of *transformation* of domestic resources only and not *scarcity* of domestic resources, development of heavy industries would have been more acceptable. What has happened is that when the basic strategy of import substitution was formulated it was not possible to foresee developments such as co-ordination of aid. Since then the whole perspective has changed; the Third Plan was formulated after taking into account aid possibilities,[2] and in the sixties the goal of achieving self-sustained growth has received less emphasis and appears to be more distant than in 1954. In criticising the decision to develop heavy industry, it is easy to forget that the Mahalanobis team were dealing with a different universe.

A factor which compounded the difficulties in integrating

---

[1] Bhagwati and Chakravarty (9, p. 7) point out that the Mahalanobis model takes no explicit account of savings, whereas economists looking at growth would inevitably have started from this end.

[2] See discussion of Indian planning in chapter 1.

external finance with domestic resources has been the rivalry among donors. The general pattern is that the East European countries give credits for manufacturing some machinery domestically, while Consortium credits are for importing machinery. Important examples are steel, coal mining machinery and fertiliser equipment. Of course, if the credits refer to different periods of time they may be complementary rather than competitive. So far, very few East European credit financed projects have been completed, but as the domestic capacity to manufacture machinery increases, the country's capacity to absorb project aid declines. In fact, a recent economic survey has made this point already.[1]

So far the general case for developing the heavy machine building industry has been discussed and the main area for concern is the fact that projects like this create difficulties in matching resource availabilities and requirements during the transitional period when external finance is necessary. The heavy machine building plant is a good example of the problems faced in utilising project aid. However, it would not be fair to call the project a mistake simply because it increased the difficulties in utilising project aid. On the other hand, this is an argument for urging a re-orientation of aid policies and programmes.

Even if it is concluded that there was a general case for setting up a heavy machine building plant, it does not follow that the particular project was well designed. The plant suffered from two serious defects – a lack of marketing and sales organisation and of designing facilities. Both these defects stem from the fact that public sector enterprises in the USSR do not face these problems and the project planners did not modify the project design to suit the requirements of a mixed economy. In addition to the imperfections in the aid programme, both these factors have contributed to the under-utilisation of capacity.

Even if the Indian Government or private firms had the financial means to purchase equipment produced by the 'machinery manufacturing' public sector plants, these plants did not have the designing capacity. In a market economy, any concern has to advertise its range of products. The heavy machine building plant, as set up, was not in a position to offer

[1] Government of India, *Annual Economic Survey, 1969/70.*

potential buyers any choice. Apparently, in the USSR, the custom is either that the concern placing an order gives the design and specifications, or that the machine manufacturing concerns have standard designs and standardised products. It is clear that the Ranchi plant had neither a designing wing nor ready-made designs to produce even standardised products. When the USSR agreed to use equipment produced by the plant, the Government of India had to sign a separate contract with the USSR to obtain the technical documentation needed for manufacturing the equipment and pay for it.[1] If the plant cannot even design a steel plant to Soviet specifications, its ability to cater for other types of steel plants must be doubtful.

Secondly, the output mix of the plant may be too specialised, in the sense it can only cater for one or two industries, and this lack of flexibility may result in under-utilisation of capacity. Unless it is assumed that over the economic life of its assets, the plant can sell a one-million-ton steel plant a year, there may be considerable waste involved. Also, depending upon the rate of technological advance, the plant may become obsolete by the time it reaches full capacity in 1975/6, i.e. it may no longer be economical to set up one-million-ton steel plants, or the production processes may have changed.

PUBLIC SECTOR VERSUS PRIVATE SECTOR

So far the question of relative priority of sectors has been discussed and the position is that the Indian Government did not provide any clear ranking for industries. All the industries for which East European credits were available were classified as high priority according to the Second Plan. But even assuming that investment in these investment goods industries was justified, should the government have expanded the share of the public sector in these industries? Most of these investments were at least potentially in sectors which private investors would find attractive. Allocating scarce public sector resources to them may be questioned on two grounds. First, if these scarce public sector resources had been reallocated to sectors which do not attract private investors, total investment and foreign exchange receipts might have been maximised.

[1] See (101) *1966/7*.

Secondly, private investors might have been more efficient in setting up projects and this would have minimised the waste of public funds.

With reference to the first question, it seems that the use of private foreign capital instead of East European credits for industrial projects in the public sector would not significantly have increased net foreign exchange receipts from external sources, for two reasons: first, the tendency of private firms to rely on other sources of capital; secondly the fact that all the East European credits were tied to projects. It is doubtful whether these could have been re-allocated so as not to clash with the interests of private investors.

If private investors were willing to bring in their own funds or obtained official credits which would otherwise not have been available, these funds can be treated as a *net* addition to funds available from external sources. The general experience of developing countries in the post Second World War years has been that private foreign investors rely mainly on official funds or local funds and that their main contribution is their technical expertise.[1] India was no exception to this rule. Private foreign firms in India relied on official sources in their own countries: financial institutions and other sources and PL 480 counterpart funds. These credits resulted mainly in the redirection of official aid and not in an addition to the inflow of official funds. The Consortium countries commit themselves to a specific amount annually or for two or three years at a time. India and the donor country negotiate the actual credits later. The credits for private sector firms come from official funds out of the original commitments and are *not* granted over and above what the country has agreed to give. There may, however, be exceptions: for example, a firm might manage to get a loan which was not included in the original commitment.

Some Eximbank loans and Cooley Amendment[2] loans were given to American firms or their affiliates in India, and it is true that these amounts would not have been available but for the presence of these firms. Private foreign firms have served a useful function by creating a favourable climate for aid. Since donors

---

[1] See Kidron (39).

[2] Cooley Amendment loans are made from PL 480 counterpart funds reserved for the use of American firms or their affiliates in India.

treated even these loans for foreign enterprises as a part of the assistance given to India, these were not funds contributed by private foreign capitalists, but official funds channelled through the private foreign firms. Considering India's actual receipts from private funds and the attitude of the private foreign investors towards the industries concerned, it does not seem that India would have been able to attract significant additional amounts of private foreign funds.

Before 1955 the total outstanding private foreign investment in India was rather less than Rs.5,000 million, and import control policies were such that, while there were heavy duties on importing finished manufactures, it was easier to set up an assembly plant in India and import all the components. India was an expanding and protected market and enjoyed political stability. Private foreign investment before 1955 was concentrated in plantations, trading, and petroleum. After 1955 the private foreign investment in plantations increased very little (except for a revision of the book value of assets), private foreign investors being mainly interested in petroleum and manufacturing industries. These were industries which required advanced technology and were highly profitable.

The gross inflow of foreign business investment in India increased by Rs.3,575 million from 1956 to 1965.[1] Of this increase, about 45 per cent was financed by external official funds. Therefore the gross contribution of private foreign investors was less than Rs.2,000 million, or 4·4 per cent of the gross receipts from external official sources.

Private foreign firms in India also received credits from local financial institutions in India, including the Industrial Finance Corporation (IFC), Industrial Credit and Investment Corporation of India (ICICI), and Cooley Amendment funds. The IFC and ICICI were meant to provide finance for industries in which the commercial banks were not interested, and these were the newer industries which attracted private foreign capital. Once a foreign firm is established in India, it can apply for any loan. There is not only no discrimination against it, but a firm with foreign collaboration receives preferential treatment from these financial institutions, because it is better

---

[1] The discussion of private foreign investment is based on RBI reports, primarily chapter 1 in (130).

8

known and probably appears more creditworthy. Those industries in which private foreign capital is concentrated receive the lion's share of finance. Moreover, the Cooley Amendment Funds were reserved for American firms or their affiliates. The total finance available to American firms from this source rose to Rs.780 million in 1965/6.

There are grounds for believing that official support to the extent of four to five dollars was necessary for each dollar invested by a firm, which furthermore has usually also to attract local capital: the gross contribution to India's balance of payments from private sources abroad was hence relatively small and the adoption of policies designed to attract more foreign collaboration would probably not have significantly increased the receipts from private sources.

Official loans for industrial development or funds from private sources would be a *net* addition to the total receipts of foreign exchange only if the East European credits could have been used for other purposes. It is by no means clear that India had much choice in the matter, both because of the lack of availability of suitable equipment, and because of the anxiety of East European countries to break the monopoly in some industries notably petroleum refining and pharmaceuticals. Since one of the avowed purposes of East European credits was to reduce dependence on foreign capital, it is unlikely that the clash could have been avoided. The only question is whether, financially speaking, the terms of the East European credits were harsher than the private firms would have offered, and that is rather doubtful.

It is argued, however, by some economists, including Mikesell, that a private dollar is worth five public dollars to developing countries, because private capital can offer something the public sector cannot – technical know-how and knowledge of the market conditions.[1] The difficulty with this line of argument is that the national interests of a developing country very often clash with the global interests of international giants. The difficulty for a developing country would be to attract private investors in the high priority industries.

[1] Mikesell and Allen (50) were perhaps overstating the benefits of private investment because they were testifying to the major decision-makers of the Joint Economic Committee of the U.S. Congress.

The case of the exploration for crude oil is interesting in this respect. The oil companies had exploited the Indian Government in the early fifties and were prepared neither to reduce their profit margins nor to explore for crude oil in India until it became apparent that the USSR had become a major oil exporter and had also offered economic and technical assistance for setting up a petroleum industry in the public sector. The USSR launched a worldwide campaign to break the stranglehold of the major oil companies on the world market[1] and a part of that campaign was to sell oil more cheaply and to help developing countries achieve 'economic independence'. The Government of India benefited both because the prices of crude oil fell following Soviet entry into the market[2] and because a public sector industry was built up. Producing and refining crude oil is an industry which is mainly in the hands of private businessmen. The Indian Government was criticised officially and unofficially for investing vast amounts of public resources and wasting foreign exchange in an industry which would have attracted private capital. The case for establishing an oil industry in the public sector was made on two grounds. First, the world demand and supply situation in the late fifties was such that neither the 'seven sisters'[3] nor the Western newcomers would have made serious attempts to exploit India's oil reserves in the fifties. Second, the profits in this industry are made in producing crude. There is a strong case for arguing that a developing country, whose government's ability to generate tax revenues may be limited, should seek other ways of increasing the investible surplus.

Let us take the second argument first. It has been argued by numerous Western spokesmen and representatives of oil companies that developing countries should not undertake exploration for petroleum because of the high risk factor, high costs of exploration and heavy overheads. Levy, perhaps the world's leading oil consultant, prepared a report on this subject. His report has been chosen to present the case, first because he lists all the possible arguments against state intervention, and secondly, because his firm did not have any investments in the

[1] The American oil companies were so concerned that the National Petroleum Council produced a two-volume report. [2] The case is discussed in 133.
[3] The major world oil companies are known as the 'seven sisters' (see 79).

developing countries and enjoys a reputation for an independent view. Subsequently, the U.N. also prepared a report on the subject of costs and financing of exploration for crude. The latter is more descriptive. Levy makes an apparently strong case against state intervention. His arguments are as follows:[1]

(1) The developing countries have a scarcity of investible resources. Among the many competing claims on public sector resources, oil exploration should have a low priority, because this is a field in which private firms are interested.

(2) International firms have the financial means, the manpower and the technical know-how and experience, which national governments do not. The implication is that private firms will be more efficient than the government or governments. In a paper presented to a U.N. seminar, Levy is even more explicit about this question of government efficiency. He says that a government often finds itself outside the main stream of technological progress, and has difficulties in staffing its operations.[2]

(3) The costs of exploration, though they differ from region to region, are very heavy and on a scale that the budgets in developing countries cannot support. The field of exploration is such that inadequate efforts may be as unfruitful as no efforts. Levy's own estimate of cost of exploration is that expenditure to establish production has averaged almost U.S. $2,000 per barrel[3] per day. On this basis 'the capital costs of building up crude oil productibility of, say, 50,000 barrels per day would run to U.S. $100 million, apart from large additional investment for transportation, processing etc. which could add up to another U.S. $150 million.'[4]

(4) The reserves, once established, become depleted so continuously that investment is necessary to sustain a rising level of operations.

(5) The investment in exploration does not bring a quick return but matures very slowly. This has been the experience of many new producing areas. For instance, in both the Rocky Mountain region of the U.S.A. and in Canada – both relatively

[1] Levy (43, ch. 1). Levy also gave a paper at a seminar organised by the U.N. on the subject of petroleum exploration, where he developed the same theme (83).
[2] See Levy (43).
[3] 1 ton of crude oil is approximately equivalent to 7.5 barrels.   [4] Levy (43).

young oil provinces – exploration and development in the post-war decade have absorbed significantly larger amounts than the funds generated by oil and gas production. In Colombia, where substantial results are being achieved in terms of establishing crude oil reserves and starting production, expenditures have aggregated more than U.S. $950 million, more than one quarter of which remains to be recovered.[1]

(6) Exploration is a very risky business and the government may not discover any petroleum, or may have to abandon the search because it does not prove profitable to produce petroleum in commercial quantities.

(7) There have been examples in the past of unsatisfactory performance, for example in Argentina and Mexico, where the oil industry has failed to keep pace with other countries.[2]

Levy is quite right to point out that exploration for crude is a very speculative, risky and capital intensive business. However, his conclusion does not necessarily follow. He emphasises one side of the coin – the high risk associated with this business. *However, unless there were equally compensating rewards the petroleum companies would not be in the business either.* Their motive is to maximise profits and the strongest objection to government intervention is precisely that petroleum companies are losing highly lucrative business. Perhaps a few figures will bring out this point clearly. In a recent book on the politics and economics of oil, Tanzer points out that in 1966 earnings on petroleum investment accounted for 60 per cent of all U.S. earnings in underdeveloped countries, and that the average rate of return on this investment was 20 per cent with a peak of 55 per cent in 1965.[3] Tanzer quotes a study by Issawi and Yeganeh, which shows that from their establishment at the turn of the century to 1960, the companies' receipts, after deducting costs of operations, amounted to U.S.$26,200 million, of which they paid U.S.$9.9 million to the governments, re-invested U.S.$1,700 million for further expansion and transferred U.S.$14,600 million abroad.[4]

In other words, over a period of sixty years the average share

---

[1] *Ibid.*   [2] J. McV. Luard has also made this point. See Sell (74, p. 81).
[3] Tanzer (94, pp. 41–2).
[4] *Ibid.* p. 44. The quotation is from Issawi and Yeganeh (34, p. 108).

of the oil exporting countries in the receipts of petroleum companies (including re-investment) amounted to less than 45 per cent. The bargaining position of any one oil exporting country is weak because the companies have alternative sources of supply and control marketing operations. Even if an exporting country nationalised its oil industry, it might have difficulty in selling its product on the world market. It therefore seems unlikely, even assuming that they make some concessions to the oil exporting countries, that the petroleum companies will settle for less than 50 per cent of the gross receipts. What this means is that out of the gross export proceeds of say U.S. $1·50 per barrel posted price for crude, the exporting country receives about 50 per cent or $0·75.

In strictly financial terms therefore the question becomes one of whether by investing its own resources the country stands to gain more than by settling for tax revenues etc. from oil companies. It is worth pointing out that in the petroleum industry all the profits are made in producing petroleum. Once the crude is discovered and facilities constructed, the costs of production are relatively low, and the spread between the selling price and the costs of production is very wide. Tanzer[1] cites estimates by Hartshorn (then employed by the West German Government) and the Organisation of Petroleum Exporting Companies (OPEC) on the costs of petroleum. Hartshorn's estimate is that the costs of supplying Middle Eastern oil have varied from 8 cents a barrel to 45 cents a barrel; OPEC's estimates are 25 cents in the Middle East and 50 cents in Venezuela. Tanzer gives his opinion that the long-term production costs might be 10 cents per barrel in the Middle East and 50 cents in Venezuela. The present author does not claim to be an expert on the economics of oil. It seems, however, even to a layman, that even accepting the highest estimate, i.e. 50 cents per barrel, the margin is very lucrative (assuming a realised price of U.S. $1·50 per barrel).

If the domestic consumption of the producing country is negligible and all the output is exported, ownership of the petroleum industry means, on the basis of existing financial arrangements, that foreign exchange receipts will be doubled.[2]

---

[1] Tanzer (79, pp. 11–13).

[2] Assuming that the net foreign exchange receipts of a petroleum producing country amount to about 50 per cent of gross export proceeds.

If the country is developing production for domestic consumption, the country benefits in two ways. First, it saves all the foreign exchange on imports. Second, the difference between the costs of production and receipts from sales is available to the government for re-investment. Theoretically, there is a good case for arguing that the developing country should consider investing in petroleum crude.

Both Levy's report and the U.N. report put great emphasis on the risks and uncertainty. Neither of them makes sufficient allowance for the fact that these risks can be reduced substantially by making preliminary surveys. An oil-company handbook[1] points out that as a result of the advances made in geology and geophysics the risk of failure in drilling can be reduced greatly. If the drilling site is chosen without any exploration, the success ratio (the ratio of successful wells to wells drilled) is 1 : 30, but with geological and geophysical exploration the ratio can be reduced to 1 : 5. A report on the oil industry in the USSR says that the success ratio in the USSR has risen very rapidly. The report says that from 1956 to 1962 the number of seismic parties in operation rose from 200 to 800[2] and that 'in the analysis of exploration (and development) data, most up-to-date electric and electronic computers, flow models, electric analogs and analysers are employed. As a result of systematic planning, interpretation and co-ordination of the geological, gravity-magnetic, seismic and structural drilling data, the success ratio of exploratory wells has been claimed to have gone up by 50 per cent. Compared to the usual world average, the success ratio of 10 per cent in wildcat exploratory drilling is a positive achievement. In production and drilling, a success ratio of 92 per cent has been claimed.'[3]

While one need not accept the Soviet figures at face value, the report does show that the risk of complete failure has been greatly reduced. In this connection it is noteworthy that the USSR's technicians did discover petroleum in commercial quantities in India after Western petroleum companies had expressed pessimism regarding the size of reserves. The initial investigation is not very costly either. The 1962 U.N. report on

[1] Royal Dutch Shell (71, pp. 71–2).
[2] National Productivity Council of India (116, p. 10).
[3] *Ibid.* (p. 9).

petroleum says that the cost of preliminary reconnaissance may be of the order of one-twentyfifth of the cost of exploration.[1]

An underdeveloped country still faces the problem of finding the means of financing investment in the petroleum industry. It is true that petroleum companies have their own means of financing investment and that there are high initial investment costs for which Levy's own estimate is somewhat higher than those which were previously being cited (although, as he pointed out, costs vary from region to region and are quite low in the Middle East). However, Leicester, a British petroleum consultant, in a paper prepared for the United Nations in 1962, concluded that the average coincided with Levy's figures and on that basis he calculated that to establish a production of 100,000 barrels per day (5 million tons per annum) the average order of investment would be U.S.$200 million.[2]

Other figures quoted are lower. For example, the chairman of Burmah–Shell estimated that the total investment needed to locate crude petroleum reserves with an annual output capacity of 6 million tons would be Rs.3,600 million (U.S.$480 million)[3] or U.S.$1,100 per barrel compared to Levy's estimate of $2,000.

Moreover, if the developing countries cannot finance petroleum investment out of their own resources, the inference is not that they should leave it to the petroleum companies, but that they should look for alternative means of financing. In an underdeveloped country, where the agricultural sector is stagnant and the manufacturing sector is small, the tax-generating potential of these sectors may be both limited and inelastic. By developing the petroleum sector first the government will be in a better position to generate the resources needed for development. The argument is not that every developing country should go in for petroleum exploration. The decision in each case depends upon its merits. If preliminary surveys show that country X has reserves of petroleum in commercial quantities and can either import or produce petroleum, the question of public investment in the petroleum industry should be examined carefully. It is assumed that the authorities in the country con-

[1] U.N. (82, pp. 5–8).   [2] Tanzer (79, pp. 127–8).
[3] See (99) for 1958.

cerned have looked into the question of alternative sources of energy and chosen petroleum as the most suitable. The case for developing the oil industry in the public sector rests on the following grounds:

(1) Given the world demand/supply situation the country concerned may be very low on the list of petroleum companies and domestic resources may not be developed for a long time.

(2) Even if it is cheaper for the company to produce elsewhere and import oil, what is relevant to the country is the difference between domestic costs of production and the import price. To elaborate upon this, let us assume that the costs of exploration and production in country X are a dollar per barrel compared to 50 cents in the alternative source of supply and that the actual c.i.f. price of crude is U.S. \$1·50. The country will be better off by producing domestically. The costs of production are relevant in making an investment decision only when they are reflected in the actual price paid. In the case of oil companies there is little connection between the costs of production and prices. So long as the domestic costs of production are lower than the import price the investing country is a net beneficiary.

(3) Depending upon the time horizon, the structure of the economy and alternatives for productive investment elsewhere, investing in petroleum may be a more efficient way of generating additional new sources needed for development, because of the high rate of return associated with this capital.[1] If the petroleum industry is developed in the public sector, there is an income redistribution in favour of the public sector. This may not be a net addition to national savings if we assume that the domestic private sector has the same marginal propensity to save as the public sector. If income is redistributed in favour of the public sector, there is an additional advantage that the government can invest the funds according to national priorities.[2]

Let us trace actual developments in India. The post-war

---

[1] Leeman (42) estimates that the profits of the petroleum companies in 1955/6 averaged U.S.\$0·82 per barrel and were even higher in the U.S.

[2] Rejecting ownership of the oil industry by private companies does not mean that the principle of profit maximisation has to be abandoned. It seems that some of the opposition to state ownership stems from a confusion of two issues – the acceptance of the principle of profit maximisation and the ownership of these profits.

world demand situation was such that neither the old established companies nor the newcomers had any pressing need to establish new sources of supply, because the newcomers faced difficulties in marketing their output and the old companies had ample proven reserves. As table 41 shows, the world's proven reserves, excluding the Communist countries, more than doubled between 1950 and 1955 and increased faster than world demand. Thus actual output could have been increased much faster if necessary, and there was no need to hunt for new sources of crude petroleum. However, the demand was not rising fast enough.

Table 41   *World proved oil reserves for selected years* (thousand million tons)

Country/Area	1950	1955	1960	1965
U.S.A.	3·4	4·0	5·0	5·1
Total Western hemisphere	5·0	6·3	9·1	9·6
Africa	—	—	1·2	3·0
Middle East	5·6	16·8	24·6	28·9
Total world, excluding USSR etc.	11·0	23·9	36·5	43·4
USSR, Eastern Europe and China	1·1	1·5	4·5	4·5
Total world	12·1	25·4	41·0	47·9

Source: British Petroleum Company, *World Oil*, various issues.

Between 1955 and 1965 world import demand for crude petroleum increased by 6·5 per cent per annum. There was a consistent surplus of production over consumption. Historically the rate of growth of oil reserves has been compatible with the rate of growth of consumption. Between 1950 and 1965, however, the world's proved petroleum reserves increased at the rate of 9·8 per cent per annum compared to world consumption, which increased at 6·8 per cent per annum.

An added factor which accentuated the world oil situation was the USSR's re-entry as a major exporter. After 1955 the USSR rapidly increased its exports of petroleum to the non-communist countries, their value increasing from 4·8 per cent of its total trade to 6·7 per cent in 1960; and petroleum represented almost 20 per cent of its total exports to the non-communist countries.[1] From 1950 to 1955 the Soviet Union's total exports to East Europe and to all other countries increased from 1·1 million tons to 3 million tons; by 1961 its total exports were 4 million tons.

It is difficult to project the future growth of the Soviet Union's exportable surplus, because adequate statistics on domestic production and consumption are not available. There are, however, indications that the Soviet Union will increase its exports only to Eastern Europe. There are grounds for doubting an NPCI view that 'the extremely high targets for energy production in 1970 and 1980 indicate immense untapped petroleum reserves within the country, and the past experience of the Soviet Union in meeting or exceeding oil production targets, all seem to indicate that the export potential will continue to rise.'[2] The East European supply situation in the late 1950s (see table 42) is unlikely to recur.

Table 42   *Excess of petroleum production over consumption* (million tons)

	World excluding East Europe and China	Eastern Europe and China	World total
1955	19·2	2·2	21·4
1956	26·4	3·4	29·8
1957	37·8	5·0	42·8
1958	8·3	8·0	13·8
1959	6·4	14·4	20·8
1960	8·2	22·2	30·8

Source: The British Petroleum Co. Ltd., *Statistical Review of the World Oil Industry* (1965).

Some Western companies might have been interested in further exploitation if very rich oil deposits had already been

[1] National Petroleum Council (54, ch. 2).
[2] NPCI Report (116, ch. 2).

discovered in India, but since this was not the case, and India's oil potential was not considered to be very high, exploration for oil in India was not a very promising proposition. Had there been no alternative to the Western firms, domestic oil deposits would not have been developed. To break the monopoly of Western firms, India had to rely on assistance from the East European countries. This question has been discussed in chapter 2. This effort cost India a total of Rs.4,030 million (post-devaluation rate) by the end of 1969.

Table 43 *Public sector investment in oil exploration and petroleum* (in Rs. million)

	Second Plan	Third Plan	Total	Total up to 1968–69
Exploration	495·0	1,025·0	1,520	1,890
Investment in refineries[a] (and pipelines)	370·0	835·0	1,205 ⎫⎬⎭	2,140
Marketing	—	160·0	160	
Total	865·6	2,020·9	2,885	4,030

[a] Includes total investment by the Government of India in Barauni, Gauhati and Koyali refineries – the three refineries built with Rumanian and Soviet assistance. The total investment in refineries was about Rs.940 million and the rest is for pipelines.

Source : Explanatory Memoranda on the Budget of the Central Government Capital Receipts and Disbursements, 1955/6 to 1968/9.

Table 43 shows that the total public sector investment in exploration, refining, pipelines and marketing amounted to Rs.2,900 million over the decade 1956–65. As India had utilised external credits worth Rs.700 million, Rs.2,200 million, or Rs.220 million annually, were raised from domestic sources. But only Rs.1,500 million out of this sum were utilised for exploration proper and as a result of this investment, the existence of reserves of crude petroleum worth 15 million tons was established in the country. Although the actual output from the new oil fields at Cambay, Ankleshwar and Naharkotia was only 3 million tons in 1966, due to the delays in completing pipelines etc., they had the capacity to produce 6 million tons per annum.

With an investment of Rs.150 million annually or less during the decade mostly from domestic sources, the accomplishments of the Oil and Natural Gas Commission (ONGC) were not unsatisfactory. Of the potential one million square kilometers of potential oil-bearing areas, more than a quarter had been aeromagnetically surveyed and seismic investigations had been conducted over 50·1 thousand square kilometers.[1] These surveys are only mentioned to show that much of the potential oil supply in India may not yet have been discovered.[2] The ONGC drilled 480 wells, of which 243 produced oil, 40 produced gas, 99 were completely dry and 80 were on test by March 1967. The commission started deep drilling in April 1957 only.[3]

The ONGC's activities were helped by previous surveys etc. Nonetheless, at least in India's case, the period spent in exploration was not very long. There were delays in actual production, but by December 1967, 7·98 million tons had been produced from Ankleshwar field and 0·04 million tons from Kalol (Gujerat).[4] From Cambay and Ankleshwar 409 million cubic feet of gas were also supplied. In 1967/8 and 1968/9 the production of crude amounted to 2·79 million tons and 2·04 million tons respectively. By the end of 1968/9 a rate of production of 3·50 million tons per year was achieved[5] and reserves equivalent to 1,638 million barrels had been established.[6] In addition, refining capacity of 5·75 million tons had been established in the three public sector refineries, Koyali, Barauni and Gauhati. Koyali's capacity was being increased by one million tons without any extra cost. In 1968/9 the three refineries processed 5·4 million tons of crude.[7]

Up to March 1969, total investment in the petroleum industry amounted to Rs.4,000 million, or to less than 2 per cent of total public sector outlay in the successive plans. About Rs.3,000

---

[1] The USSR gave credits for exploration of petroleum crude.
[2] (99) for 1967/8, pp. 10–11.
[3] Ibid. p. 12.   [4] Ibid. p. 12.
[5] Annual Report of Public Sector Undertakings, 1968/9 (101, p. 73).
[6] (99) for 1967/8, Statistical Appendix; see table on world reserves of crude petroleum.
[7] See Annual Report of Public Sector Undertakings, 1968/9 (101, p. 81).

million was raised domestically and the foreign exchange component of the programme, Rs.1,000 million, was financed from external sources. The question is whether India would have been able to obtain more external finance by turning to private capitalists rather than to the East European countries. The private oil companies, as they showed by their behaviour in the fifties, were not interested, since they already had more than enough to sell. It was only in response to the competition offered by the East European countries that they changed their tactics and offered India credits for oil exploration, building pipelines and setting up refineries in the public sector, which were accepted. Though the oil companies were seeking concessions for exploration in India in the sixties they might not have started production on a large scale because the world supply situation had not changed. Even when they offered to set up refineries in the public sector they reserved the right to import crude. Philips Petroleum reportedly had this clause in its refinery agreement.

If an investment is justified by the results, investment in exploration was worthwhile for the Indian Government. It is doubtful whether vast amounts of foreign exchange would have been saved, because in any case the foreign exchange component was met from the USSR's credits. On grounds of performance alone, investment in petroleum production yielded much better results than some other investments, such as the Rourkela and Durgapur steel plants where the government invested Rs.4,000 million and made substantial cumulative losses.

It has been argued that because the East European credits were tied to an enterprise in the public sector, the result was over-expansion and an increase in inefficiency, and that this inefficient utilisation of resources should be treated as a cost of borrowing from the East European countries. Two points should be clearly distinguished here: the ownership of an enterprise, and its establishment and management. The objection to an enterprise being in the public sector may be either that it cannot be run as a commercial enterprise motivated by profit considerations, or that the firm in a centrally planned economy is not as efficient as its private partner.

The argument that public sector enterprises cannot be run on a commercial basis is not valid. It is true that in Western countries, such as Great Britain and the United States, nationalisation or development in the public sector took place either because the private sector did not consider the investment worthwhile, or because the government felt that these industries should not be run on a commercial basis. After 1945 many industries, as well as certain services, were nationalised in the U.K. because the government wanted to offer certain goods and services at low prices. As a result of inexperience in handling such enterprises, and of a certain confusion and misconception about the role of the public sector, many of them were badly managed and were running losses. In a developing country, however, a different approach can be adopted, to make these enterprises commercially viable. The idea is not to reject the principal tenet of capitalism – profit maximisation – but to ensure that the state earns these profits.

The question of relative efficiency of the private firms and the East European countries is discussed here with special reference to the thirteen public sector enterprises which were at an advanced stage of construction in 1968/9.[1] As a general observation it is fair to mention that the enterprises financed by East European credits do not have a good record, even compared with other public sector enterprises. In 1968/9 23 out of the 85 units under construction declared dividends, but apart from ONGC and India Oil, none of these were constructed in collaboration with the East European countries. In fact, a sample survey of enterprises financed by East European countries shows that all made financial losses between the period 1965/6 to 1968/9.

Many of the public sector enterprises undertaken in collaboration with the East European countries did suffer from bad planning, inadequate preparation, escalation in costs and delays in implementation. However, India's experience with other collaborators has shown that private foreign firms are not necessarily better. Some of the problems of public enterprises are due to inexperience in industrial planning, the complexity of the projects and the collaborators' ignorance of local conditions. The criteria for measuring relative efficiency would be the costs of production and the time required to set up a plant and to produce the same output. To make a meaningful comparison,

[1] See the financial accounts of the enterprises in the Annual Reports (101).

however, the two projects should be similar in all essential respects. In comparing two steel plants, for example, the costs differ according to the location, the raw materials used, the production processes and the output. Therefore a proper comparison is only possible where two or more bids are offered for the same type of project. One such case is the Bokaro steel plant, for which American private steel firms and the USSR presented proposals.

BOKARO STEEL PLANT

The comparison between the two proposals covers the total cost, the cost of production facilities provided at the two plants, technology, foreign exchange cost, and raw materials and manpower requirements. To do full justice to anything as complex as a steel plant, it is necessary to cover both investment and production costs. Table 44 provides the cost estimates for the two projects. Since the Americans worked out the costs in detail and the Russians did not, the totals may not be exactly comparable, but the general experience with Soviet project estimates is that they leave out many items; hence there is no question of overstating the Soviet figures.

Table 44   *Total costs of construction of the Bokaro steel plant projects*

	Stage i	Stage ii	Stage iii	Cumulative
U.S. (m. $)	827·3	237·8	316·9	1,504·8
(m. Rs.)	3,939·6		1,506·2	7,147·8
USSR (m. Rs.)	4,860·0		6,940·0	10,273·32

Notes: The figures for Stages i, ii and iii are only construction costs for plant and related items. The cumulative figures include capitalised interest, technical assistance before starting ($17 million), personnel, recruiting costs, raw materials, stockpiled and miscellaneous items. These costs were given in the U.S. report. Dastur and Co. worked them out for the USSR plant from the information given in the detailed project report presented by the USSR.

Sources: For the USSR: Dastur and Co. (19, p. 3 and table 4). For the U.S.: Elliot and Wagner (26, p. 57).

On the basis of these estimates, the cost of a four-million-ton plant built by the USSR would be 25 per cent higher than that of an American plant. These were first estimates and India's experience generally has been that the costs of public sector projects are revised upwards later. Since the American project was never implemented, there is no way of judging the accuracy of American estimates. But Soviet costs were not even worked out in detail and only indicative costs for Rs.5,400 million for the first stage were given. These were soon revised upwards to Rs.6,200 as table 45 shows.

Table 45   *Total project costs of Bokaro, Stage* i

U.S. ($m.)	891·5	(Rs.4,234·6 million)
USSR as shown in the detailed project report		
(Rs. m.)	5,400	
Technical Committee Estimate (Rs. m.)	6,018	
Steel Ministry (Rs. m.)	6,265	
Annual Report of Public Sector		
Undertakings, 1968/9 (Rs. m.)	6,200	

Source: Same as table 44, and *Annual Reports of Public Sector Undertakings,* (101) 1968/9. The figure of Rs.6,200 million excludes Rs.510 million estimated for off-site facilities.

This escalation of costs within a year was due partly to devaluation and partly to the omission of many items. The cost of imported equipment increased and the Soviet credit had to be increased accordingly by 10 million roubles, because the foreign exchange component of the project cost was only 20 per cent. The Soviet estimates had left out items such as the cost of land, design engineering, commissioning, training, recruitment, construction facilities and machinery, main administration offices, township, interest on investment and customs duty.

The last figure – as shown in the *Annual Report of Public Sector Undertakings* – includes the cost savings suggested by Dastur and Co. and accepted by the Soviet Union, although these were only minor suggestions, amounting to Rs.95 million. Dastur and Co. had suggested that the Steel Ministry's revised estimate could be reduced by Rs.1,075 million, while simultaneously raising the capacity to 2 million tons.[1]

[1] Dastur and Co. (19, p. 2).

Dastur and Co.'s report on the Soviet proposal concludes that the costs of the Soviet project were too high. Thus it says, 'from the time in early December 1965 when these estimates became known, they have been generally considered high, even after taking into account the increase in import duties and escalation of equipment and construction costs during the last two or three years. It is also known that steel plants designed to produce flat products with facilities comparable to Bokaro are under construction or have been completed during the past few years in Britain, France, Italy and Japan at less than one-half the estimated cost of Bokaro.'[1]

The study points out that the Bokaro cost estimate includes Rs.300 million for an additional blast furnace and related facilities, which the Indian consultants considered to be unnecessary. Nonetheless even after removing that difference, Bokaro costs per annual ingot ton would be around Rs.2,760.

Table 46   *Estimates of total plant costs of different steelworks*

Steelworks	Year of completion	Initial ingot steel capacity (million tons per year)	Total plant cost (million tons per year)	Plant cost per annual ingot ton Rs.
Fukuyama (Japan)	1966	1·50	1,488	992
Spencer Works (U.K.)	1962	1·40	1,638	1,170
Taranto (Italy)	1964	2·50	2,153	860
Dunkirk (France)	1963	1·50	1,440	960
Bokaro (USSR proposal)	Stage I	1·70	4,860	2,860

Source: Dastur and Co. (19).

Though the facilities in all the plants listed in table 46 and their production programmes are similar, there are important differences of location and raw materials. So perhaps a more accurate comparison would be between the costs of producing steel at Bokaro estimated by the American survey and the detailed project report from the Soviet Union. While costs in the

[1] Dastur and Co. (19, p. 3).

Soviet plant are still higher than those in the corresponding U.S. plant (see table 47), these two are much closer than the costs of production in different countries shown in table 46.

Table 47 *Comparison of Bokaro plant cost per annual ingot ton: the U.S. and the USSR*

	Step I	Step II	Step III
U.S. ($)	522	381	311
(Rs.)	(2,479)		(1,477)
USSR (Rs.)	2,860		1,735

Sources: For the USSR: Dastur and Co. (19, p. 3, table 4). For the U.S.: Elliot and Wagner (26, p. 57).

The report goes on to say that the comparable U.S. cost for Step I would be Rs.2,140 per annual ton ingot and that constructing this plant in India would push the costs up by Rs.342 per annual ingot ton.

In the American proposal, the foreign exchange component was $512·6 million, or Rs.2,435 million. The entire foreign exchange cost was to be financed by a loan for 20 years at $5\frac{3}{4}$ per cent. The foreign exchange component of the Soviet proposal was much smaller – 190 million roubles – later revised to 200 million roubles, or Rs.1,058 million at pre-devaluation exchange rates. The foreign exchange component was to be financed by a Soviet credit to be repaid in 12 years at a $2\frac{1}{2}$ per cent interest rate.

From the point of view of keeping the foreign exchange costs to a minimum, the Soviet proposal was certainly superior to the American. The amount of loan was also correspondingly smaller than the amount of the American loan and the donor agreed to utilise any equipment available in India. The Americans were not consulted about using equipment produced at Ranchi, but they would probably have been reluctant to do so, since any delays in procuring supplies from the heavy machine building plant would have jeopardised the success of the steel plant and Ranchi might not have been able to produce equipment according to American specifications. The Ranchi plant was suffering from an underutilisation of capacity, so the Soviet Union's willingness to utilise this equipment was an additional advantage.

Both India and the USSR were taking a big risk in deciding to use equipment from Ranchi. It meant an added responsibility for the latter – to make sure that the plant, which was built by them, was producing the equipment on time and not holding up Bokaro. The plant's weakness has already been exposed, in that it could not even produce equipment for a Soviet steel plant and a special contract had to be signed for technical documentation.[1]

A comparison of costs is only meaningful in relation to the facilities provided. The basic assumption underlying both projects was that Bokaro should be designed for rapid expansion. In fact, the American consultants acknowledge that 'in planning needs, only modern units of large capacity have been considered. This will result in some of the equipment being lightly loaded in the first steps, notably the universal slabbing mill and continuous strip mill'.[2] Therefore, during the fixed stage the costs of production in both the units are higher than in the subsequent stages.

Table 48 shows the main facilities provided in both projects. According to the engineering experts, the facilities provided are comparable. Dastur and Co. thought that the Soviet costs could be reduced or at least postponed by cutting down on unnecessary facilities. The U.S. report says that the selections are based on 'maximum achieved performance on the best equipment installed today in the U.S.'[3]

Dastur and Co.'s specific recommendations for reducing costs were:

(1) To use three pig-iron casting machines instead of the four proposed in the Soviet report for the blast furnace.

(2) To use four blast furnaces, instead of the five proposed in the Soviet report, and to eliminate one blast furnace on foundry iron.

(3) To use 250-ton converters in the steel-melting shops instead of the 100-ton converters proposed in the Soviet report. The advantages of this arrangement are: investment is lower,

---

[1] *Annual Report of Public Sector Undertakings*, (101) 1967/8.   [2] See Levy (43).
[3] Elliot and Wagner (26).

operations are no more difficult than with smaller vessels, and operating costs are lower. By using 250-ton converters, it was possible to save Rs.220 million. The Soviet contractors did not want to do so during the first stage, because the operations of such converters had not been fully established in the USSR itself.

(4) To modify the design of the rolling mill. The cost of the rolling mill was more than the cost of the complete steel plants at Bhilai, Rourkela and Durgapur. It could be reduced substantially by modifying the designs.

Table 48 *Comparison of facilities at the two steel plants*

	U.S.	USSR
Coke plant	Sizes according to needs	5 × 69 (coke ovens)
Blast furnaces	0·6 m. tpa to 1·0 m. tpa	× 2,000 (cum one on foundry iron)
Oxygen steel-making vessels	sizes according to needs	
Universal slabbing mill	4 m. tpa of ingots	50 in. universal
Continuous wide hot strip mill	3·5 m. tpa of slabs	80 in. continuous
Tandem cold-rolled steel mill	1 m. tpa of coils	80 in. four-stand tandem
Wide plate mill (Step II)	0·4 m. tpa to 0·7 m. tpa of plate	

Note: m. tpa = million tons per annum.

(5) To reduce the capacity of the slabbing mill. Recent developments had shown that a conventional slabbing mill ran the risk of technical obsolescence and the 5·5 million tons per annum slabbing mill should therefore be reduced.

(6) To reduce the capacity of the hot strip mill. The proposed hot strip mill's maximum capacity could only be realised in about 1980 and since the large investment would be only partially utilised for 15 years (from 1965), the mill could be reduced in size. By reducing the number of stands from 12 to 11 and by modifying electrical systems, costs could be substantially reduced.

(7) Instead of relying on its own refractory plant, the facilities

should be cut down and the plant should rely on the refractory industry in the country.

(8) Since a significant part of the equipment was to be produced locally, Bokaro could rely on local suppliers for spares and components so that the investment of Rs.316 million in a repair shop was not justified.

The USSR rejected most of these recommendations, with some justification. Setting up a repair shop and its own refractory plant would have meant duplication of facilities and at the time Bokaro was planned refractory plants were lying idle. However, the question is whether quality control could have been exercised and whether the refractory industry would have been able to deliver the goods. Similarly, having to close down the steel plant due to the lack of repair facilities may be more expensive than setting up a repair shop on the spot. Unless repair facilities are located near the steel plant, transporting heavy equipment may also be problematic.

When commenting on the Soviet response, the government representative conveyed the same impression: that the USSR had good reasons for not accepting Dastur's recommendations. Shri T. N. Singh said in a statement made in Loksabha: 'The Soviet agencies in their final reply have accepted some of the proposals put to them, resulting in a net reduction in the cost of plant and equipment of Rs.95 million, apart from further consequential reductions in engineering, service facilities, customs duty, etc. They have given sound techno-economic reasons for not accepting some of the other important proposals. In addition, they have pointed out that acceptance of other proposals would involve not only the redesigning of those particular units, but also the redesigning of the entire general layout and utilities. This, they anticipate, would result in delay of about one year in the establishment of the first stage. Bokaro steel management will also be liable to pay redesigning charges for any modifications desired, which the Soviet agencies have not agreed to in terms of the Memorandum of Acceptance.'[1]

One serious criticism to be made of Bokaro is that, though Dastur and Co. had been working on this project since 1958 and had accumulated considerable data, their services were

[1] Press Information Bureau (120).

not utilised by the Soviet contractors, who insisted that they would prepare all the drawings, designs etc. themselves. They prepared another detailed project report, which the Government of India accepted. If Dastur and Co. had been associated with the contractors from the beginning, project costs might have been reduced considerably.

The fact that the Soviet proposal included facilities such as a big refractory and repair shop throws some light on the working of Soviet enterprises. In the Soviet Union, each enterprise is treated as an entity and is as self-sufficient as possible. When there are no other enterprises to provide spares and components, the repair shop is a necessary part of the project. As pointed out before, the contractors may have been justified in not trusting the Indian industries to deliver the goods on time, but it is a telling commentary on the Soviet view of the heavy machine building plant, which was built with Soviet collaboration, specifically to provide machinery and equipment for steel plants. Bokaro could have utilised the plant's services to a greater extent than was done.

The proposal for Bokaro brings out another feature of Soviet project planning. The problem is not approached as one of achieving the given target with minimum costs and units of optimum size, by phasing out investment. The dimension of timing in investment seems to have been neglected and many units were of a larger size than initially needed. If the units had been of a smaller size initially there would have been two advantages. First, the total costs would have been lower initially. Secondly, when planning future expansion, the latest techniques of production could have been absorbed. The risks of technological obsolescence would therefore be smaller.

To a layman, it is not clear whether it is cheaper to set up big units at once, as the Soviet Union did, than it is to phase investment. However, it would appear that if some units were under-utilised for five or six years there is a *prima facie* argument for postponing some investment and phasing it. These questions of minimising costs and maximising technological flexibility may not have received much attention because the structure of Soviet industry is not competitive. The key to Bokaro's successful functioning is its ability to compete. It is too early to say whether Bokaro will pass the test.

One of the criticisms levelled against Bokaro was that the slabbing mill was too large and ran the risk of technological obsolescence. It is interesting that the Americans also chose a slabbing mill rather than the continuous casting facility. The American consultants' report says: 'The key unit of the plant is the 4,000,000 tpa universal slabbing mill. The plan for Bokaro is based on the development of this single primary mill to its full capacity. An alternative to the slabbing mill would be a continuous casting facility; however, this was rejected by U.S. Steel as being too complicated and sensitive an operation for an Indian plant at this stage.'[1] Since the size of the American mill was smaller (4 million tpa) compared to the Russian mill (5.5 million tpa) the former was less costly and hence waste was minimised.

Apart from the facilities, the Bokaro steel plant has also been criticised for the decision, inherent in the Soviet proposal, to use as input the best quality coal available domestically, but the Dastur report points out that 'our national policy requires that these coals be conserved by using some proportion of a third component at our steel plants. Moreover, even if it were possible to divert these coals from existing steel works to Bokaro, the total quantity available is itself physically short of Bokaro's requirements'. The report therefore suggests a slight modification of the coal preparation system. Whether this recommendation was accepted or not is unknown.

The requirements for iron ore were very rigid, i.e. the variation limits from the norm were very stringent. The Soviet report admits that 'with variations up to 3 to 4 per cent the blast furnace performance will be worse than that assumed in the Detailed Project Report'.[2] These problems should have been tackled at the designing stage together with necessary adjustments to machinery and equipment. The American experts showed more awareness of the problem and concluded that 'it will take two years or more to find satisfactory long-term solutions to basic raw material problems'.[3]

The Soviet contractors offered no solution, but those from the United States suggested that the Kiriburu mines be owned by

---

[1] Elliot and Wagner (26). The continuous casting facility was being adopted in the early period and U.S. Steel was operating a continuous casting slab plant by early 1967.   [2] Dastur and Co. (19, pp. 5–9).   [3] Elliot and Wagner (26).

Bokaro. To make the iron ore suitable to Bokaro's requirements, it was proposed to improve iron ore handling, reduce aluminium content and produce crushed ore of uniform mesh size. The Americans had also decided to conduct research on coke to make the coal blends suitable for Bokaro, and this as far as cost was concerned was treated as a part of the project. The case of the Barauni oil refinery was similar. The Detailed Project Report stated that the oil produced would not meet Indian specifications, but neither party did anything about it until oil stocks had been accumulated in the plant. An extensive modification of the plant was then necessary. The same thing might happen in Bokaro if the raw materials problem is not sorted out before the equipment is installed.

The complexity of this project can be appreciated from the magnitude of technical assistance offered. In the American scheme, the technical expenses are as high as $139 million (Rs.660 million), including a provision for $5 million (Rs.23.7 million) a year for ten years as a technical assistance fee. The foreign exchange component of technical assistance is $50 million (Rs.237.5 million) and the rest is in local currency. Though the report does not give a detailed breakdown of technical assistance fees, it seems that this $50 million (Rs.237.5 million) was for working drawings, technical know-how and detailed project reports, and the rest was for paying the salaries of foreign technicians and for training Indians abroad and in India.

India would have had to pay the Soviet Union Rs.184 million for the first stage only. The breakdown is shown in table 49. The corresponding figure for U.S. technical assistance payments for Stage 1 would be Rs.220 million, one-third of the total. However, Rs.184 million is not the total amount for Stage 1. When the cost reduction study was written, another contract for the payment of Soviet specialists had not been signed, and this figure does not include the training of Indian engineers in the USSR.

The contractors from both countries planned elaborate training programmes. The U.S. report had concluded that in the light of the expansion programmes going on simultaneously in other steel plants, the number of experienced people available from them would be small, so that most people would have to be trained. Thus it was assumed that only about a thousand Indians from other plants would be available for Bokaro and 5,400 would have to be trained specially, with the cost of training being borne by the Government of India. In the Soviet

Table 49   *Technical assistance fees paid to the USSR*

Item	Amount (Rs. million)
Detailed Project Report	25
Working drawings for Stage I	25
Technical assistance in construction (1,719 man-years) – specialists, suppliers, representatives etc.[a]	123
Total	184

[a] Estimated by Dastur and Co. (19).

report, the exact number of Indians to be trained has not been agreed upon. Each nevertheless assured adequate numbers of experts in the field. For example, for the first stage alone about 400 to 500 Soviet experts were expected to be at the site during the construction peak, apart from suppliers' representatives and service personnel.

In summary, the costs of producing steel in Bokaro are high by international standards in both the American and Soviet proposals and may be treated as the cost of tied credit. Furthermore, for the facilities provided the Soviet plant proposal was costlier than the American one, as reflected in the higher costs of production. It would, however, be misleading to use the difference between national costs of production (in table 47) as representative of that between foreign-trade prices, because the USSR was in a monopoly position and charged what the market would bear. This is in sharp contrast to Bhilai, which was advertised as the cheapest of the three plants built during the Second Plan.

Both American and Soviet proposals shared the possibility of being technologically obsolete – because of not using continuous casting. The American plant was smaller and less costly and because of this losses due to obsolescence would be minimised. Another factor which increases the loss from possible technological obsolescence is the time needed to put up the Soviet Bokaro plant. From the time of signing the agreement on 25 January 1965 the original schedule called for the first blast furnace complex to be commissioned by September 1970 and for the entire plant to be completed by December 1971. The last available annual report on public undertakings conservatively estimated that there would be a delay of six months in commissioning the first blast furnace.[1] Since then Bokaro has had severe labour troubles and a delay of another year or so cannot be ruled out. In fact a recent article in the London *Times*,[2] based on the report of a parliamentary committee on steel and heavy engineering, says that because of the USSR's failure to produce final plans and drawings, the completion of the plant would be delayed by nearly two and a half years, causing the Indian Government to lose Rs.325 million. If Bokaro's equipment and products are obsolete or non-competitive by the time it reaches full capacity it may not be financially viable.

From the point of view of utilising domestic capacity created, the Soviet proposal was definitely superior in that the Ranchi plant was given a chance to prove itself. However, the plant's inability to deliver the goods – and the present reports are not encouraging – may further compound the error and Bokaro's success may be jeopardised.

Bokaro is a representative example of the projects financed with East European credits in the sense that it raises all the questions associated with these projects. Perhaps the most important is the competitiveness of these enterprises. A bird's-eye-view of other public sector projects shows that irrespective of the collaborator there were similar problems in planning and implementation.

The Loksabha Committee on Public Sector Undertakings conducted an inquiry into the management of public sector enterprises. The report says, 'Reports of the Estimates Committee provide a number of instances where the projects were

[1] *Annual Report of Public Sector Undertakings*, 1968/9 (101, p. 8).
[2] *The Times*, 19 October 1970.

not planned and executed properly ... leading to delays, wastages and loss to the undertakings. The mid-term appraisal of the Third Plan has pointed out the same thing. According to this report the stage is yet far from being reached where it can be claimed that time schedules, cost estimates, flow of benefits and returns on investments generally conform to the basic assumptions made when industrial projects are approved.'[1] The memorandum on the Fourth Plan has also observed that 'from studies which have been carried out so far, it is apparent that a larger proportion of projects in the public sector have been unable to adhere to time schedules and cost estimates on the basis of which they were first approved.'[2]

In planning a project, the planner should investigate the location; the source, cost, and consumption of new materials; the manpower requirements; the costs of construction and operation; the profitability of the venture; the demand for various products and the suitability of the output to the Indian market. The East European aided projects are characterised by the omission or miscalculation of many of these items, leading to delays in construction and loss of output. For instance:

(1) In the case of two projects, the foundry forge and the Barauni oil refinery, the soil had not been investigated properly and the foundations had to be strengthened before construction could be started.

(2) The Detailed Project Report on the heavy machine building plant and foundry forge at Ranchi did not discuss the question of availability of raw materials. This caused considerable delays in the implementation of the projects. Moreover, since domestically fabricated steel was not available on time, the programme of commissioning the plant and equipment in various shops was delayed by two to two and a half years. The heavy machine building plant was to use castings and forgings produced in the foundry forge, and as these were not available India had to import castings worth Rs.15 million from 1965/6 to 1969.[3] It is true that the delay was caused by Indian suppliers, but an investigation of the industry's capacity

---

[1] Committee on Public Sector Undertakings (102, pp. 1–2).
[2] *Ibid.*
[3] Ministry of Finance (114, pp. 186–7).

to supply steel at the planning stage could have prevented the fiasco.

(3) Many of the projects were based on inadequate data, a failing which was especially evident in the field of pharmaceuticals. The Committee on Public Sector Undertakings (CPU) gives the impression that neither Indian nor Soviet officials had enough data to be able to decide whether projects were profitable. Thus the CPU's report on pharmaceuticals says, 'technical and economic feasibility studies in respect of the five projects were conducted by the Soviet team which visited India in 1958. The Committee went through their report and found that most of the data were based on very rough estimates. It is as a result of this cursory data, on which assumptions regarding economic feasibility were based, that the Phytochemical Project at Neriamangalam had ultimately to be abandoned. It was found by the government that the data relating to the availability of raw materials and their cost bore scant relation to the actualities. Based on this meagre data, government had proceeded with the Project, incurring a loss of Rs.3·30 million (out of which the Kerala Government's share was Rs.1·99 million), before the Project was abandoned as an unworkable proposition. In the other three Projects also the assumptions in regard to cost of raw materials etc. have not proved accurate in higher costs of production and less profitability than originally assumed.'[1]

The Committee's statement about the manner in which these reports were prepared shows that it was not only the price estimates which were treated casually. In a report on public undertakings of December 1965 the Committee gives another reason why the project was abandoned. The Committee says, 'it was explained to the Committee during the evidence that the techno-economic study of the Phytochemical Project formed part of the study of the entire complex of five projects which the Russians had prepared. Taking the whole complex together, it was a profitable proposition, but when the government examined each project individually it was not found so.'[2]

(4) The practice of writing Detailed Project Reports with the help of cursory data resulted in serious marketing problems also.

[1] EC (108).   [2] Committee on Public Sector Undertakings (102, p. 8).

The problem here may be that in a centrally planned economy the demand is given and market study may not be an important part of project planning at all. In a mixed economy, however, even though the particular enterprise concerned is in the public sector, its customers are most likely to be the industrial private sector or final consumers. Unless output is geared to the needs of the market, these enterprises may not be able to sell their products. The heavy machine building plant and other machinery-producing units may run into this difficulty and the oil refineries may already have done so. If the equipment had not been modified and redesigned they would not have been able to produce crude according to Indian specifications. The Indian Drugs and Pharmaceuticals Co. was producing drugs for which there was no demand, or in quantities far in excess of what was required domestically.[1] If the drugs were being manufactured at competitive prices and there was a demand for them overseas, the lack of internal demand would not have been fatal, but so far the plants have been unsuccessful in exporting their products.

All the criticisms listed above are really special cases of one general criticism – bad project planning. This was manifest in other ways, such as the lack of coordination between the arrival of equipment and its construction (Ranchi and Bokaro).[2] The report on drugs and pharmaceuticals did not even work out time schedules for delivery and construction.[3] Another example of inadequate preparation is the modification in designs and equipment after starting construction on the project. The equipment in oil refineries had to be modified because the crude processed would not have been according to Indian specifications.[4] The changes may be justified or not. The point is that by making all the necessary investigations first, changes during construction can be minimised. Such changes cost both time and money.

One cost of delays is the loss in production and the consequently higher import bill, i.e. if a plant reaches full capacity two years later than the plan projections, equipment has to be imported, and this may cause delays in other projects which

<hr>

[1] From an article on Soviet-aided enterprises in *The Times*, 19 October 1970.
[2] *Annual Report of Public Sector Undertakings* (101).
[3] Committee on Public Sector Undertakings (106).
[4] Committee on Public Sector Undertakings (103, p. 30).

were supposed to use the equipment. A concrete example would be Bokaro. If the heavy machine building plant cannot deliver the goods on time Bokaro will be delayed because this equipment cannot be obtained from an alternative source. Of course the secondary bottleneck-creation effects of a project depend upon the short-term supply rigidities.

The other cost of delay is that it costs more to set up the plant than originally proposed. In most cases, the projects financed with East European credits cost more than originally estimated (see table 50). However, project costs did not escalate to the

Table 50   *Original and revised cost estimates for selected public sector enterprises receiving credits from the East European countries* (in Rs. million)

	Original 1961	Revised 1964	Revised 1965	% increase of the last figure over the initial
Pharmaceuticals				
Rishikesh	122.5	183.5	201.5	66.0
Hyderabad	115.0	170.4	193.0	58.3
Madras	21.5	34.8	35.6	65.0
Refineries				
Gauhati	130.6		177.0	35.5
Barauni	382.1		444.1	11.6
Gujarat	302.1		275.0	9.0
Mining and engineering				
Bhilai Steel	1,100.0		2,023.4	83.9
Heavy Electrical Corporation	1,259.5		2,113.02	67.7
Heavy machine building plant	281.5		461.6	63.9
Foundry forge	584.6		1,117.0	91.1
Coal mining	175.0		293.0	67.4
Heavy machinery	185.0		244.6	32.2
Total	3,443.3		5,462.6	63.0

Note: Revised estimates refer to: Bhilai 1963, heavy machine building plant 1965/6 (pre-devaluation figures), Heavy Electrical Corporation excluding Rs.310 million for township and common charges. The latest estimates available for each project have been taken.

Sources: Estimates Committee Report CP No. 5736.30 and Annual Report of Public Sector Undertakings. Original estimates for the heavy machine building plant are from the Detailed Project Report.

same extent in the case of all projects. The escalations are relatively lower in the case of oil refineries than other projects, but this is probably due to political rather than economic factors. After Barauni was built, Western firms offered to set up a refinery with the same capacity at half the price. The USSR was very sensitive about its image and, rather than be accused of overpricing and exploitation, it decided to lower the price. Revision of costs is not unusual for a public sector project,

Table 51 *Revision of projects estimates of selected public sector enterprises receiving credits from different donors* (in Rs. million)

Name of undertaking	Original estimate	Actual anticipated expenditure	Percentage increase
(1)	(2)	(3)	(4)
Durgapur steel plant (U.K.)	1,150·0	2,052·5[a]	78
Rourkela steel plant (West Germany)	1,280·0	2,034·8[a]	80
Bhilai steel plant (USSR)	1,100·0	2,023·4[a]	83
Hindustan Teleprinters Ltd.	15·0	16·5	10
Gauhati refinery (Rumania)	130·6	145·1	11
Hindustan Antibiotics Ltd.			
Pimpri unit	115·0	1·59	38
Penicillin expansion	4·5	6·1	36
Streptomycin unit	17·3	20·8	20
Hindustan Photo Films Manufacturing Co. Ltd.	73·8	85·3	15·5
National Mineral Development Corporation Ltd. (Kiriburu iron ore project, Japan)	90·6	112·2	24
Hindustan Machine Tools Ltd. (many collaborators) (watch factory, Japan)	25·0	36·8	47
Fertiliser Corporation of India Ltd.			
Trombay unit (U.S.)	243·4	334·0	37
Nangal (West Germany)	209·0	312·0	49
Heavy Electricals Ltd., Bhopal (U.K.)	352·5	493·0	39·9
Heavy Engineering Corporation Ltd. (USSR and Czechoslovakia)	1,259·5	2,065·0	64

[a] Revised estimate 1963.
Source: Committee on Public Sector Undertakings (102, p. 55).

but table 51 brings out that the revised estimates for projects financed with East European credits are much higher than other projects. However, it is not possible to conclude from this table that the former are necessarily more expensive. The fact is that East European countries did undertake some projects of the sort not financed by Western firms. A comparison is only possible in the case of steel plants and to some extent in the case of oil refineries. All the public sector steel plants seem to have had similar troubles – delays and cost escalation.

The West German steel plant at Rourkela was characterised by all sorts of troubles, including the failure of equipment to arrive on time, lack of coordination between the various contractors, and delays in construction and commissioning. The situation was so bad that the West German Government sent a special team of experts to review and remedy the situation.

The Durgapur steel plant, built by a consortium of British firms on a turnkey basis, has been criticised for 'inordinate delay in commissioning of several units, delays in reaching the rated capacity and the high costs of production'. The delays in construction were caused partly because of unsatisfactory ground conditions calling for stabilisation of foundations, such as piling, and changes in design during the process of construction.[1]

Compared to Rourkela and Durgapur, the Soviet plant at Bhilai was completed as scheduled and reached its rated capacity as planned. There was some trouble even at Bhilai, when the plant was being expanded. But on the whole the Soviet contractors did better in erecting and commissioning the plant than the Germans or the British. On the other hand, the American proposal for a steel plant was more attractive on paper than the Soviet proposal, as described below. However, the difference may be that the latter had to show greater efficiency in comparison with the Germans and the British. When they agreed to finance Bokaro, there was no competition.

The contrast in these instances was between enterprises financed by different countries but within the public sector (although the building was in some instances undertaken in collaboration with private foreign firms). The comparison was

[1] Committee on Public Sector Undertakings (105, pp. 4–5).

not extended to include enterprises in the private sector, because there are very few similar enterprises in the two sectors except for oil refineries and steel plants. The other public sector projects were more complex than the ones ordinarily attempted by the private sector. It is perfectly fair to say that many of the public sector projects were badly managed, but private firms had similar problems. Examples are discussed below to support this contention.

The first example is that of a World Bank loan for the private sector coal companies. This loan was meant to meet the foreign exchange requirements of the coal companies for the import of machinery to carry out their programme of expanding facilities and opening new mines to increase their annual production from 44 to 61 million tons.[1] But the loan was not utilised for some time and eventually the amount of the loan was reduced from Rs.167 million to Rs.138 million.

The second example is that the World Bank gave Tata Ltd. a loan of Rs.360 million to meet a part of the cost (Rs.750 million) of the programme to expand the output by 70,000 ingot tons. The company concluded an agreement with Kaiser Engineers for the provision of the engineering, procurement, supervision, and construction services necessary. The Kaiser organisation had undertaken to complete the project in two and a half years, i.e. by 31 May 1958.[2] Even though Tata Ltd. is the oldest engineering firm in India, with 50 years' experience, it decided to invite foreign collaborators rather than undertake an expansion programme. In spite of this the company experienced several difficulties, including delays in the arrival of equipment, partly due to the Suez crisis. The main part of the programme – coke-oven batteries, blast furnace, steel melting shop etc. – were completed by the beginning of 1959 rather than by June 1958 and the merchant mill and re-equipment of the old sheet bar and billet mill were only expected to be completed by the end of 1960.[3] The construction was completed in 1960.

Tata explained the delay on three grounds: the complexity of the task undertaken and delays in importing and in transporting equipment. The explanation has a familiar ring. Many

[1] Tata Iron and Steel Ltd. (80), *1954/5*, pp. 10–12.
[2] *Ibid.*   [3] Tata Iron and Steel Ltd. (80), *1958/9*, p. 12.

public sector projects also suffered from delays in importing equipment and had similar internal transport problems. Tata adjudged the expansion of a steel plant to be very difficult, 'A construction project of the scale and complexity of the two-million-ton programme, covering every phase of operations from the winning of ore to the rolling of finished steel, would have represented under the most favourable circumstances a complex undertaking in any country.'[1] It is hence evident that they must have considered setting up a new steel plant, including site preparation and construction of a new township, a still more complex task. By contrast Bhilai was completed on schedule.

The example of steel mills shows that in forcing the pace of industrialisation some inefficiency and delays are unavoidable. The question is how far the intangible experience gained should offset monetary losses. If the process of development is treated as one of the better exploitation of a country's natural and human resources, training personnel in design, construction and the operations of an enterprise is an integral part of industrialisation, but it does not preclude the propriety of minimising these losses by trying an alternative strategy.

Such a perspective is the general one of resource allocation. From the point of view of the actual project selected, two more considerations are relevant – quality and prices of equipment.

If a credit was tied to a project and no other source of finance was available, India might have had to buy equipment or maintain a production process which was not exactly suitable to her requirements. On the basis of the information available, this problem arose only in the case of oil refineries. Soviet crude oil is of different density to Indian or Persian crude oil and refinery equipment made in the USSR is designed to process domestic crude. To use this equipment for producing refined products elsewhere it is necessary either to adjust the equipment or to suffer heavy losses because the products are unsuitable. In the case of the Barauni refinery, the Soviet contractors stated in the Detailed Project Report that furnace oil could not be produced according to Indian specifications. However, the government decided to accept the report and to

[1] *Ibid.* p. 13.

9*

leave the question of furnace oil to negotiation. When this question was discussed with a Russian specialist, Mr Glagavidov, the Director of the Institute of Research on Petroleum, he recommended that the specification of the furnace oil should be changed and that it should be mixed with other products, as the alternative was to change the design of the plant. Thus he says: 'We have considered this question thoroughly and do not find a suitable process which could give a fuel oil of low pour point and high viscosity. In order to make fuel oil more suitable for the requirements of consumers, we are decreasing the pour point to the extent of 14 °C by diluting it with kerosene extract. In our opinion this is the best solution and the refinery should approach the government for getting exemption for paying diesel oil duty on this furnace oil. This product will not meet the specifications of diesel oil because of carbon content and its pour point. Besides, as a fuel oil, this product is of much higher grade than what is available at present in the market. We, therefore, see no difficulty in marketing this product.'[1]

The Director had a good reason for suggesting a new specification for furnace oil but it involved a loss for the Indians. The Central Board of Revenue rightly objected to the new specification on the grounds that it would 'result in a considerable loss in revenue to the government as this product could not be distinguished from and may be abused as, L.D.O.'[2] (low duty oils).

Since the coking unit was defective, the actual furnace oil produced was different from that indicated in the Detailed Project Report. The report describes the troubles thus: 'After the coking unit was actually commissioned in August 1964, within a short time it became apparent that it would not be possible to produce furnace oil in accordance with specifications laid down in the Detailed Project Report. The result was that the off-specification furnace oil component produced at the unit accumulated to the maximum of storage capacity available and brought the refinery operations to a standstill in December 1964. It was found that both the quality and quantity of the furnace oil component (coker fuel oil cut) obtained from the coking unit differed considerably from that given in the Detailed Project Report, thus aggravating the situation and making it

[1] Committee on Public Sector Undertakings (103, pp. 28–9).   [2] *Ibid.*

impossible to dispose of the coking unit products on specification finished products.'[1]

Regarding the prices of machinery and equipment provided by the East European countries, the proper comparison would be with other credit financed imports, and not with purchases from the cheapest source. In the case of tied credits from different sources the question of costs is only relative, i.e. were tied credits from East European countries more expensive than those given by others? Here again only the oil refineries and steel plants can be discussed. Concerning the three steel plants built at the same time it seems that the costs of constructing Bhilai, Rourkela and Durgapur are comparable. However, the proposed American investment costs of production per annual ingot ton of steel in Bokaro are much lower than the corresponding Soviet costs (see table 48).

The total costs of refineries and the refining costs of crude per ton are given below in tables 52 and 53, which show that the costs of production in the refineries built with private sector collaboration are lower than the costs of production in the refineries built with East European credits.

Table 52   *Costs of public sector oil refineries* (Rs. million)

Name	Capacity (million tonnes)	Township	Total cost	Foreign exchange component	Collaborator
Madras	2·50	—	440·0		ENI (Italy)
Gauhati	0·75	17·2	159·8	64·3	Rumania
Barauni	2·00	34·4	434·5	178·1	USSR
Koyali	3·00	25·0	307·0	150·0	USSR
Cochin	3·56	4·84	293·3	177·8	Phillips Petroleum (U.S.)
Haldia	2·5	—	460·0	230·0	Technip ENSA Industrial Export (Bucharest)

Notes: (1) The costs for all refineries exclude the costs of townships associated with them, but a detailed breakdown showing whether depreciation and capitalised interest payments are included or not is not available. (2) The costs of Madras and Haldia are high because as a result of devaluation the foreign exchange component increased.

Sources: Annual Report of Public Sector Undertakings (101), *1965/6*, ch. 1, and Bureau of Petroleum Information (100), ch. 3.

[1] Committee on Public Sector Undertakings (103, p. 23).

Table 53   *Refining costs in various refineries* (Rs. per ton)

Name	Final estimates[a]	Figures given to the CPU[b]
Public sector		
Gauhati	21·3	21·60
Barauni	21·7	37·93
Koyali	10·2	37·46
Cochin[c]	8·0	—
Haldia[c]	18·4	
Madras[c]	17·6	
Private sector		
Burmah Shell		18·02
Esso		12·19
Caltex		19·98

[a] Estimated from table 52.
[b] The figures of Indian Oil Corporation refineries are exclusive of interest charges on loans.
[c] Estimates included in the project cost.
Sources: Table 52 and Committee on Public Sector Undertakings (103, p. 65).

The author's estimates are lower than the estimates given to the Committee on Public Undertakings because the Committee's figures include the costs of associated townships. The margin of difference in the case of Gauhati is small. In the case of Koyali, however, the Committee's estimates of costs of production are three times the estimates shown here. This is because the Committee's estimates show the costs of production at the two-million-ton stage, whereas the author's estimates are based on later figures for the three-million-ton stage. The extra outlay for the three-million-ton stage was only Rs.30 million, while the output went up by one million tons. The same explanation applies to Barauni. The Committee report on Indian refineries points out that when the Barauni refinery reaches full throughput, the refining cost is expected to come down to Rs.23 per ton.[1]

The rapid decline in the refining costs at Koyali cannot be explained merely by high overhead costs and built-in capacity for expansion. The Soviet contractors may have had to

[1] Committee on Public Sector Undertakings (103).

revise the costs for political reasons. When the costs were revised, no extra outlay was necessary. A report on Indian refineries says, 'The estimate for the two-million-ton stage was Rs.302·1 million. The actual expenditure amounted only to Rs.275·0 million. The third million-ton stage was expected to cost only Rs.29·1 million. As such, this expenditure would be met from the savings of the second million-ton stage.'[1] However, most refineries have a built-in capacity for expansion so the cost reduction may be just scoring a propaganda point.

The unit costs for refining clearly indicate that the Soviet and Rumanian plants were dearer than the plants built with the collaboration of the private sector. But it is not possible to give an exact comparison because of the differences in production processes, product composition, location and timing. All the private refineries were built in the 1950s and near sea ports, unlike public sector refineries.

Yershov[2] tries to explain the difference in costs with reference to the factor of location and the cost of providing off-site facilities, which private sector refincries did not. This is, however, both misleading and inaccurate. Each refinery has to provide the facilities necessary for the operation of the plant. In comparing the unit costs of production, the costs of townships were excluded from this analysis, so the figures relate to the actual investments for production.

Goldman quotes N. M. Silouyanov, the Soviet Counsellor for Economic Affairs in New Delhi, as saying that Barauni has a lubricating-oil plant, a kerosene unit and an electric power plant, which other plants do not have.[3] But the Cochin refinery does have a kerosene unit and an electric power plant costs only Rs.19 million. According to Yershov, the lubricating-oil plant costs Rs.50 million. If these costs for special facilities provided – Rs.69 million – are deducted from the total costs of the two-million stage for Barauni to make Barauni and Cochin comparable, the total costs for the former are Rs.130 million higher than those for the latter.[4] The output of the Cochin refinery is, moreover, expected to be 0·50 million tons more than that of Barauni. So even after making allowances for poor location,

---

[1] *Ibid.*   [2] Yershov (98, pp. 100–4).   [3] Goldman (28, p. 33).
[4] These cost estimates were given in the Loksabha in 1964 and hence are slightly different from those quoted in table 52.

Barauni was an expensive proposition. The refinery at Cochin
was cheaper than the public sector refineries built by the USSR
at about the same time.

Since petroleum is an integrated industry, and all the profits
are made in producing crude, the deal should be examined as
a whole. In order to gain a foothold in India, the petroleum
companies may even have accepted a loss on the price of the
refinery. The Madras refinery for example was going to refine
crude from a Persian oil-field.[1] Similarly, Phillips Petroleum
made its own arrangements for importing crude. Neither of
these companies had a market or marketing arrangements in
India. Since they entered into collaboration with the Government of India they did not have to set up a distribution network.
The addition of a new outlet for their crude was a net gain for
them, even though they could not charge monopoly prices as
the old established companies did in the 1950s. Taking into
account these factors, the 'cheap' refinery may prove to be an
illusion if it is shown that crude could have been obtained at
cheaper rates from other sources.

From the study of oil refineries, it appears that the Russians
charged higher prices than the private sector. India's general
experience was that whenever suppliers could charge a high
price for credit-financed goods they did so. During a recent
inquiry into this problem in Loksabha the representative of the
Ministry stated that, 'We have to confess that whenever we
invited limited tenders from a single source, whether it is East
European country or any other source, we are not able to get
always a competitive price. In the case of East Europe, they are
sensitive to our finding that prices are not competitive. According to the Agreement we buy only when the prices are competitive in relation to world prices. They have always shown
willingness to reduce price.'[2] One example of this habit of
charging monopolistic prices is the heavy machines tools project
at Ranchi. The original cost estimate was Rs.185 million and
was revised upwards within six months by Rs.75 million. This
is a familiar story. But the interesting part is that the Czechs
were persuaded to bring the prices of equipment and machinery
and services down by Rs.27 million because it was discovered

---

[1] Bureau of Petroleum Information (99), 1967/8, ch. 1.
[2] Goldman (28, p. 93).

in the meantime that the prices charged were too high.[1] Kidron has pointed out that there is a tendency when the lender and the supplier of equipment are the same for a price to be quoted which is higher than when they are separate. He estimates that 'India may be normally paying anything between 6 and 15 per cent, sometimes as much as 20–30 per cent, above the ruling prices for aid supported imports'.[2]

Goldman mentions another case, where an American firm, the Chemical Construction Co., had charged an exorbitant price for a fertiliser plant. He says, 'Because its system was unique and the Indians had no one else to turn to, the Chemical Company at first quoted a price of $19 million to build a fertiliser plant at Trombay. Subsequently, the Indians found that the same firm had constructed a similar plant in Florida for $4–5 million. The price of Indian plant was lowered to $9 million, still double the price of the Florida plant.'

The most glaring example of monopolistic pricing is the pricing policies of petroleum companies. According to the agreements signed with these companies in the early 1950s, they had complete freedom to choose the source of supply and price of crude oil. India was supposed to pay the posted Gulf price. After the Suez crisis, however, the prices of crude oil started coming down as a result of the world supply situation and the pricing policy adopted by the Soviet Union. The prices were brought down by offering wide discounts on the posted Gulf prices. India was not, however, given the benefit of this de facto lowering of prices until the USSR offered to sell crude at 15 to 20 per cent below the Persian Gulf price. The Oil Price Inquiry Committee, appointed by the government to inquire into the question, accepted that the Soviet offer was definitely an important factor in the revision of oil prices by the oil companies. The report summarised the situation thus: 'The oil companies consider it a coincidence that their offer of discount on crude oil was made at about the same period when the offer of Russian crude oil for processing at the coastal refineries in India was being discussed with them by the Government. The oil companies did not accept this offer on account of the freedom allowed to them in the Refinery Agreements in regard to the choice of source of supply of crude oil. One cannot fail to recognise that

---

[1] Data personally collected by the author.   [2] Kidron (39, p. 123).

the competition generated by this offer influenced the suppliers in their final decision to allow discounts at the current rates bearing in mind the traditional nature of the discounts off posted prices with their suppliers long before the offer of the Russian crude was made to them. We are supported in this belief by the statement of Mr E. G. Lindroth, Senior Vice President for Finance and Director of Esso Export (quoted in the article entitled "Discounts Break Middle East Prices" appearing in the *Oil and Gas Journal* of 15 August 1960) to the effect that the study of the market made by his company indicated that discounts were being granted for large and increasing volumes of oil and the amount and duration of discounted sales contracts were increasing along with the size of the discounts.'[1] The report goes on to quote articles and instances to show that discounts had become a normal feature of the international scene in the late 1950s and even that the discount offered to various countries depended on the bargaining position of the country concerned.

There is little information available on the quality of the machinery. When the government representative was asked about this he said that where quality was concerned it was not possible to make a correct assessment of East European products.[2] The equipment for oil refineries was not suitable for Indian conditions, but an engineer who visited these plants thought that the Soviet equipment at Ranchi and Bokaro was very good and on the whole satisfactory, though it was not always of the most modern technology.[3]

Another cost of project tying, which has perhaps received less attention than possible distortion of investment priorities and higher prices, is that of unnecessary imports of skills and under-utilisation of skills locally available. The creditor, being concerned with the successful implementation of the project, may insist on a turnkey contract or at least on associating foreign consultants and managers with every stage of project implementation.

The Soviet contractors were generally willing to use whatever local skills were available, if only because of the relative scarcity

---

[1] Indian Oil Price Inquiry (133, pp. 22–3).   [2] Ministry of Finance (114, p. 230).
[3] Data personally collected by the author from an Indian engineer who worked with Dastur and Co.

of skilled indigenous manpower. But in all Soviet projects, the credit agreement is comprehensive so that Soviet staff take the responsibility for everything – employing large numbers of their own nationals as necessary. This arrangement has its advantages, because there have been less delays in these projects than in the Czechoslovak foundry forge, for instance. In the foundry forge, the Czechoslovak contractors provided only the foundation drawings and left their Indian counterparts to elaborate the detailed working drawings. That willingness to let the Indians undertake a larger share of responsibility than did the Soviet contractors was one of the factors that caused comparatively more delay in the construction of the foundry forge than in the cases of the heavy machine building plant and the coal mining machinery plant.

A comprehensive training programme was provided on the Soviet projects of a kind which a foreign firm would not have found profitable. For a private firm it may be cheaper to import the technicians needed for a job than to train them. The USSR, however, seems to have treated it, at least in the case of Bhilai, as a policy objective to ensure that the plant could be operated and maintained by Indians. The USSR trained a total of 426 engineers and 387 operators for Bhilai, out of a total of 2,141 personnel for all the Hindustan Steel Ltd. plants trained abroad by the end of 1963.[1] But in January 1964 there were 280 foreign technicians on Bhilai's payroll, compared to 57 in Durgapur and 258 in Rourkela.[2] If the training job had been successfully accomplished, the number of technicians should have been reduced. There may be two possible explanations. First, the number of foreign technicians on Hindustan Steel's payroll was higher for Bhilai because others paid for their technicians. The technical assistance programme was separate from the financial credit, whereas everything (including technical assistance) is charged against a project credit. There are two criticisms of Soviet methods; one is that while they adopted the right approach – trying to build up a local reservoir of skills – they did not do a thorough job. When the expansion of Bhilai ran into difficulties, the explanation given was that the number of Soviet technicians had been reduced to one-third of that used for

[1] Hindustan Steel Ltd., *Statistics for Iron and Steel in India, 1964*, p. 77.
[2] *Ibid.* p. 77.

setting up the plant. The difficulty again partly lies in transferring technology and skills, but these troubles are probably unavoidable in the process of industrialisation.

The second criticism is that, being concerned with the success of a project, the Soviet contractors have insisted on doing all the pre-investment appraisals, Detailed Project Reports, drawings and designs. The outstanding example is Bokaro. Even though there was a Detailed Project Report and the Indian consultant firm of Dastur and Co. had already done some preparatory work, the Soviet partners did not use it. Their viewpoint is understandable: they stepped in after the negotiations with the United States broke down and they wanted to make sure the project was a success.

CONCLUSIONS

Among the possible costs of tying discussed here it appears that:

(1) Utilising East European credits for industrial development was not a cost in the sense that it involved a significant potential loss of funds from other sources. India could not have increased her net receipts of foreign exchange from external sources significantly by a different allocation of credits.

(2) Accepting the East European countries as partners in these enterprises rather than private firms may have involved some cost because: (i) in some cases, such as petroleum refining, the equipment and production processes which they could offer were not suitable to India's requirements; and (ii) the costs of production in the Bokaro steel works and the Gauhati and Barauni refineries were higher than the private sector refineries and the United States proposal for Bokaro. This was not an avoidable cost because India did not have other sources of finance for the projects concerned. The general experience, however, is that public sector enterprises, whether planned and implemented in collaboration with the East European or other (private) partners, have run into difficulties and are characterised by bad planning and implementation.

(3) Whether tying to the 'public sector' itself involves a cost is very difficult to say. It is true that the bureaucracy is still not able to cope with the problems of public enterprises. However,

considering the stage of development reached in India and the nature of these projects, it is clear that even when some of the enterprises, such as steel and fertilisers, were being built in the private sector, the private firms had problems. The objections against public sector enterprises can be dealt with by treating them as autonomous corporations rather than as extensions of government departments and by giving special incentives to the management and workers by a profit sharing formula. It is perfectly true that the management of public sector enterprises leaves a lot to be desired. However, this is not due to the fact that the East European countries tied these credits to the public sector.

The costs of credits tied to East European countries, therefore, include in varying degrees unsuitable equipment, high prices, inexperience in planning projects with a view to keeping the costs to the minimum, inability to produce the goods needed and lack of marketing expertise. Since the East European credits were tied in so many ways the costs of tying are high, even though they cannot be quantified. However, a meaningful comparison would be with a credit equally tied, an Eximbank credit to an American private sector firm to set up a diesel factory, for example. In such a case the relevant consideration is the price of the equipment. Such a credit might even be more expensive than a credit from the USSR. Other countries, however, gave some untied assistance in various forms. Since the possibilities of switching were greater (in the case of other countries), the effective costs of tying were lower. In the case of East European countries, however, there was little room for lowering the costs of tying.

6

CONCLUSIONS

India was one of the few countries which received development assistance from both East European and other countries. Her experience is that while the former gave only 8 per cent of the total assistance utilised, and 17 per cent of the credits for industrial development, their credits were useful beyond their actual contribution in two ways. First, they gave credits for building up heavy industry in the public sector when other donors were reluctant to do so and thereby helped to break the monopoly of the private sector. Second, because of cold war rivalries, other donors responded to the USSR's aid programme by increasing the amounts of aid, softening the terms of loans, and broadening the end use of credits.

The late Nikita Khrushchev put it neatly: 'This aid which the capitalist countries are planning to extend to the states which have recently won their independence should also be viewed as a particular kind of Soviet aid to these states. If the Soviet Union did not exist, it is unlikely that the monopolies of the imperialist powers would aid the underdeveloped countries.'[1]

It is interesting to note that the USSR has not reacted in a similar manner to new initiatives taken by other donors. While other donors have responded to the changing requirements of the economy by granting debt relief and non-project assistance, the East European credit programme has been characterised so far by its relative rigidity. If the East European countries do not introduce flexibility in their programmes, the difficulties in finding projects to utilise their credits will increase. Their willingness to give credits may not mean very much unless the scope of these credits is broadened to accelerate the process of utilisation.

The East European credits are all tied to projects as well as to the country of origin. However, since the repayment arrangements are comprehensive, the criterion for measuring the cost

---

[1] Quoted by Tansky (78, p. 5).

of these credits is not import prices, but the difference between terms of trade with Eastern Europe and others. On the whole, it appears that the East European countries paid comparable prices for exports to those India obtained from others. Similarly, for imports of raw materials and semi-manufactured goods the prices were comparable.

The two case studies of imports of equipment (Bokaro and oil refineries) show that prices set by the USSR were higher than those offered by the alternative sources of supply. Imports of machinery and equipment constituted more than 60 per cent of total imports from East European countries until 1965/6. However, due to the lack of data, no definitive conclusion about import prices of machinery from East European countries is possible. Hence a quantitative comparison between Indo–East European and Indo–non-East European terms of trade is not possible.

Since the prices of exports to the East European and other markets are comparable, the usual criterion for measuring costs of tied credits can be applied to give a rough indication. It was pointed out in chapter 5 that the prices of East European machinery may in many cases be 15–20 per cent higher than the cheapest source. However, there is no evidence that the prices charged by East European credits are higher than in the case of tied credits from other sources. But there are some special disadvantages associated with tied credits of Eastern European countries.

One such disadvantage is limited choice. In theory, East European countries declare their willingness to finance any project. It is not known whether the Indian Government initially wanted different projects, but changed its decisions in order to take advantage of the aid available from East European countries. The hypothesis that East European countries can provide only certain types of equipment is supported by the fact that it takes a long time to earmark a credit for a project. Another example, though not of the same kind, illustrates the same point. If there was any fertiliser equipment to spare in the USSR, it is likely that it would have been offered on credit terms to break up the monopoly of private firms in a politically sensitive industry.

Another disadvantage is the lack of experience of the East

European countries in planning for a mixed economy. In a centrally planned economy domestic buyers have no choice because all the production is centrally planned. In a mixed economy such as India, the buyers can turn to alternative sources of supply within the country, or import the goods. In planning many of these enterprises, customers' preferences were not taken into account. This difficulty is not insurmountable and a marketing wing can be developed. Had a proper market study been made at the beginning, the composition of output might have been different.

Only a few enterprises implemented in collaboration with the East European partners are complete, but the need to tackle the problem of marketing is already apparent. Most of these projects are suffering from an under-utilisation of capacity for a variety of reasons (including bad planning on the part of the Indian authorities). The lesson to be drawn is that cooperation with East European countries is not very useful for building up marketing organisation and techniques.

Another disadvantage, not so much of East European aid as of utilising funds from different donors, is that of matching availability with requirements. If two credits are offered, one to produce some equipment in India, and the other to import that equipment, India might be in an unenviable position. This has happened in two cases – coal and steel. The choice is either not to utilise the capacity created at home or to forgo a credit. Because all donors look upon development loans as an export promotion device, they are reluctant to use locally produced equipment. Private foreign firms take the same line because usually their contribution consists of imported equipment.

The problem is further complicated when the firm which produces equipment for production in a particular industry is receiving credits from an East European country, while the industry which buys equipment is receiving a credit from a Western firm or government. For example, even if an American firm received a Cooley Amendment loan – a rupee loan – it would not be anxious to buy equipment from the heavy machine building plant at Ranchi. However, if an Indo–American enterprise in India was producing that equipment locally, AID officials might be more sympathetic about using Cooley funds to buy it.

In importing different technologies in the same or inter-dependent industries, India has taken a big risk. If these industries use different specifications in their products they may not be able to use each others' output. This indirect cost of borrowing from different countries may prove to be high. It is too early to say whether this will be a serious problem, because most of the Soviet-aided projects have not reached their full capacity, but it has already emerged.

Tying credits to imports very often results in an under-utilisation of local skills, because donors insist on using their own technicians etc. to design a project. The Soviet contractors were generally willing to use local talents but in the case of Bokaro they insisted on doing everything themselves.

The discussion on costs and benefits of East European credits would not be complete without examining whether repayment in kind has worked, and whether it can be recommended as a general policy.[1] Until recently, India has not had great difficulty in repaying credits in kind. India's exports to the East European countries have been generally additional. It could have found markets for 26 per cent of the total exports to the East European countries elsewhere during the period 1960–5. Moreover, India was not building up new markets to the extent indicated by the export figures, because the East European countries were re-exporting a part of the goods they imported from India.

Indian experience is, however, a special case. But for three favourable circumstances in the past, India's exports to these countries might not have been additional. First, there were difficulties in the way of increasing traditional exports to hard currency areas. Second, India's exports to the East European countries, before India started borrowing from them, were negligible. Third, the trade policy of the East European countries was reversed, from no trade to promotion of trade with the developing countries. Since external trade is regulated by the state, it can be assumed that India would not have been able to expand her exports in the absence of the trade and pay-ments agreements.

In the absence of such special circumstances, it might not be desirable to adopt the policy of tying repayment in kind. In

[1] At the UNCTAD-II meeting in New Delhi some representatives of developing countries advocated this.

dealing with Indo–U.S. or Indo–U.K. trade for example, the first problem would be to make sure that the borrower's repayment exports were additional to normal exports in two senses: (i) the borrower's exports to country A are additional to its exports elsewhere; and (ii) repayment exports to country A must be additional to what the borrowing country would have exported originally to A (in the absence of any special concession agreement etc.).

The first question has been discussed in chapter 4. In dealing with the free market economies the second is equally, if not more, important. It is not an easy task to project the normal range of exports over the next decade or two to country A. Supposing, for the sake of argument, that such a range of exports can be projected on the basis of certain assumptions about the rate of growth of demand for that commodity, and the borrower's share in the market A; some special mechanism will be necessary to make sure that the purchases of private importers are not affected by the additional quantities bought for repayment. The government can only do this by giving the borrower some special concession and possibly curtailing imports from others. In other words, to import additional quantities over and above what would have been purchased otherwise from the borrowing country, a deliberate change in the trade policy of country A would be necessary. Unless the aid givers are prepared to liberalise their trade policies, a commitment to accept repayment in kind may not be a net gain to the developing country concerned.

There are some additional problems in the selection of commodities from particular developing countries, both for the repaying country and for other major exporters of these commodities. Depending upon the proportion of repayment exports to normal exports, the repaying country might find that when the special marketing arrangement ends, it has difficulties in exporting these commodities elsewhere. If the quantities involved (of repayment exports) are very large and the lending country is an important market for other exporters of the same commodity, their exports will be affected. If a lending country is giving credits to various countries simultaneously, it faces an additional problem of increasing its imports from all these countries in such a manner that all the borrowing countries are better off as a result of the change, i.e. their respective exports are over and above what they would normally have sold.

So far one aspect of the Indo–East European economic relationship – aid – has been examined in the period covered by this book. Net receipts of development credits financed only 29 per cent of India's imports from the East European countries. Trade or exchange was much more important than the 'transfer of resources' from them to India. Their assistance was more in the nature of honourable cooperation – helping India to find markets for its goods and providing it with much needed development imports in return, rather than allowing India to accumulate a huge trade deficit on account of credit financed imports.

India's experience shows that these countries can indeed provide additional markets for exports of agricultural commodities. In the past they have also supplied essential machinery and equipment for various industries. The main difficulty in expanding trade is the lack of coordination between the partner countries. Unless a developing country such as India is prepared to coordinate its production and trade plans with the centrally planned economies, there are difficulties in finding the imports needed. If, however, quantitative targets are fixed for certain goods, there is no flexibility.[1] The biggest problem for a developing country therefore is how to combine the advantages of assured sources of supply and tied markets without creating excessive dependence on them.

While the past rate of growth of this trade has been very high, the scope for further expansion along the same lines is rather limited. The commodity composition of exports must be widened if the policy of repayment in kind is to be beneficial to India. Equally important is the further extension of convertibility within the group. This will make it easier for India to find the goods needed.

The commodity composition of Indian imports will be a key factor in deciding the future of Indo–East European trade relations. It was mentioned previously that India had had difficulty in finding the goods it required most. A good illustration of this difficulty is the long delays in utilising credits. In

[1] Nove and Donnelly (58) and Kaser (37) make the point that bilateralism implies coordination in planning.

September 1969 the share of East European countries in external assistance authorised and utilised was 12 and 8 per cent respectively. In the coming years the problem of finding suitable imports will be accentuated for two reasons. First, the imports of machinery and equipment are becoming less important. Second, a greater proportion of export earnings will be needed for repayment and less will be available for current imports. Therefore a change in the trade and credit policies and/or payment arrangements with the East European countries will be called for. Under the present arrangements, their desirability as trading partners may diminish.

A turning point has been reached in Indo–East European relations. The choice is between moving closer and letting trade build up rapidly, or treating this trade merely as an instrument to repay credits. In the latter case, the rate of expansion of Indian exports will be governed by two factors: the repayment burden and the demand for current imports (including defence equipment). In other words, export promotion will not be treated as an independent objective. The choice between the two should depend upon the pace of diversification of exports and imports. Exports of manufactures should become general, rather than making headlines in the newspapers.

The current Indo–USSR trade agreement definitively undertakes the diversification of both exports and imports, but it has to be recalled that under the previous treaty (of 1965) the USSR agreed to export products of Soviet-aided raw materials and to import Indian manufactured goods. Even quantitative targets had been agreed upon, but in practice the commodity composition of trade did not change as rapidly as was expected. It remains to be seen whether the new agreement will be used as a blueprint for action or will remain a declaration of intent.

In making a policy decision about future trade relations with East European countries the Government of India might give more attention to the other East European countries rather than to the USSR. In the past, the former have proved to be more reliable suppliers than the USSR. Moreover, they might be more suitable trading partners as sources of raw materials and semi-manufactures and markets for manufactured goods. The East European credits have been a useful though relatively small supplement to domestic savings. The availability of this assistance has enabled India to build an industrial structure in the public sector in accordance with India's own policies and for this reason was very welcome. The experience of the East European countries in building industrial enterprises has not helped India to set up the enterprises at the minimum cost, and in reasonable time. However, without undertaking individual case studies, it is not possible to attribute the blame to them.

The gains from the East European 'trade and aid' experiment have fallen short of what was originally expected of it by the less developed countries. While it has strengthened India's bargaining position *vis-à-vis* other aid-givers and helped India to break the monopoly of foreign firms, it has not much reduced India's dependence on other sources of finance or other markets. While the past rate of growth of trade has been very high, India still relies mainly on other countries for both exports and imports and will continue to do so for some time to come.

While the magnitude of their assistance to India was small, the new aid giving policies introduced by the East European countries – loans at concessional rates and loans for industrial development – have had considerable impact on other donors. One might say that nowhere has such a small substance cast such a great shadow.

BIBLIOGRAPHY

Agrawala, A. N. and Singh, S. P. (eds.)
1 *The Economics of Underdevelopment*, Oxford University Press, New York, 1963.

Ahuja, K.
2 'India's Trade with Eastern Europe', *Indian Economic Journal*, January 1962.

Allen, R. L.
3 *Soviet Economic Warfare*, Public Affairs Press, Washington D.C., 1960.

Arnold, H. P.
4 *Aid for Developing Countries*, Bodley Head, London, 1962.

Arora, V. K. and Girja, K.
5 *Documents on Indian Affairs 1960*, Asia Publishing House, 1965.

Arya, P. N.
6 *A Study of India's Bilateral Trade and Payments Arrangements*, U.S. Aid mission, New Delhi, 1968.

Benedikov, I. A.
7 'A Good Example of Economic Cooperation', *Eastern Economist*, 2 March 1962.

Berliner, J.
8 *Soviet Economic Aid: the New Aid and Trade Policy in Underdeveloped Countries*, Council on Foreign Relations, New York, 1958.

Bhagwati, J. and Chakravarty, S.
9 'Contributions to Indian Economic Analysis: A Survey', *American Economic Review Supplement*, Part 2, September 1969.

Bhatt, V. V.
10 'Savings and Flows of Funds Analysis – A Tool for Financial Planning', *Reserve Bank of India Bulletin*, September 1969.

Billerbeck, K.
11 *Soviet Block Foreign Aid to Underdeveloped Countries; An Analysis and a Prognosis* (trans. J. Bolkamper), Hamburg Archives of World Economy, Hamburg, 1960.

British Petroleum Co.
12 *World Oil Review*, 1965.

Brown, W. A. and Opie, R.
13 *American Foreign Assistance*, Brookings, Washington D.C., 1953.

Carter, J. R.

14 *The Net Cost of Soviet Foreign Aid*, Praeger, New York, 1971.

Chenery, H. B. and Clark, P. G.

15 *Inter-Industry Economics*, Wiley, New York, 1962.

Clay Committee

16 *Report of the President's Committee to Strengthen the Security of the Free World*, USGPO, Washington D.C., 1963.

Cohen, B.

17 'The Stagnation of Indian Exports', *Quarterly Journal of Economics*, March 1964 (based on *A Study of Export Policies of the Indian Government 1951/2 to 1962*, unpublished dissertation, Harvard, 1964).

Columbia School of Law

18 *Public International Development Financing in India*, Report No. 9, New York, July 1964.

Dastur, M. N. and Co.

19 *Cost Reduction Study on Bokaro Project*, Calcutta, May 1966.

Dave, S.

20 'India's Trade Relations with the East European Countries 1952/3 to 1959/60', *Indian Economic Journal*, July 1961.

21 'India's Trade with the East European Countries – A Rejoinder', *Indian Economic Journal*, April 1962.

Deshpande, S. N.

22 'The Fourth Five-Year Plan', *Reserve Bank of India Bulletin*, July 1970.

Divetia, V. V.

23 'An Operational Technique for Financial Planning', *Reserve Bank of India Bulletin*, September 1969.

Domar, E.

24 *Essays in the Theory of Economic Growth*, Oxford University Press, New York, 1957.

Eldridge. P. J.

25 *The Politics of Foreign Aid in India*, London, 1969.

Elliot, R. and Wagner, R.

26 *Synopsis of a Techno-economic Survey of a Proposed Integrated Steel Plant at Bokaro*, Washington D.C., 1963.

Friedmann, W. G. and Kalmanoff, G.

27 *International Financial Aid*, Columbia University Press, New York, 1966.

Goldman, M.

28 *Soviet Foreign Aid*, Praeger, New York, 1967.

Goldwin, R. A.

29 *Why Foreign Aid?* Rand McNally, Chicago, 1963.

Harrod, Sir R.
   30 'An Essay in Dynamic Theory', *Economic Journal*, March 1939.
Hartshorn, J. E.
   31 *Politics and World Oil Economics*, Praeger, New York, 1962.
Hejmadi, J.
   32 'Volume of Indo-USSR Trade Rises', *Journal of Industry and Trade*, May 1966.
Hoblik, K.
   33 *The U.S., the Soviet Union and the Third World*, Hamburg, 1968.
Issawi, C. and Yeganeh, M.
   34 *The Economics of Middle Eastern Oil*, Praeger, New York, 1962.
Jackson, R. J.
   35 *The Case for an International Development Authority*, Syracuse University Press, Syracuse, N.Y., 1959.
Karunakaran, K. P.
   36 *India in World Affairs 1947–50*, Oxford University Press, London, 1952; and *1950–53*, 1958.
Kaser, M.
   37 *Comecon: Integration Problems of the Planned Economies*, Oxford University Press, London, 1967.
   38 'East European Development Aid: Comparative Record and Prospects', *The World Today*, November 1970.
Kidron, M.
   39 *Foreign Investments in India*, Oxford University Press, London, 1965.
Knorr, K. F.
   40 *Ruble Diplomacy*, Center of International Studies, Princeton, 1956.
Kovner, M.
   41 *The Meaning of Co-Existence*, Public Affairs Press, Washington D.C., 1961.
Leeman, W. A.
   42 *The Price of Middle Eastern Oil*, Cornell University Press, Ithaca, 1962.
Levy, W. J.
   43 *The Search for Oil in Developing Countries*, Report prepared at the request of IBRD, New York, 1960.
Little, I. M. D. and Clifford, J. M.
   44 *International Aid*, Allen and Unwin, London, 1965.
Lubell, H.
   45 *Soviet Oil Offensive and Interblock Economic Competition*, RAND Corporation, Santa Monica, California, 1961.
Mahalanobis, P. C.
   46 *The Approach of Operational Research to Planning in India*, ISI Statistical Series No. 18, Calcutta, 1963.

47 *Talks on Planning*, ISI Statistical Series No. 14, Calcutta, 1961.
Malenbaum, M.
48 *East and West in India's Development*, National Planning
Association, New York, 1959.
Martynov, V. A.
49 'Soviet Economic Aid to Newly Liberated Countries' in
Problems of Foreign Aid, Proceedings of the Conference on
Public Policy sponsored by the University of East Africa at
University College, Dar-es-Salaam, 1964.
Mikesell, R. and Allen, R. L.
50 *Economic Policies Towards Less Developed Countries*, Joint
Economic Committee, U.S. Congress, USGPO, Washington
D.C., 1961.
National Council for Applied Economic Research
51 *Export Prospects of Black Pepper*, New Delhi, 1965.
52 *Export Prospects for Vegetable Oil and Oil Seeds*, New Delhi,
1965.
53 *Export Prospects for Mica*, New Delhi, 1958.
National Petroleum Council
54 *Impact of Oil Export from Soviet Block*, vol. II, Washington D.C.,
1962.
Nehru, J.
55 *Independence and After, Speeches*, vol. 1, 1946–9, Ministry of
Information and Broadcasting, New Delhi, 1949.
56 *Speeches*, vol. 3, 1953–7, New Delhi, 1958.
57 *Speeches*, vol. 4, 1957–63, New Delhi, 1964.
Nove, A. and Donnelly, D. C.
58 *Trade with Communist Countries*, I.E.A., London, 1960.
Nurkse, R.
59 *Patterns of Trade and Development* (Wicksell Lectures, Stockholm, 1959). Blackwell, Oxford, 1962.
Ohlin, G.
60 *Foreign Aid Policies Reconsidered*, OECD, Paris, 1966.
Organisation for Economic Cooperation and Development
61 *Flow of Resources to Developing Countries, 1956–63*, Paris, 1964.
Overstreet, E. and Windmüller, J. P.
62 *Communism in India*, University of California Press, San
Francisco, 1959.
Pant, P. and Mehra, K. S.
63 'Prospects of Exports in the 4th Plan', *Foreign Trade Review*,
January-March 1969.
Patel, S.
64 'Export Prospects and Economic Growth: India', *Economic
Journal*, September 1959.

65 'Trade of Developing Countries with Socialist Countries', *Foreign Trade Review*, April–June 1967.

Pincus, J. A.

66 *Costs and Benefits of Aid: An Empirical Analysis*, UNCTAD, Geneva, 1967.

67 *Trade, Aid and Development; The Rich and Poor Nations*, McGraw-Hill, New York, 1967.

Prebisch, R.

68 *Towards a New Trade Policy for Development*, Report by the Secretary General of UNCTAD, U.N., New York, 1964.

Rajan, M. S.

69 *India in World Affairs 1954–56*, Asia Publishing House, 1964.

Roy, H.

70 *Tea Price Stabilisation; The Indian Case*, World Press, Calcutta, 1965.

Royal Dutch Shell Ltd.

71 *The Petroleum Handbook*, London, 1959.

Rudra, A.

72 'Trade between Developing and Socialist Countries', *Foreign Trade Review*, January–March 1962.

Schultz, T. W.

73 'Economic Prospects for Primary Products', in Ellis, H. S. and Wallich, H. C. (eds.), *Economic Development for Latin America*, Macmillan, London 1961.

Sell, G.

74 *The Competitive Aspects of Oil Operations*, Institute of Petroleum, London, 1958.

Singh, M.

75 *India's Export Trends and Prospects for Self-Sustained Growth*, Clarendon Press, Oxford, 1964.

Singh, R. K.

76 *Prosperity through Exports*, Engineering Export Promotion Council, Calcutta, 1965.

Spulber, N.

77 *Soviet Strategy for Economic Growth*, Indiana Univ. Press, 1964.

Tansky, L.

78 *U.S. and USSR Aid to Developing Countries*, New York, 1967.

Tanzer, M.

79 *The Political Economy of International Oil and the Underdeveloped Countries*, Beacon Press, London, 1969.

Tata Iron and Steel Ltd.

80 *Annual Reports*, 1953/4 to 1960/1

United Nations
81 *Economic Bulletin for Europe*, Geneva, 1957–69.
82 *Petroleum Exploration, Capital Requirements and Methods of Financing*, New York, 1962.
83 *Interregional Seminar on Techniques of Petroleum Development*, New York, 1962.
84 Official Record of the Security Council, New York.
U.S. Congress House Committee on Foreign Affairs
85 *Staff Memorandum on the Communist Economic Offensive*, 4 March 1958, Washington D.C.
U.S. Congress (Senate Special Committee to Study Foreign Aid Programme)
86 *Foreign Assistance Activities of the Communist Bloc and Their Implications for the United States*, a study prepared by the Council for Economic and Industrial Research Inc., Washington D.C., 1957.
U.S. Department of State
87 *Communist Economic Policy in the Less Developed Countries*, No. 7020, USGPO, Washington D.C., 1960.
88 *The Communist Economic Threat*, No. 6777, USGPO, Washington D.C., 1959.
89 *The Sino–Soviet Economic Offensive in the Less Developed Countries*, No. 6632, USGPO, Washington D.C., 1958.
90 *Communist Governments and Developing Nations, Aid and Trade in 1967*, USGPO, RsE–120, Washington D.C., 1968.
USSR Mission to the United Nations
91 *Economic and Technical Cooperation between the USSR and Developing Countries*, New York, 1967.
Varma, D. S. N.
92 *Aspects of India's Foreign Relations*, Indian Council of World Affairs, New Delhi, 1957.
Vassilev, U.
93 *Policy in the Soviet Bloc on Aid to Developing Countries*, OECD, Paris, 1969.
Watts, N. and Datar, A. L.
94 'The Development of India's Trade with the Soviet Union and Eastern Europe', *Bulletin of the Oxford University Institute of Economics and Statistics*, February 1968.
Westwood, A.
95 *Foreign Aid in a Foreign Policy Framework*, Brookings, Washington D.C., 1966.
Wilber, C. K.
96 *The Soviet Model and Underdeveloped Countries*, University of North Carolina Press, Chapel Hill, 1969.

Wiggins, J. W. and Schoeck, H. (eds.)
  97 *Foreign Aid Re-examined*, Public Affairs Press, Washington D.C., 1958.
Yershov, Ya. A.
  98 *Neft i borba Indii za ekonomicheskuyu nezavizimosti*, Moscow, 1965.

INDIAN GOVERNMENT PUBLICATIONS AND REPORTS
OF PUBLIC UNDERTAKINGS

  99 *A Handbook on the Petroleum Industry in India*, various issues.
Bureau of Public Enterprises
  100 *Lukudyog* (monthly publication).
Committee on Public Sector Undertakings
  101 *Annual Reports*, 1965/6 to 1968/9
Bureau of Petroleum Information
  102 *Management and Administration of Public Undertakings* (Third Loksabha), 13th Report.
  103 *Indian Oil Corporation Ltd. Refineries Division* (Third Loksabha), 36th Report.
  104 *Bhilai Steel Plant of Hindustan Steel Ltd.* (Third Loksabha), 22nd Report.
  105 *Durgapur Steel Plant* (Third Loksabha), 29th Report.
  106 *Indian Drugs and Pharmaceuticals Ltd.* (Third Loksabha), 32nd Report.
Department of Commercial Intelligence and Statistics
  107 *A Guide to Official Statistics of Trade, Shipping and Customs and Excise Review of India*, New Delhi, 1965.
Estimates Committee
  108 Third Loksabha, 32nd Report.
  109 Third Loksabha, 48th Report.
  110 Third Loksabha, 52nd Report.
  111 Third Loksabha, 53rd Report.
  112 Third Loksabha, 57th Report.
Institute of Foreign Trade
  113 *India's Trade with Eastern Europe*, New Delhi, 1966.
Ministry of Finance
  114 *Utilisation of External Assistance* (Fourth Loksabha), 11th Report.
  115 *Economic Survey* (annual, 1967/8 to 1969/70).
National Productivity Council of India
  116 *The Oil Industry in the USSR, Czechoslovakia and Rumania*, NPC Report No. 18, New Delhi, 1962.

Parliament
117 Loksabha Secretariat, *Loksabha Proceedings (Questions and Answers)*, vol. I, 1953/4.
118 *Loksabha Proceedings* (excluding questions and answers), vol. II, 1953/4.
119 *Foreign Policy of India: Texts of Documents 1947–64*.
120 Press Information Bureau, *T. N. Singh's Statement in Parliament. Cost Reduction of Bokaro Project*.
121 Text of the Finance Minister's Statement on his Return from his Visit to Canada, U.K., U.S., laid on the table in Loksabha.
Planning Commission
122 *Papers Relating to the Formulation of the Second Plan*.
123 *Papers Submitted by the Panel of Economists*.
124 *The First Five-Year Plan*, Planning Commission, 2 vols., New Delhi, 1952.
125 *The Second Five-Year Plan*, Planning Commission, New Delhi, 1956.
126 *The Third Five-Year Plan*, Planning Commission, New Delhi, 1961.
127 *Draft Fourth Five-Year Plan*, Planning Commission, New Delhi, 1966.
Reserve Bank of India
128 *Annual Report on Currency and Finance*.
129 *Monthly Bulletin*.
130 *A Survey of India's Foreign Assets and Liabilities*, 1961, 1964.
Statistical Sources
131 Indian Jute Mills Ltd., Calcutta, *Annual Report*.
132 Indian Refineries Ltd., New Delhi, *Annual Report*.
133 Indian Oil Price Inquiry Committee, *Report*, July 1961.
134 Ministry of Commerce, *India's Trade Agreements, 1967/8*.
135 Ministry of Commerce and Industry, *Report of the Muddliar Export Promotion Committee, 1963*.
136 Ministry of Finance, *Report of the Committee on Utilisation of External Finance, 1964*.
137 Ministry of Finance, *External Assistance* (annual).
138 Ministry of Finance, *Explanatory Memorandum on the Budget of the Central Government* (annual, 1951/2 to 1967/8).
139 Ministry of Agriculture, *Annual Statistics of Production, Yield and Acreage under Principal Crops*.
140 Commonwealth Economic Committee, *Industrial Fibres* (annual).
141 FAO, *Commodity Year Book*, Rome (annual).
142 Office of the Chief Controller of Imports and Exports, *Brochure of Foreign Trade Statistics of India*, New Delhi.

143 *Monthly Statistics of Foreign Trade – Shipping Customs and Excise Revenue*, New Delhi.

144 Office of the Economic Adviser to the Government of India, *India's Trade with Rupee Payment Countries*.

145 *India's Export Trade with U.S. and Canada 1961*, Indian Chamber of Commerce.

146 *India's Export Trade Review 1961 and 1964*, Indian Chamber of Commerce.

147 *Annual Reports*, Indian Coffee Board.

148 *Tea Statistics*, Indian Tea Board (annual).

149 *Commodity Trade Statistics*, OECD (annual).

150 *Annual State of the Trade of the U.K.*, vol. II, H.M.S.O., London.

151 *U.N. Year Book of International Trade Statistics*, New York.

152 *Imports of Merchandise – Merchandise for Consumption*, Annual Reports, U.S. Bureau of Census, Washington D.C.

153 *Vneshnyaya Torgovlya Soyuza SSR* (subsequently SSSR); *statistichesky sbornik*, annual issues for 1955 to 1965, Moscow.

INDEX

Adamjee, G. M., 143
Ahuja, K., 173
aid, to India; conditions of, 9; definition of, 2; matching availability with requirements of, 258; policies, 1, 3, 7, 9–12, 55, 66–7, 74–5, 207; real value of, 4; terms of, 3–4, 42–55, 66–83 *passim*; volume of, 1, 33, 37–9, 40, 41, 42, 43, 48–9, 50–1, 53, 65–6, 74, 76–83, 256
AID (Agency for International Development), 44, 258
Allen, R. L. 4n., 11, 166, 212n.
aluminium, 191
Ankleshwar oilfields, 38, 73, 222–3
Argentina, 11, 94, 98, 166, 215
asbestos, 190–1
Australia, 51, 78, 83, 150
Austria, 50, 76, 80

balance of payments: of India; 13, 84–107; statistics concerning, 108–25
Barauni oil refinery, 33, 34, 38, 39, 49, 63, 199, 223, 238, 241, 245, 247–8, 249–50
Belgium, 44, 50, 76, 80
Bennet, H., 6n.
Bhagwati, J. and Chakravarty, S., 20n., 21, 58, 202, 207
Bhatt, V. V., 23n.
Bhilai steel plant, 33, 37, 39, 45, 63–4, 98, 100, 105, 125, 199, 205, 241–7, 253
bilateral trade, 4
Billerbeck, K. 45, 64
Bokaro steel plant, 33, 39, 45, 63, 65, 69, 125, 198–9, 226–37, 241, 243, 247, 252, 254, 257
Brazil, 154, 155
Brown, W. A. and Opie, R., 6
Bulganin, N., 27, 28
Bulgaria: exports to Western Europe, 159; trade balance with India, 85, 87, 89n., 92, 115, 118–24; volume of aid, 1, 40, 41, 78, 82
Burma, 11, 94, 98–9

Cambay oilfield, 38, 73, 222–3
Canada: in Consortium, 16n.; project aid, 47; technical assistance, 62; trade with India, 150, 172; volume of aid, 50, 52, 53, 76, 79, 80
capital: accumulation and investment, 201–3; receipts, 91
Carter, J. R., 2n.
cashew nuts, 139, 149–51, 156, 160–2, 170, 172, 174, 179–81, 184–8, 194, 196
castor oil, 154, 160, 172, 174
centrally planned economies, 1, 61, 128–31, 165, 168, 207, 240, 258, 261
Ceylon, 140, 141
Chakravarty, S., *see* Bhagwati, J.
chemicals, 164, 175–6, 189–90
China, 25, 26–7, 183, 204
Clay Committee, 69
Clifford, J. M., *see* Little, I. M. D.
coal mining industry, 198, 244; in iron manufacture, 234–5; machinery, 37–8, 199, 241
Coates, S. E., 204
Cochin oilfield, 73, 247–8, 249–50
coffee, 129, 134, 136, 139, 148–9, 159–60, 171–4, 179, 184–8, 193, 196
Cohen, B., 140–1
cold war, 1, 5, 18, 65–6, 256
Committee on Public Sector Undertakings, 65n., 237–40, 242, 246n., 247n., 248
competition, affecting diversion of exports, 136–42
compressor and pumps project, 199
Consortium, Indian: members of, 16n.; organisation of, 9; statistics concerning, 76, 80; terms of aid from, 52, 53, 55–6, 59–61, 67, 208, 210
consumption, theories concerning, 21
convertibility: of currency, 3–4; of repayments, 46–7, 84–101 *passim*
Cooley Amendment loans, *see* PL 480
copper, 189, 191
cottage industries, 22
coverage: of exports, 110; of imports, 111–14

273